Legend's Legacy

The Hand at Our Shoulder

Legend's

By Mike Gaddis

Legacy

Published by Sporting Classics

LEGEND'S LEGACY –
THE HAND AT OUR SHOULDER
is published by *Sporting Classics.*

Copyright ©2009 by Mike Gaddis

Publisher & Editor: Chuck Wechsler

Cover & Inside Art: Dan Burr

Printed in the United States.

First Edition

Library of Congress Control Number: 2009924829

ISBN 978-0-9794853-6-7

Dedication

To my maternal Aunt and Uncle, Louise and Sidney Walker, who taught me I'd find the secret of life somewhere between a doodlebug hole and a mountaintop. They were right.

VI

Contents

VIII

X

Preface

For everyone who ever scaled the height of a dream, there's another who stood on the ground and steadied the ladder.

So it has been with my sporting life. At many times and in many places. From modest beginnings in rural Carolina, where a loving mother once suffered a boy to decorate a bedroom wall with bird skins and butterfly wings, and a tolerant father once unwrapped what he thought was link sausage from the deep freezer only to discover a freshly defunct rattlesnake. To bucolic upbringings in the little country Community of Cedar Grove, where an encouraging aunt and uncle taught me the valued parable of the owl and the butt-fly, introduced me to the adventure of a 35-acre summer wheat field, showed me how to shoot a .22 rifle, pointed out the spoor of a coon, when to pick a persimmon, and made me to look for the world's gold standard of devotion in the eyes of a dog. From a grandmother whose knees cracked when she knelt to show me the delicate white beauty of the first trillium along a secluded oak-bottom stream, to a cane-toting grandpaw who blew smoke rings while he taught me how to turn a catalpa worm.

To the old man who trusted to me my first real shotgun, to another who took me under wing and tutored me about a bait-casting reel and how to trick a bass, to the other one still, who with the magnificence of his skill brought me to yearn for the grace and glory of a fly rod. From the Zulu tracker in the African Natal who taught me that what would be taken in blood must be given back in spirit, to the professional hunter who said to me in a most wonderful moment, "Sir, you may touch your animal now," and brought me to remember that triumph will never be sullied by remorse.

To life itself, the eternal teacher, days outdoors, their never-ending fascination. To old friends, old friends and constant companions. Woods, waters and wild things, each with a story, each with a song. Beseeching me to learn them all.

Not the least of my mentors was a 37-pound wisp of English setter,

1

indomitable of spirit and relentless of heart. I draw on her strength and courage every day that I live. And much that I am, much that I can ever hope to be, I owe to her.

Father-daughter, aunt and nephew, grandfather and grandson. Friend and befriended. Master and hound. No matter the affiliation, among the greatest, most beautiful, and validating gifts of the hunting and fishing traditions are mentorship, heritage and legacy. Find if you will, any other aspect of human existence, that has had as profound, nurturing and perpetuating influence upon the health and happiness of the human spirit. If ever there has been a national treasure, if ever there will be, here it is

Now more than ever it is my hope that this nation will cherish and cling to these centuries-old tenets of the peoples' mores, will embrace them as unfailingly as the Constitution. When, in these embattled years of the 21st century, their very tap-roots are wont to wither by egocentric factions who would rejoice at a social coup and so irrelevantly cast them aside. They have rested in esteem and harmony at the cornerstones of humankind for untold generations, and we must hope, for the sake of this Republic, the many more. The caring, sharing, and discovery, amid the ancestral schoolroom of Nature, that happens at the crossroads of wisdom and wonder.

So here, in hope and celebration – past, present, and future – are a few humble parables from meetings at that happy juncture. Including the title novella, reminiscence of friends and family, days with dogs, caring people and hopeful dreams. With the faith that the millions of others like them, happening day-to-day among you and yours, shall endure.

Six or sixty, our fascination for woods, waters and wildness is fathomless. I am thankful that I have walked this path. Me and mine. Most of all, I am thankful for the kind and caring souls who have seen me there and back. I am reminded that among the most inspiring of these, there stood one great common denominator. That, of the greatest of my many mentors, all remained replete with awe until the day they died.

Wisest of all is wisdom that never ceases to wonder.

November Farm
Creedmoor, North Carolina
January 3, 2009

3

Chapter 1

Tell Me

Tell me.

Do kids somewhere still grow up with Cochise, Robin Hood and William Tell rather than the Terminator and Robo-Cop? Do they still forge blood-brother pacts with the Ogalala Sioux? Ride paint stick ponies with feathers streaming from their manes?

I hope so.

Do perfect slingshot prongs still grow in dogwood trees? Green snakes still habit scuppernong grape vines? Can you still whittle a little makeshift waterwheel from basswood, put it on an ash spindle . . . make it sing true among the rocks in the creek wash?

Can you recreate, now that you're a man or woman grown, the same sense of accomplishment you had when you spied a large bright eye and then the hidden body of your first bedded cottontail? Or tracked it home a second time the morning after snow? Do you still remember the old man and tobacco smell of your grandfather as he sat along side you on a mossy bank and waited for the redbreasts to spend themselves on a bream hook? The words of his stories?

If so, no matter where you lived, we came along together. Does it still happen?

Can boys still read the spoor of mink, muskrat, otter, fox and bobcat? Do they know when the hazelnuts ripen along the slopes of the meadow? When it's safe to eat a persimmon?

Would they recognize the drumming of the grouse? The love antics of the woodcock? Has someone told them that snapping turtles won't turn loose 'til it thunders? That the proper word for a retriever fetch is "Back!"?

I worry about these things nowadays.

The world is full of lessons, and the most important, it seems to me, start at Earth level – with four feet on the ground, two big ones and two little ones. With the scent of the woods, the ripple of water, the caress of the wind, the meaning of the seasons, the meanderings of wild things, with grown folks and kids and the simple words, sharing and caring it takes to explain them. At the natural crossroads of wisdom and wonder.

As the years travel by, I find ever growing cause to be thankful for my boyhood, for the stepping stone it gave me to the world. Most of all, for the people who made it possible. It was a dream crammed full of loose, happy days with friends, along a creek or through a woods, with a .22 rifle or fishing pole, and a dog, of clamoring happily after the grown folks who showed it all to me, who taught me where I fitted and made me know I mattered. In the 60-odd years since, it has never let me down.

Expeditions were boundless, forever exciting. Some, particularly the Sunday afternoon excursions through the mountains for rattlesnakes, were high adventure. We'd muster midday – me, my brother Joe and the Bingham boys – bristling with assorted weaponry, amid a cheerful caravan of family and friends in old CJ-3 jeeps. Following the ancient woods paths, little more than wagon-rutted pioneer trails, we proudly rode vanguard, straining for the peculiar sheen of sunlight on timber rattler hide. The hapless serpent that befell our vigil never troubled Eden again. And if it wasn't unduly punctured or trail-worn when we made home, we tacked the skin out on a board and posed for the Kodak.

Learnings were homespun, spontaneous, cleverly devised. Easy parables, something like the owl and the fly. My aunt and uncle tendered that one, calling me from play. I was ten years old and had just shot it out with the Durango Kid. I still wore my twin cross-draw pistols when I rushed into their little house in the pines.

A small whet owl perched on my uncle's arm. The owl turned its head backwards and stared at me. Captivated, I stared back. Smoothing his feathers with my finger, I talked to him for a while, working up to the question.

"Can I keep him?"

"No. He wandered down the chimney," my uncle said. "We'll send him back.

"You wouldn't want somebody to latch onto you just cause you happened down their chimney, " he said, noticing my sagging lip.

"No, sir," I said dutifully, beginning to drift.

"Wait now," he beckoned, "look here."

He turned the owl on its back. "See?" he said, pointing with one finger.

There was a tiny black fly clinging stubbornly to the bird's feathers, just below its vent.

"All owls have a little fly that kinda hangs around there and cleans up," he explained. "For doing that the fly gets to keep company with the owl. Something you might want to remember."

I glanced at my aunt for confirmation. She was smiling wryly.

For a long time I examined owls. Sure enough, most of 'em had a fly. Some had several.

It was later, when I got out in the world and around people, that it all made sense. There're a hell of a lot more flies than owls.

Many times, this humble country allegory has made the revelation ridiculous enough to tolerate. I suppose they knew that.

In the eyes of a black-and-tan hound I first discovered loyalty. By way of a vixen with kits, I learned the meaning of devotion. In the death of my first squirrel I came to know remorse. Watching my aunt and uncle stroll an autumn woods path, with the painted leaves sifting down, I first observed the wonder of love. In each instance, someone led me there, and brought me back. And taught me what was genuine.

I know now that it was not easy for the folks of my upbringing to wrest loose the time to tutor a green-eared kid, yet I cannot recall that anyone did it grudgingly or that anybody ever got in a hurry doing it. The only thing I remember is that we did it together and that "it" and they became one and the same.

On a high knob on Ridge's Mountain where we stopped with the coon dogs in the small hours one morning long ago, weary, worn and happy, popped corn over an open fire, and then slept 'til the pink of dawn, I can still find my uncle. Wherever I listen to a bawling pack of 13-inch beagles taking a hare to ride, my father is there, steering me and a single-barrel twenty safely toward the path they will cross. When I discover the fragile pink pedals of a lady's-slipper in a woodland, and hear the nearby babble of a brook, I see the small, gentle countenance of my grandmother, pulling me close to shoulder and stooping to show me its beauty.

Words and values were their greatest legacy – the outdoors their greatest gift. Beyond these, they left me to fill in the blanks.

Tell me it still happens.

Chapter 2

Bless This House

The storms ran late that year. Two weeks into November, a hurricane hopped the dunes, battering its way inland with pummeling winds and pelting rains. Schools shut down. Towns drowned. Folks were put to high ground.

Apologies to the souls who suffered, but it was the best Thanksgiving of my life, because Taylor's Creek bloated and relocated out into the woods the bridge to the old Coble house on my Uncle Sid's farm.

We went there, you see, us and ours, to the house where Jacob Coble raised up a passel of young'ns, a turnip patch and a few hogs – afore the Yankees came uninvited – and Ma Coble sent the boys warn't off to war down to hide at the Buzzard's Rock that stood over the branch where, almost a hundred years later, I would shoot my first wood duck. Where old Rock treed my first coon. Went there, you see, to thank the Lord. And nothing, not even Noah's flood, was left to stand in the way.

That was the year I was 9 years old, and Uncle Sid called on Uncle Sam, just like Uncle Sam had called on him and a lot of other boys a few years before. The year he borrowed Doc Hayworth's half-track, an armored troop carrier from the Big War. The time he and I mounted a recon mission, whang and clang, three miles down the shoulder of Old Highway 49, two more through the woods, to breach the gap between us and a table blessing. Uncle Sid was cap'n and I was first mate, and my 15-inch beagle Jack was bo'sun. The good ol' U.S. of A. was emblazoned against our olive-drab flanks and Old Glory flapped proudly from the bridge-staff. And everybody that passed would honk and salute.

"Stand smartly, Boy," my uncle ordered, as he nudged her nose over the brink. It wavered there like an inch-worm measuring space, then dropped steeply into the creek bed – squishing and sliding down the near side and grunting and banging up the far – while the brakes scrinched and Jack yowled.

That was the year we spruced up the house extra-special, the November I went to the woods with my new sheath knife and brought back oak and hickory boughs, dried-blood red and tobacco yellow, and hung them gaily about the walls and mantels. While Uncle Sid pushed aside the shutters and flung open the doors, aired the kitchen, swept off the porches and dusted the floors. And afterwards, once we'd hauled up the kindling' and stove bolts, knocked the soot out of the pipe, and laid the chimney fire . . . that was the year we walked the hardwood ridge above the swimming hole, and I took the .22 to warn the squirrels about a grateful stew.

That was the year all was made ready, when it seemed it couldn't possibly be, and we took the undaunted carrier back across the inky creek bottom that night by the light of the stars, me and Uncle Sid, and left her standin' watch by the other side. While eerily from the bottom the big owls grumbled "Who?"

"Tell 'em," Uncle Sid said to my Aunt Louise that evening, "me and the boy have laid Thanks."

We gathered there the morning after, at the pink of sunrise, us and ours. Me and Jack and Uncle Sid fired up the ship and with a roar, a wallow and a fog of diesel fumes we shuttled across the gaping maw of the creek, a dozen to the time, to the top of the white flint hill and the knoll where the old house lived. While menfolk whooped and women squealed, Jack yowled and young'ns howled – folks held for dear life to platters and plates, pots and tins, jugs and jars, and bowls and bins, crocks full of chicken, tubs full of lamb, cookers of beef and turkey and ham, taters in tow sacks and fat-back in beans, biscuits in baskets with molasses between, sweet tea in barrels and cakes in a box, pies in a stack and corn on the cob, dumplings on knees and cobblers on bellies, watermelon pickles, berry jams and jellies.

That was the year I was given a stick match and a chunk of fat pine, and trusted to light the hearth fire for the first time. The year I thrilled as the little flame whispered timidly from the kindling, crept up through the dry oak and green hickory, gaining courage as it went, until it found its voice and swelled to a roar. By then, you could hear the old cook stove humming too, and together they hurried the house close and cozy. Comforting the womenfolk, busily over the fixin's, chattering along softly above the thump of the percolator, that was beginning to belch periodically a spurt of black coffee into the little glass bulb on top of the pot. While from the AM radio that lived in a cabinet in the corner, seeped the homey baritone of Ernie Ford:

"Bless this house, Oh Lord we pray; make it safe by night and day, Bless the roof and chimneys tall, let Thy peace lie over all . . ."

I remember maybe most now how I felt, how infinitely happy I was, safe from want and warm with the world – a world still with all its pieces.

In an hour or so the hot coals had grown under the fire and Granny raked a few out on the hearth and sat the Dutch oven on top of them, before shoveling a few more onto its lid. So that on its insides the sweet cornbread would bake and make the room smell like 11 shades of Heaven. In unison with the buttery beckon of the turkey and oyster dressing roasting in the side bins, the brown-sugar-and-cinnamony scent of the steeping yams, and the cloying, spicy breath of the desserts. Behind them would come the hearty waft of the soups, the bacon-peppery spoor of the baked beans, the scallion-and-crème bouquet of the squash, the sizzling, breaded exhalation of the okra, each in its time before the fire. Joining with the cheerful, fruited pant of the puddings within the good-humored snugness of the little house, to be orchestrated into a swelling chorus so fragrantly symphonic your mouth ached and slavered.

I suppose we weren't as sophisticated then, not like now, cause after dinner was set and we gathered round the table we all joined hands and offered the Lord's Prayer. Asked him to bless the house and thanked him for rich bottomland and summer rains and good health, and each other, and the half-dozen other things necessary to all that rested before us. In the momentary quiet after the Amens, while each soul added a personal, silent echo, you could hear Ol' Ernie once over, *"We gather together . . ."* A local tradition, just after noon, every Blessing Day. The same time the siren went off at the Asheboro Fire Station.

T he best was last. After dinner and stories had ruminated, menfolk and boys went huntin'. Cause back then hunting season came in on Thanksgiving Day. All year we waited. To stomp the thickets and start a rabbit. To spy a squirrel in the tip-top of a tulip tree. Or if we got especially lucky, to step in an explosion of quail, or twist loose a coon. All year we waited to wander through the woods, gathering like gypsies black walnuts and persimmons, chinquapins and hic'ry nuts. The hazelnut kernels that waited in cuspy pods on low-growing bushes along the hillsides. The purple grapes, shriveled, cool and sugary, hidden under the fallen leaves beneath the suggestion of a barren muscadine vine.

Until twilight fell, and tired and complete we made our way back to the yellow lamplight growing behind the windows of the old house. Where inside the fire had died, all the beautiful smells had faded to the odor of gray ashes, and the womenfolk were packed and waiting for the trip back across the creek to the far side of the hill.

That was the year, after Uncle Sid and I had delivered the last of them safely over, had posted the carrier at the bottom of the hill and were walking slowly back to its crest to join them, I learned what melancholy meant. The year he said to me, "Remember this day, Boy, as it has been, for in this way it can never be again."

And this is the year I wish with all my heart that I could give it back to every kid in America.

Chapter 3

Ashworth Sundays

The bleached, disheveled timbers of the old house protrude above the honeysuckle like the scattered bones of a forsaken corpse. The cedars that once soldiered the fencerow straight and full are mostly gone, the few remaining, shabby and gnarled. Garden and grounds I knew so well in the green breath of summer lie in sere anomaly under the leaden December sky. The desolation assails the innocence of my memory and punctuates the years of his absence, yet it cannot displace his legacy. Gazing along the threadbare suggestion of the wagon path, I still sense the splendid baritones of his presence.

The proud script penned by his father into the worn, leather Bible on the parlor secretary pronounced him William Manly Ashworth. The year was 1890 and it was the 22nd day of the Christmas month.

For three generations of us who arrived afterwards, he was simply and dearly "Uncle Manly."

He was a large man for his day, standing six-feet-three in his prime and scaling maybe 220 pounds. A gentle person, blessed with a lusty voice and a ready smile, his generosity was well fitted to his stature. In a normal conversation he could be heard in lucid, resonant tones at Union Grove Church, a good half-mile west. There were clear, still, go-to-meeting mornings, with the windows opened, when the enthralled congregation mistook the preacher's desperate peaks of inflection as an augury of conviction. On a summer Sunday, in the years I knew him, his perennial attire was a long-sleeved white shirt under a pair of clean, but well-worn overalls. In an era when most men of his generation religiously wore hats, he went bareheaded, his full thatch of silver hair wetted and neatly groomed.

He lived on the family homeplace, a small farm of 90-some acres in the red clay, white flint and buck-tallow of Cedar Grove Community in Randolph County. The house, clapboards over logs, stood on a gentle swell at its center, overlooking meadows of butterfly weed, zephyr lilies and goldenrod, and the cool, shadowy bottomland skirting Taylor's Creek. It was a place of simple grace and charm, from the strength of the oaks bordering the farm path to the harmony of the blue gingham curtains behind the blown glass windows. When his nine siblings left to find their fortunes in the world, Uncle Manly discovered his in the place he was raised.

Uncle Manly was a confirmed bachelor. Whether by choice or happenstance, he lived alone. Maybe he loved and lost. I never knew. There were, no doubt, times he was lonely.

But never on a Sunday. On Sundays, he welcomed the gathering of an extended family, which found its way back to its ancestral beginnings, drawn by taproots and tranquil memories into a mutual search for renewal. Uncle Manly was forever at its epicenter, the cornerstone of its commerce.

To the grown folks he was the herald of simplicity and country values in a world increasingly complex and urbane.

To us young'ns he was a companionable mentor, oftentimes accomplice. Forever young at heart, he would welcome us with boyish anticipation, never tiring of our endless questions, rejoicing at the eagerness of our insistence.

He knew the hidden woodland where the first trillium grew, the secret of a butterfly chrysalis, how to trick the door shut on a freshwater mussel with the stem of a straw. Deftly, he'd unravel the mystery in a quail roost, find the cool, cloying muscadines that hid themselves safe from frost under November leaves, fashion a pop gun that shot gumballs.

Do you know when the hazelnuts ripen along the slopes of the meadow? How the king snake gets its name? When it's safe to eat a persimmon? How buckeyes look when they first peek from their husk? He could explain.

Would kids today recognize the lyrical music of the wood thrush, the bubbling trill of the wren, the whipsawing of the whippoorwill? Has someone told them that snapping turtles won't turn loose 'til it thunders? That a bobcat jumps tree? That you can squall a coon? Has somebody explained about bee trees? Stinging nettle? Molly-pops? Have they been taught to pick a bird when the quail rise?

Can they fashion a bow and arrow from a hickory sapling and some Dominecker feathers? Skin a snake? Turn a catalpa worm?

"Come," he would say in simple phrases, "the world is full of fascinations," revealing each in turn.

Along the alders that shadowed the creek banks in the shimmer of summer, where the brown water snakes resided, we wandered in a cluster, relishing the old man and tobacco smell of him, the words of his stories. By his side we sat with the fishing poles he had whittled from a stick, catching redbreasts on hook and line from his overall pockets. About the painted meadows, through the dusky bottoms, deep into green forests we followed his reverent footsteps, gaining respect first for the world around us, and then for ourselves.

In the wonder of a wren's nest in a discarded sunbonnet we learned legitimacy . . . in the honesty of tumblebugs on a mound of cow manure, we were brought to humility.

In a thousand ways, in a hundred places, we were taught that the least is as important as the greatest, and that a boy, or a girl, is simply one creature in a Kingdom.

Uncle Manly was the lesson the sixth grade forgot to teach.

In the grace of the old house, when Aunt Bessie instigated parlor hymns around the wheezy pump organ, we reveled in the comforting strength of his song. In an acapella anchored by his rich baritone, 20 strong and four generations deep, we shook its moorings with strains of *Will There Be Any Stars In My Crown*, *Amazing Grace* and *Rock of Ages*. When Aunt Rachel railed in from Mississippi, and Baxter Skeen hauled in George Pegram and the Boys to renew his smoldering courtship, we waited anxiously for the Boys to blow into *Rocky Top*. By then, inebriated by the feeling, Uncle Manly would explode into a spirited buck dance. Enthralled with his exuberance, we would clap and whoop, spirits soaring.

At the scuppernong vine in September, he would throw himself into an industrious frenzy, picking from the top of the scaffold for the smaller of us, and generally watching out for the womenfolk. On the return trip to the big house, he was ever vigilant for that year's round of Christmas trees.

"I'll be doggone if that ain't a pretty one, Joe!" he'd proclaim to my grandpa, calling us kids around to see.

Before the flickering firelight on the Eve of Noel, the room inundated with the scent of red cedar and baking sweet potatoes, the beagles kenneled and the rabbits hanging silvered and frosted by moonlight on the side porch, with the promise of the long-awaited morning dancing in our heads, he was old Father Christmas . . . the eternal countenance of gentility, giving and goodwill, the essence of innocence and sincerity, the harbinger of peace and joy.

I remember him most vividly at this season. But always he is there, reminding me of how I began, how I should strive to live, and why I love equally both mistletoe and doodlebugs.

He was a constant in a hundred childhood evenings. In the gathering twilight, when it came time for farewells, he was everywhere at once, it seemed, clinging to the last fleeting minutes as a child clings to the hand of his mother, sincerely and anxiously taken with the notion that the day would only end in success if he could extract a promise of return, "God willing," from every departing soul.

He would be standing by the path as we left . . . a lantern in hand against the growing night . . . amid the fragrant amalgam of lilac, jasmine and honeysuckle that had melted onto the cooling air of the rising evening, the clack of the cicadas and katydids in the foreground, the long, throaty *yeeeaannnks* of the toads, the whipsawing of a distant whippoorwill. For as long as he could see us, he would wave, entreating again and again, "Come back, Joe. Come back, Joe."

Dusk is falling now as well, almost 60 years later, as I turn from the lifeless old home place and make my way back along the faint wagon path, yet I hear him calling still, ever so clearly in the quiet, cold air.

Chapter 4

Thirty-Five Acres Was The World

T he law had been out for a good while on big game like rabbits, squirrels, ducks and quail, but I was hard into a Saturday of sorting and cleaning tools of the hunt for another opening day come Tuesday.

Laid around for inspection were a Daisy BB gun, two slingshots, magnum and small-bore respectively, a hawkbill knife with a broken handle, several tubes of Red Top BBs, a leather pouch stuffed with choice creek pebbles for the slingshots, and a small can of 3-in-1 oil. If you're wondering about the oil, BB guns commonly developed performance problems with barrel friction, and a dollop of the 3-in-1 did marvels to restore the desired ballistic properties. Knowing that kind of thing at the time was of similar magnitude to the knowledge you acquired later that you had to compensate a mite for the first shot from a clean rifle barrel.

It was mid-June, school had been out long enough to forget, and the wheat harvest was at hand. I knew, because my close surveillance of the crop, seed to tassel, was only slightly less exacting than that of those whose livelihood rested solidly on its success or failure. By mid to late May, the green stalks had begun to exhibit the yellow mottling that led with sunny days and warm nights to deep golden maturity during the wedding month. Now the heavy whiskered heads beckoned, rippling and furling over the earth at the whim of the winds.

Of the vast array of adventures awaiting a foot-loose boy of nine in rural Randolph County, circa 1951, combining wheat held stature near the pinnacle. It wasn't the cutting of the wheat itself; that was only the means to an end. For the adults, it was mean, sweltering, exhausting work. When conditions were right, it was hot and dry, and the heat demons danced maniacally atop the heads of the grain. The dust billowed in constant clouds about the man on the combine, busy with bagging the chutes and loading the ramp, and the chaff was an unrelenting irritant to sweaty skin. When the combining was done, the heavy bags had to be loaded onto the truck, and later the straw bales.

But I enjoyed the immunity of youth in a season of unbridled spirits. My job was to ride armed on the combine once things got underway, dismount for high-mettled rabbit chases and generally ward off the varmints that had taken residence in the unknown depths of the grain stalks.

I have often wondered since if anyone has ever truly studied the ecology of a Piedmont wheat field; that is, if they're the way they used to be. An idea says it would be self-contained, for there was vertebrate and invertebrate, insect and mammal, vegetarian and carnivore, predator and prey. Most of the native species we knew were well represented. Small bugs and beetles, spiders of all descriptions, grasshoppers by the score, terrapins, toads, leopard frogs, snakes, voles, indigo buntings, mice and field rats. Rabbits were in profusion, foxes red and gray were present in one collection, with even an occasional weasel or deer. It was the only time I could ever expect to discover the combined fascinations of my boyhood in one place at one time.

My mentor and guardian for the associated happenings, as well as most other outdoor pursuits of the era, was my maternal uncle, Sidney Walker. A day began pre-dawn. I'd walk down the hill, run past the bridge the troll harbored under, double-time through the pines the big owl guarded, to my uncle's back steps. The yellow glow of the kitchen beckoned an ever-welcome and faithful haven from the intimidation of the dark. Over cereal and fruit, a morning ritual now 60-odd years on, my lead questions always concerned the present reliability of the combine. I had little tolerance for errant machinery, and the hateful thing was forever devastating me with broken belts, cracked conveyor slats, broken cross-shear teeth, or some inexplicable malady of its internals.

Uncle Sid was a craftsman. Whether it involved the intricate woodwork of an antique restoration or building a woodshed, he was meticulous. It carried over to his farming. Most of it was wasted on me at the time, I regret, for it all meant *slow*. By the time we made the equipment shed, well after daybreak, I had little appreciation for the ordered sequence of the work process, but a lot of understanding about what professional people now call occupational stress.

It was up in the morning, after the dew was off, when we'd finally get started. The metal flap on the exhaust stack of the big Case tractor sprang open with the initial, blue-fumed belch of engine ignition, then settled into a tinny dance in concert with the combustion rhythm. The old tag-along combine had little choice but to follow, disengaged but protesting, to a final shakedown fieldside.

Moody Hoover was our combine man, all six-and-a-half towering feet of him. When he swung his lanky frame onto the riding platform, the check was complete and the morning's work could begin.

Whup-boooh.

His hail to my uncle was the long-last signal when it seemed the day would be sacrificed to unending preparation. Hung with assorted weaponry, I'd scramble to my designated station beside the drop chute.

The forward lurch of the tractor started the shearing blades, and, as the first cut of the tawny stalks fell with the reel to the ribbed intake conveyor, the whole machine shook and vibrated itself to life with a deafening roar. Separated from the heads, the clean grain cascaded into the burlap bags waiting on the spreaders, and the mouthful that came from the first run was always sweetest. The dust grew in billows, grasshoppers rose in armies, and the air was pregnant with anticipation. All senses alerted, the vigil was on.

Fields were judged largely by size and the character of the crop. The big, dense fields were best as they offered additional shelter and harbored more game. Problem was, you had to cut them in one day, otherwise the cloak of darkness presented escape opportunity for the inhabitants. It was a personal tragedy when we engaged a big field mid-afternoon. The small fields could be cut quickly, which kept you on edge, but you saw less and the rabbits nearly always beat you to the woods.

The thing about cutting wheat was the farther you went, the better it got. The first several turns around a field didn't create a lot of excitement, cause all the residents simply migrated toward its center. But as you kept whittling away on the perimeter, the general population became reconciled through an increasing state of alarm to unavoidable departure. From then on the pace of the affair was torrid.

"Snake!"

It seemed the snakes were among the earliest refugees. A holler and beckon from the tractor brought me on the run. I was left to my own means with the shiny, black racers, big chicken snakes, the musky garters and possum-playing "puff-adders." These were usually pinned to the ground with a stick behind the head and captured alive to suffer integrated incarceration in a burlap sack, for tally and closer examination the end of the day. But the sinister, cat-eyed and pregnant-bodied copperheads commanded the attention of all parties. Barring breakdowns, it was the only time Uncle Sid stopped the tractor.

It was here the slingshots came into play, the vipers given no quarter. "They might show up later when you reach for a piece of lumber," Uncle Sid said, "or bite one of the dogs come fall."

If my eye was good, I'd send them into a writhing demise with a flattened head, in which case my stock and reputation was compounded considerably. If I missed, I endured the humiliation of watching Moody or Uncle Sid deal an undignified end to a respected foe with a whippy sapling. Whap. Whap. I always figured I owed them better than that. Either way, the hapless creature came to bag, later to be removed from its hide. The beautiful hourglass markings of the skin made for the prettiest kind of belt-cover or hatband, demanding no less respect among my peers than elk ivory among the Iroquois.

Then came the rabbits. Most of all, there were the rabbits . . . from the fragile young of the year to the grown bucks and does with the big, deep, liquid eyes, capable of expressing fear and hurt but never anger or threat. Watching closely, you could spy them when they first broke the wheat cover in front of the tractor and threw themselves into a desperate race for the sanctuary of the woods line. All year they had eluded me with their fleetness on fair terrain, but now the loose, layered straw countered the thrusts of those powerful hind legs and vengeance was mine. Finding their driving legs of little advantage, they became terrified when pursued and would eventually dart under a pile of leavings, lulled into false security. It was then I would stalk and pounce, bringing them struggling to hand. With the exuberance of a puppy, the joy of the chase unparalleled, I'd run them until I lay panting, cotton-mouthed and streaming in the steamy summer sun, waiting for my legs to hold me again – to resume once more.

We never harmed the rabbits. They were admired and petted awhile, and then released. With boyhood defiance, against my Uncle's counsel, I tried to keep some now and again. But I found quickly and harshly they are tender creatures, less the will to live. More than most wild things, they languish rapidly into a comatose state when robbed of freedom and soon will die. I had five in a box one time and they became so distraught they chewed each other's ears to the skull. They were just sitting there in complete depression, no longer beautiful and without dignity. I had to destroy them and the experience left me with very deep feelings for the value of freedom a long time before I ever studied the Constitution.

You expected the rabbits, but you could usually count on something more. We were making the last few rounds on a secluded field near a slab pile one morning when three young gray foxes fled the combine.

"Fox!" Moody yelled, and we both leaped off the combine and took in after them. One became so confused it laid down on top of the straw in the wide open field. I was strong for catching it alive, but Moody took to gathering rocks.

His daddy had chickens that fell victim to the foxes now and then, and like most farmers of the time, he grew up at war with Reynard. But Moody was excited and the fox would live for another day. He threw five rocks point blank, only to watch the fox clamber up, untouched, and bound away. Not altogether without my blessing.

Another time we saw two deer leave, which back then was an epiphany. I gave their story to my aunt later with much drama and importance. There was an Eastern diamondback that caused quite a stir, because we didn't see rattlesnakes very often. After dragging its carcass around on a stick for most of the day, I cut the rattlers off with the hawkbill and carried them handy for enforcing respect at opportune moments, particularly in Sunday school with the girls. And we nearly ran over a five-foot chicken snake that had caught a half-grown rabbit and was in the process of swallowing it. The lower jaw was unhinged and the neck skin so distended the white showed between the scales.

When the last swath of stalks no longer stood over the field, and the fat grain bags lay in pattern, marking the passing of the combine, I gathered up the BB gun, stuffed pockets with Red Top tubes, and disembarked upon the waning afternoon hours to foot-hunt in the ground cover. It was a grand safari, wholly my own, while Moody and Uncle Sid, bound with the shackles of responsibility, labored the harvest sacks onto the flatbed Chevy. The straw was alive with field rats and big lubber grasshoppers, and a brisk kick produced either a challenging ground target scurrying for fresh territory, or a fast, crossing wing-shot that demanded my best. Lead and follow-through were no strangers when I graduated to the shotgun the next year or so.

I took most of them fairly, but succumbed to the temptation of a sitting shot here and there. When you're nine, you ain't as old as you are later, and the ethics haven't kicked in. I shot the BB gun hot, counted coup unmercifully, and laid my assorted bag for unabashed display before my elders.

Whiling away the time so, it was rare I heard my uncle's first summons near nightfall, for I was in a land and place beyond his reach. We had endured a lot of geography that year, drilled into us in Mrs. Rice's fourth grade classroom. I would come to see much of it later and the dimensions of the world would change irretrievably.

But just then, for all its reported vastness, it lay totally within my grasp, within a 35-acre Carolina grainfield.

Chapter 5

Rock & Rye

Dust clouds lingered along the now empty street and the sun was a molten ogre in a brassy sky. There was cotton in my mouth and care in my step as I walked toward the livery stable at the edge of town. Somewhere behind me a horse nickered and, in the distance, a dog barked. I was a man adrift in a dangerous land, shortly to face death eye-to-eye with no one to back me. I carried a Winchester '73, and two short guns, one rigged for a Colorado cross-draw, the other under my waistband. Beads of sweat trickled down my forehead and tumbled down my face, leaving drunken tracks in the trail grime. I glanced ahead to the alley between the watering hole and the dry-goods emporium. The time was at hand.

The Durango Kid had stepped to the boardwalk from the alley, his back to the store-front. Like a wraith, he moved to a post under the porch, took a last drag on his cigarette and swung down into the dust. He was tall, lean and coarse, and the scar that was his trademark lay in proud flesh across his cheek. He was reputed to have gunned down 16 men by way of Texas, Arizona and New Mexico. He had been making bones about number 17 . . . my bones! We were 30 feet apart now. At this range, somebody was going to die. His right hand hung over the Colt in a tied-down holster.

"You've lived too long, Pike," he growled.

"If you think you can waltz," I spat back, "start the music."

He grinned and the fingers on his gun hand quivered.

Then Mama called.

I tried to ignore her, but it was no use. So that's the way it was. I had to back away from my set-to with The Kid, him standing there leering at me like I was a piece of dirt under his boot.

It must be a basic law of nature. Mammas always call at the wrong time. You can prospect around for hours undisturbed, but get in a good gunfight, corner the cat or draw a bead on the mockingbird, and it happens.

I ran to the house, agitated.

"Yeah. What do you want?" I snapped.

"Don't take that tone with me, young man."

"Yes-ma'am."

"Your Uncle Sidney is on the phone and wants to talk to you."

Impromptu calls from my uncle came rarely, were usually special. The Kid could wait.

"Hello," I said.

"Boy," my Uncle Sidney said, "you might ought to come over. We've got something to show you."

I didn't even ask. Whatever it was, I needed to see it. I shucked my guns in the middle of the floor and hit the screen door running, leaving it to slam hard against the frame. Mama yelled something at me, but it was lost in the wind. I ran down the hill and across the bridge where the trolls lived, and sprinted into the midst of the pines where the small frame house rested. The door was ajar and I hollered. From somewhere beyond my Aunt Louise beckoned me in.

They were on the living room floor, these two grown-up people that, fortunately for me, had never quite grown up. Between them were two black-and-tan hound pups, and maybe it was only June, but my eyes lit up like Christmas candles. The pups lifted their heads momentarily to question my presence, then the male returned to worrying my uncle's boot-straps, and the little female sank her teeth back into my aunt's dress hem.

"They're beautiful," I said wistfully. "Whose are they?"

I dropped to my knees and both pups came with a rush.

"Well," my uncle teased through a grin, "we thought maybe, if you approved, we might call 'em ours."

I shot a big smile back at him. "Then call 'em ours," I clamored.

The male pup had a broad head and muzzle, with good, wide paws under him and great, pendulous ears. He would make a big, strong dog. His chest would be deep, and his wind would be long, and he would have a deep, rolling bawl that would reverberate off the hills and echo through the hollows. But for now he was busy washing my face. The female was petite, with bottomless hazel eyes and clean features. She would be lithe and lean, with staying quality. She was sitting there, looking at me with those eyes, stealing my heart.

"Course you'll have to help take care of 'em, and help train 'em," Uncle Sid continued. "With a little luck, we might make a pair of decent coon and possum dogs out of 'em. Come October, we'll see."

We named them Rock and Rye.

I rounded the corner of the house in an extended gallop, a green coon hide kicking up dust behind me, and ran full-throttle into a gaggle of chickens. In a wild scramble and tumultuous din of squawks and cackles, a riot of ponderously flapping poultry beat it for the safety of the mulberry tree and the smokehouse roof. All save one fussy, old, red hen. She dawdled just long enough for me to arrive, gathered up her petticoats, and clamored right in under my feet. We piled up in a cloud of dust and feathers, and the last thing I saw before I hit the ground was a monstrous load of fresh chicken manure, all heaped up and twirled at the top like soft-serve ice cream. When I got up, I had a big gooey mess on the front of my shirt and my knee was bleeding. I would have wrung the old biddy's neck, but I couldn't tarry.

"Here, Jughead!" my Uncle Sid had said, with a twinkle in his eye. He called me that sometimes after the cartoon character in Snuffy Smith. He had Rock and Rye on a double-snap leash. He had teased them with the coon hide and they were going crazy.

"Tie this rope to your belt. Drag that hide around the house and down the branch a-ways. Leave it up a tree where the dogs can't reach it. Hurry back now, but don't come the same way."

So, I left the red hen for another time and ran on down the branch. I found a small poplar with a bare trunk and limbs starting about eight feet up. I dragged the hide to the base of the tree and rubbed it on the trunk far as I could reach. Then I shinnied up, pulled the rope over the lowest limb and tied it off. The coon hide dangled enticingly. All set, I raced back.

My uncle took an appraising look at me when I came up and kinda smiled. The chickens were still raising Cain in the back yard. The pups were six months old now and three-quarters grown. They had reached a frenzy and were lunging hard against the leash.

"Alright, dogs," Uncle Sid said, rubbing each in turn. He unsnapped the leash. "Get 'em!"

"Both dogs tore out for the corner of the house, us in behind. Uncle Sid let out a loud squall. "_WHOOAAGGH!_ Git 'em, dogs!"

The dogs were giving tongue as they rounded the house. Then suddenly they went quiet. When we got there, they had their noses to the ground. They had reached the point of the chicken collision and trying to untangle the trail. After a minute, Rock picked up the scent and announced to the world in a long, throaty bawl. Rye bayed tentatively a time or two, then fell in with her mate in a series of high-pitched yelps. You would have thought somebody was wailing the daylights out of her. Away again they flew down the branch.

Uncle Sid and I looked at each other and grinned. *"Whoooaaggh!"* I yelled. And we took out running.

When we got to the poplar, Rock was fussing about on my return trail, confused with the loss of the ground scent. But little Rye was trying to climb the tree. She had found the dangling hide and meant to have it. The poplar was almost vertical, but she'd get a running start and try to run up the trunk. Her jaws were missing their mark by mere inches. When she fell back, she fell hard. But she was right back up, barking every breath in a steady chop.

Uncle Sid called Rock in and grabbed Rye by the collar while I climbed the tree. Then he turned the dogs loose again.

"Shake that hide and blow that squaller," he ordered.

Rock saw the hide jump and went berserk. Rye was standing on the tree, whining and growling.

"Throw it down," my uncle said.

It never hit the ground. The dogs growled fiercely as it fell and lunged for it, grabbing it in mid-air. Uncle Sid let them fight and worry it for a few minutes, then took it away and put it in a sack, out of sight. We made much of both pups, praising them in encouraging words.

"They're a-comin' on," Uncle Sid said. "We'll borrow that pet coon of Sheriff Mason's a time er two, and repeat this with him, 'cept we won't kick him out. Then we'll take 'em to the woods."

September was near, and school, and I was dreading that. But you can endure most anything as long as you've got a little something to look forward to. Close behind September would be October, and then November, the best month of the year. It would bring clear, crisp nights and the Harvest Moon, and the coons would walk. And we'd be there, Uncle Sid and me, with ol' Rock and little Rye. I was shivering, and it wasn't cold at all.

The autumn moon was on the make and it bathed the woods in a sort of eerie, perpetual twilight. There was a chill in the night and you could see your breath on the air. The sky was clear as a wishing well and the stars sparkled across the heavens like a thousand diamonds thrown by wistful sweethearts.

We stood on Buzzard Rock on Taylor's Creek, uncle Sid and me, listening. Deep down the Wooliever Hollow, a hound dog was bawling, in long, sorrowful notes that lingered mournfully in the dark like lost souls begging salvation.

"We'd better get in after them," Uncle Sid said. "Rye's already out o' hearin'."

Off the rock and down the hollow we ran, through the clawing cat-brier and alder thickets. I fell off a log into the branch and skinned my chin. Later, I caught a rebounding limb across the face. It left a big, ugly welt that looked mean in the lantern light. But I was so excited I hardly noticed. After a while, we left the branch run and climbed to the top of the hill that stood east of the sprawling cornfield bottom. Pausing, we caught our breath and listened again.

The coon had turned up the bottom and the dogs were hot in after him. The tempo of their music was quicker now, and steady. They were telling the news and moving on fast.

Taking out after them again, Uncle Sid fell into a stump hole up to his knee and hit the ground with a grunt. But he was right back up and running before I could ask if was he alright. Ahead, we could hear the all-out urgency of the dogs. They were in full cry, givin' Br'er Coon what for. Rye was wailing like a tormented banshee.

"*WHOOOAGGHEE!* Talk to me, dogs," my uncle hollered.

He turned to me. "Won't be long now," he shouted. "They've got his address."

About that time the dogs barked tree, and the hair stood up on the back of my neck.

"*Yaaooahh!* I hollered and left out.

The dogs sounded about 200 yards up the bottom and I was dodging stumps, ducking limbs, and bouncing off trees in a mad rush to get there. I could hear limbs rattling and sticks breaking, and I knew my uncle was hard in behind me. The dogs were barking incessantly, in staccato chops.

The dogs had set down on a massive gum tree behind Clement Luck's pond. They said he was here, and no gripes about it. It was hard to understand how they could chop that way and still breathe. I felt like barking too, and probably would have, but along then uncle Sid burst onto the scene.

He said something about the biggest gum tree in Randolph County, but I couldn't get it all over the racket the dogs were making. Better a gum, I thought, than an oak with a bunch of leaves. I knew about those big oaks. They kept most their leaves until December and were usually full of hollows.

The lantern lit up a little arena around the great trunk of the gum. In its faint illumination, the dogs looked demonic, jumping and snapping out of the night. Above the small circle of light, it was pitch black. Uncle Sid unlimbered the long, seven-cell flashlight from its shoulder sling. He pointed it up in the gum tree and pushed the switch. The brilliant beam lanced the darkness and the lower limbs of the giant gum stood starkly white in the reflected light. Bright as it was, it faded considerable in the upper reaches of the tree. Uncle Sid backed away and began slowly circling. We were straining to see shining eyes. The dogs were choppin' high cotton.

In the very top of the tree, barely visible in the fading beam of the flashlight, was a dark lump on the trunk that might be a coon. But if it was, he wasn't in any hurry for us to know it.

"Cut loose with that squaller," Uncle Sid said. I hit it a time or two. Whatever was up there didn't move. We eased around the tree a bit more.

"Hit it again, like you mean it," my uncle yelled. He hollered at the dogs to keep them high. He didn't need to. I laid down hard on the squaller that time, and it sounded like the meanest varmint in three counties. On its dying note, two burning eyes lit up in the lump in the top of the gum.

"WHHOOOAAAGGHH!" Uncle Sid squalled. "There he is, boy." I was feeding cartridges into the tube of the little Remington Sportsmaster, and I was so excited I dropped half of them on the ground.

"Take a rest on a limb, now, and take your time."

I moved around until I had a shot at the lump in the tree and propped the barrel over a dogwood branch. I was trying to get the sights lined up, but I was shaking and they kept dancing around as if they harbored a mind of their own. I tried to squeeze off a shot, but I knew it was wild when I pulled the trigger. The sound of the gun sent the dogs into a renewed fury. I missed twice more.

Uncle Sid smiled, with a half laugh. "Settle down, boy, these dogs are dependin' on you."

Mustering my resolve, I took a deep breath, let out half, and settled back under the gun. I waited until the sights quit jumping and squeezed the trigger. The crack of the rifle was instantly followed by a hollow thud. For a moment, it seemed I had missed again. Then the lump in the tree unfolded into a coon and bailed out, catching limbs momentarily on the way down and falling among the frenzied dogs. There was a frightening minute of fierce fighting. Rock yelped and jumped back. His ear was torn and his muzzle was bloody. He shook his head, snarling and biting at the air, and the blood flew. Then he tore back into the fray. Rye had a death grip and was shaking the coon like a rag doll. Then both dogs clamped down for keeps and the coon was quickly finished. We pulled them off. The fight was draining out of them, but they were still whining.

Uncle Sid picked the coon up by a hind leg, held it aloft for inspection. It was a big boar, maybe 15 or 16 pounds. He handed him to me. I admired him for a while, then dropped him in the sack my uncle held open. The hide would fetch a half-dollar or so, and I would be back in ammunition for the .22, which was always my foremost concern.

Uncle Sid slung the sack over his shoulder and we cast the dogs off anew. We treed two more coons before midnight, took one, and left the other in the tree. Along about one o'clock in the new morning, we passed a muscadine vine and stopped to rest. Uncle Sid showed me how to dig around under the leaves and find a few lingering grapes, somehow overlooked by the forest creatures and now all shriveled and mellowed by the recent frost. Insulated under the damp leaf cover, they were deliciously cool and burst all sugary sweet in my mouth.

The dogs struck again shortly afterward, and ran strong for an hour, but then trailed off and never treed. Uncle Sid took the hunting horn from his belt and blew them in.

"It's been a good night," he said. "No use overdoin' it." Another time I might have argued, but I was getting tired and sleepy.

Our hunting round had taken us to the Hale Place bottoms and not far away was a mossy knob overhanging a quiet, secluded pool on the creek. We made our way there and Uncle Sid raked back the leaves and built a small fire, while the dogs and I sank exhausted onto the leaf-mottled carpet of moss. He pulled a wrinkled, little brown sack from the pocket of his jacket and poured out a handful of popcorn. He dropped it into the pan of an old, blackened wire popper from his game pocket, along with some butter he had scraped with his knife from a wadded up piece of wax paper. From another little roll of paper he sprinkled in a measure of salt. Then he settled back on his elbow and held the pan of the popper over the fire, moving it back and forth now and again to keep the corn from sticking. My eyes were heavy and the rhythm of his motion in the fire-glow lulled me into a trance.

After a few minutes there was a half-hearted sputter from the pan of the popper, and a few seconds later a muffled thump. Then another, heavier, thump and another. Soon the thumping had increased, rising in cadence until the popping of the individual kernels became indistinguishable. The fluffy, white popcorn swelled against the screen lid. Its aroma was sweet and enticing. Uncle Sid opened the lid and sat the popper between us. The first mouthful was so good it made my mouth hurt.

We ate slowly, savoring it kernel by kernel, talking of the night's events and studying the pulsating coals of the dying fire. Below, the silvery reflection of the moon rested on its back on the placid surface of the pool and overhead the constellations were boldly drawn against the sky. I lay on my back looking for Orion – the mythical hunter, whom Diana had loved but accidentally killed and placed in the heavens forever. My aunt had told me the story, and it was one I liked. I felt the kinship, for I was a hunter too.

Rye lay close beside me, her muzzle on my leg, and Rock lay close by her, his big head in the hollow of her flank. My uncle was a comforting presence a few feet away. I felt good all over. Then I drifted off to sleep.

We woke near dawn and in the gathering of day, walked at leisure toward the Coble House, our point of departure the night before. The dogs were in front, content to stay close and travel at a comfortable pace. Uncle Sid followed, the sack with the two coons carried loosely across his shoulder, and I brought up the rear with the rifle resting muzzle down over my forearm.

As we neared the house, my uncle hesitated mid-stride, and I almost ran into him. He turned and looked at me. Then he smiled, and handed me the sack from his shoulder. "Here, Jughead, you carry this and walk in front with the dogs."

I shifted the rifle to my left hand and heaved the sack over my right shoulder. The heft of the coons felt good on my back. I saw my Aunt Louise standing on the front porch. She would see the sack and ask for the story. I could feel the pride swelling.

She was waiting with a cup in each hand, the steam from the freshly brewed coffee lifting gently into the chilly morning air.

We still went occasionally, but it was not the same. In the song of the November nights, the high notes were missing. We had lost little Rye to distemper the year before, and were reminded each time of the lingering sadness. Rock felt it too. He often lay listlessly in his kennel, a look of loneliness in his eyes. Sometimes I would hear him from my bed deep in the night, baying slowly and mournfully for hours. His spirits would rebound when we took him to the woods and the long strains of his soulful bawl would roll down the sprawling bottoms as before. But it was difficult to rekindle the life of the hunt, for now it seemed more like a eulogy.

The world pushed me on. I survived Mrs. Lancaster's tenth grade Latin class, and Ruby McCallister's advanced algebra exam, and left for college. The first autumn was hard. When it wore into November, I would often sit at my desk in the dorm in the small hours of the morning, sick with thoughts of home, longing for the things I had left behind. For a while, I would succeed in transcending the present, and my spirit would wander back to the Uwharrie woods to join others that must be waiting there.

Gradually, the loneliness was forced aside as I fell into the rigors of an education. By my junior year, other corridors of life had opened to me, and I was plunging ahead with concern for little other than the present and the future. The geography might have been the same, but the distance to home had grown considerably. So what happened that February night, I was not expecting. I had studied at the campus library until midnight and was late returning to the dorm. It was a dreary evening. Fog loitered along the streets and sidewalks, and gathered around the street lamps in faint halos. An icy drizzle was falling, and the wet barren limbs of the oaks and elms glistened coldly in the refracted light. I opened the door and stepped inside the warm dormitory.

As an afterthought, I decided to check the mail before I retired. Stuffed into my narrow postal box was a lumpy, manila envelope, soiled and worn from its journey. On its face in fading handscript, it bore my name. My eyes jumped to the return address. It read Sidney Walker. It was from my uncle. It had been several months since I had seen him. It hit me that this was the first written message I had ever received from him. Premonition tightened my throat as I opened the envelope. Inside were two leather dog collars, one well field-worn, the other blackened and smooth with age. There was a slip of paper, torn from a yellow, ruled pad. On it were a few scribbled lines. I got no further than the salutation, which read, "Dear Jughead,"

It had been a long time, and the emotions came cascading back like water down a dry branch after a summer storm. I left the dorm and went back out into the rain and the cold. It was where I belonged. I crossed to the city park and sat under an oak tree. Big, cold drops of rain dropped spasmodically from its limbs, on my shoulders and down my neck. It didn't matter . . . it really didn't matter at all. After a few minutes had passed, I pulled the dampened slip of paper from the sodden envelope once more.

"Dear Jughead,

"Old Rock died yesterday. We buried him under the moss by the spring run, alongside Rye. Your Aunt Louise etched an inscription for them both on a scrap of copper. It should weather nicely. You'll have to see it when you come.

"I thought you might want their collars to keep as you grow older.

"Love,

"Your Uncle Sid"

I was rummaging around among some old record albums recently and found a long-playing 33 cut by a singer named Paul Ott some years back for the National Wildlife Federation. One of the songs on the label was *Ol' Blue*, a venerable country ballad about a coonhound. I wiped the dust off the record, put it on the turntable and sang along.

I had an ol' dog, and his name was Blue,
Bet-cha five dollars he's a good'un too.

I had forgotten how good Ott's version was, and I was enjoying it again, immensely.

Many and a-many of an early morn,
I've heard Ol' Blue a-runnin' thru the corn,
Good Ol' Blue, you're a good dog, you.

In the background, there's a coon dog a-bawling, and some banjo and guitar accompaniment. But it's that lonesome coonhound, bawlin' his very soul out on the ground, that makes the song.

O" Blue he died, and he died so hard,
He shook the ground in my back yard.
An' I dug his grave with a silver spade,
An' laid him down with a silver chain.
Dear Ol' Blue, you're a good dog, you . . .
I'm a comin' there too, I'm a comin' there too.

Whenever I hear that tune I'm reminded of Rock and Rye. You could substitute either for Ol' Blue, and it might not rhyme, but the song would still work. I was 12 years old that night we stopped on the knob over the creek at the Hale Place and popped corn, and slept in the leaves with the dogs until dawn . . . and my Uncle Sid was almost 50. The years have slipped by. Uncle Sid's gone along to join the dogs, and I reckon they're all treed by now under some big gum in the Bottom of the Ages.

Hang on, you . . . I'm a comin' there too.

Chapter 6

Only Girls and Grown-Ups Grumbled in July

Summer came in a rush that year. Spring blushed
past and suddenly it was July. The sun grew more
oppressive with each new morning and soon the heat
monkeys were dancing feverishly at the bottom of a
hazy blue sky.

Folks talked constantly of it during the day and
suffered with it at night. It rivaled the worst of Dog-
days and you lay sweating in bed against sticky sheets in the unending,
stifling stillness of it. It was blackberry time in Randolph County
and aggravated chigger bites from early morning forays added to the
torment, stinging like mischief from the sweat. A washbowl and a wet
cloth for moping hot foreheads became a bedside mainstay, but relief
was elusive in those forever hours between midnight and dawn.

For the grown-ups there was little escape. Maybe a few stolen
moments under the shade of a maple tree, but there was livelihood
to be won and always a thing to be done. Decency in those days
demanded more of adults in attire than now and there wasn't a lot

that could be shed. The girls had the same problem, cause once they got past six or so, the buds blossomed and bare chests were no longer proper. One of the blessings of boyhood was freedom from such convention. We promptly stripped to cut-off pants, less when out of sight, and relegated hard-soled shoes to the hall closet.

For us, the curtain was rising on another joyous season, and we answered it almost instinctively. The shaded coolness, damp earth and meandering creeks of the bottomlands were beckoning.

We were country boys, by spirit if not altogether by location. Our main haunt was Taylor's Creek, from the southwest corner of Billy Walker's farm to the Union Church Bridge. Its enticing flow coursed our most favored spots. There was the big pool below the Coble House, where most of us learned to swim, the rapids and the large rock with the cedar tree growing out of it at the Hale Place. There was the fiord at Uncle Manly's where we wallowed across with the jeeps on wild night-rides, the Flat Rock stretch and the fishing hole above the church. Each was unique in its own right, but similar in attraction, a place to amortize time into something special.

From first light until the screech owls began their eerie whisperings we followed our every whim, never at a loss for excitement.

That was the summer we started the grist mill on the tailrace of the Hale Place "rapids." That is, we carved waterwheels from ash and dogwood as my uncle had shown us and set them in the three narrows of the terminal chute. They were fun to make. You took your pocketknife and carved five or six flat blades and notched them so they'd lock together in the center. Then you cut the axle from a good straight limb, and slit it in the middle so you could push the blades through with a tight fit. The axle rode forked sticks on grooves that kept it laying true when you propped it in the rocks at the right height. It took some doing sometimes, but when you got things right the little wheel would virtually sing. We had all three right just one time, as I remember. We set up some accompanying machinery on the axle ends, built a mill house out of mud and sticks, and christened her the Walker-Gaddis-McCombs Feed and Flour Company.

We cut access roads into the banks of the creek and added a loading dock. Took orders and set up a delivery route. "Grist" we hauled from an upstream sandbar after building a trammel bridge over an intervening tributary. It might not have been recognizable to just anybody, but it was a thriving enterprise for about a week. Then one evening a bad thunderstorm washed the whole thing off to oblivion. There was no trace the next morning. We figured it ended up somewhere below the Union Church Bridge. It was a bitter loss, but a valuable lesson. Profit's usually a matter of margin.

We spent other happy hours on that same stretch of fast water. During our fall wanderings we gathered the seed husks from the trumpet vine, squirreling them away in the house somewhere for winter. Shaped like dug-out canoes, they made the finest kind of racing craft when dried. Usually on a challenge, we'd start them at the head of the run and see whose canoe got to the bottom first. Each man was allowed a stick for navigation purposes, and its indiscriminate use brought clamors of protest from the balance of the field. It was a precarious trip amid the rocks and swampings were common. Or you'd get caught in an eddy, going nowhere while the others shot by on the mainstream current. We had special rules for that, so you wouldn't fall completely out of the race. But it cost you in time and you had to count on an equal calamity with the opposition to stage a comeback. You lost more than you won and somebody usually slipped off a rock and busted his noggin. For sheer excitement, it was tough to beat.

Near midday, we'd often follow the spring run below Uncle Manly's to the deep, cool pond at its head. Cherished as all springs were, it was neatly rocked and covered, with a speckled tin dipper hanging by on a nail. The water was pure ecstasy on a hot day. Clean, clear, tooth-numbing cold.

There was a wooden spring box in a trough below the head pool, where the cold water could flow through. Along with a fresh milking, there'd be a few summer apples, all firm and chilled. He would leave them there, knowing we would come. Junes or Pippins, the flesh so crisp it would pop when you bit into it. Crawfish, mud puppies and dusky salamanders were regular occupants, as well. We usually rounded up an old fruit jar and left with an assortment.

There was a leopard frog that lived there, too. Leopard frogs were rare. Bullfrogs and toads were good sport, but a leopard frog was a quest. We tried everything we could to catch him, given the sanctity of his domain. But spring holes were to be unmolested. It was one whipping you couldn't beg out of. The leopard frog took our full measure and we could never catch him. He taunted us unmercifully each visit, until we could take it no more. One day we took the BB guns and got him, but the lifeless form in hand was a hollow victory. We wished him back almost immediately and faced our abysmal incapacity to do so. Being boys, we didn't dwell on it, but trips there weren't the same afterward and we knew we had cheated ourselves of something even more valuable than the frog.

Afternoons were for fishing. Years since, I've fished fresh and salt, from the Florida Keys to the smallmouth streams of Maine, the salmon waters of the Bonaventure to the Madison and Yellowstone of Montana, with a lot of stops between. There's a lot of excitement out there, but nothing more delightful, I believe, than the hours we wiled away lying on the bank of Taylor's Creek a short trek from home, waiting for a six-ounce sunfish to take a cork to ride on the lazy, brown surface waters of a hole you couldn't guess the bottom of. Maybe it was relatively the same, and the difference is in time and dimension, and I am the one who has changed, for I find it difficult today to find that same freshet feeling. Then, it seems, the world was sufficiently vast to permit escape, vibrant with new discovery, scarce the constant dilemma of choice between renaissance and responsibility.

Be that as it may, it is a sweet memory that below the fiord and beyond the rock dam at Uncle Manly's was a long, deep pool some 200 yards in length. Its intrigue and promise as a fishing destination was long-since anchored by both appearance and reputation. It was said Joel Ashworth had caught a five-pound chub within its reaches one time or another, and had seen larger. While we never came close to rivaling that, I can attest it was a peach of a bream hole, and we came to love it. Robins, yellow-bellies, green-ears and fliers were common, and we were about as happy with the horny-head suckers, yellow bullheads and snapping turtles that rounded out the catch.

Fishing then was a lot simpler than now. You could walk into any country store and come out fully equipped for 35 cents. There'd be a hank of line, a cork-stopper, a long-shank #10 hook, and a split-shot to anchor it down, all neatly wrapped around a little green wooden frame with the hook run back into the cork so you didn't need to worry about it when you put it in your pocket. You could buy a few extra hooks for a nickel, and along then Pfleuger was packing them in a little wooden cylinder about two inches long that you could carry a few BBs in once the fishing was gone. Store-bought poles were unheard of. When we got ready to fish we cut one out of the woods, of ash or hickory. And if you got a particularly good one with just the right backbone, you carved your initials in it and hid it somewhere you could find it again.

We fought granny's rooster and the local wasps for bait. The rich damp dirt of the chicken lot was home for juicy, gray earthworms big as a pencil and an occasional wiggler. The wasp nest larvae were unbeatable as bream bait though they often cost a sting or two and were the devil to keep on a hook. You carried them in the nest and peeled back one compartment at a time to get at the fat grubs inside.

About two o'clock, we'd nestle into a well-chosen spot along the bank somewhere amongst the green ferns and the poison ivy (don't recall we ever worried about it), thread a worm and drop her in. We'd move it around a little now and then and anticipation rode every jiggle of the cork. If a dragonfly lit on your set, it was best luck.

It was easy to fool yourself. You'd get lulled off, twitch and brush the line; the cork would jump and you'd all but fall in, trying to grab the pole. All for naught. What you hoped for was to see it bob right good a time or so, then set sail clean out of sight. When that happened, you were almost sure of hooking a pretty decent fish. But most of the time we were hoodwinked by the little stuff you could never catch.

Once in a while we would manage something spectacular. Richard McCombs caught a three-pound catfish one evening after a big rain and I had a bass that fell off just before I got him in. We took turns fighting an immense snapping turtle to a standstill and then didn't know what to do with him. He broke off while we were trying to decide.

We didn't get to ponds much on our own. There were some around, but we were warned away from them – the grown folks figuring we would manage to fall in and drown – all the more reason to go, but there was the thing of getting there. There was no denying the attraction of the bigger waters. Though we often did no better than on our creek holes, the ponds were inaccessible and therefore uncharted and promiscuous.

One sultry afternoon in August Aunt Louise and Uncle Sidney took me to Danny Bell's pond. It was only an acre or so, vast and mysterious. I got to use a cane pole for the first time that trip and thought I had truly arrived. We started near the corner of the dam, a spot I have favored on any pond since. I shook up the worms in the can, found the biggest, fattest one I could, and threaded him on carefully so the hook didn't show. There was a log lying about ten feet from the bank and I dropped my hopes close beside it.

The cork had hardly come to rest when it popped under one time, surfaced, popped again, then left for good. I jerked hard and the little cane bent to the water. The line sang as it zipped sideways and whatever was on the fighting end was looking for the bottom of the pond.

I was trying as hard as I could to pull the fish up – yelling and crying the same time – and couldn't. My aunt and uncle came on the run, got caught up in the excitement and shouted orders, but I was doing all I could. Nothing I had encountered on the creek held a candle to the behemoth that trying to wrestle me under the log. My arms and wrists were aching, and my legs were weak. From fright so much as fight. Fortunately, about then the fish was tiring too, and I began to gain line. Encouraged, I put my whole body into the effort and heaved him out on the dam.

There, against the green grass, speckled yellow, orange, purple and red, the iridescence sparkling under the afternoon sun, lay the sunfish to end all sunfishes. He looked big as a softball glove! I was flushed, hot, and trembling as I picked him up. He was bigger than my uncle's double handspread. It was a shellcracker, about 24 ounces worth, the biggest any of us had ever caught. Including the grown-ups. My spirits soared as high as the nighthawks riding the evening breezes. I put him in a bucket of water to keep him alive and we took him to my uncle's pond at the Coble Place where I turned him loose.

"That way," my uncle said, "you'll catch him again someday."

For years I tried, but never did. I was a long time adopting catch-and-release. But it was hopeful, knowing that, somewhere, he was there.

The Coble Place pond was the locus of another discovery that August. It had bullfrogs galore and we spent hours trying to capture them. With slender success. Until we learned a trick that was their total undoing.

It happened quite by accident, really. My brother Joe, Don and Stanley Avent and I were fishing. Things were slow, so we had turned to frogs to fill the cracks between bites. In the horseplay and confusion that always accompanied such aspirations, Stanley got his hook caught in my brother's new red shirt. Mama had just bought it for him, from Woolworth's in Greensboro, for the considerable sum of three dollars. Fearing a reprimand, we worked hard to free it without damage to Joe or the shirt. Failing, it became necessary to amputate – the shirt, that is. I managed it with my pocketknife, but also whacked loose a small piece of cloth that stayed with the hook.

Shortly afterwards, Stan got within pole range of Ole-Under-The-Root and was trying to snag him with the hook. He didn't have to. The frog took one gander at the dancing bit of red cloth and lolloped it in.

"Whoo-haw." Stanley let out a victory-whoop, and from there it was on. We sacrificed another bold swath of brother's shirt, Hattie hang the consequences.

It was too good to be true. You could sneak up on a frog on a pad, squatting like a green Buddha on a throne, dangle the cloth a few inches from his nose, and *loll-up,* he'd lick it up like hard candy. First, he'd shift a little for a better look, then cock his head, studying it a moment. Then *zzziittt,* the tongue would shoot out and he'd nab it. Setting the hook was pure reflex. There wasn't a lot you could say about their fighting ability, but they were game through and through. We caught some real giants, and for the spatter in the frying pan that evening, we defrayed the price of a wailing.

I had the duel with the two big snakes at the Coble Place bridge that year. We stopped to get the tractor a drink one day and my uncle spotted one of them lying on the rocks sunning. It was the biggest of its kind we had ever seen. Snakes held a fascination nothing else mustered. This one was about four feet, heavy, dark and blunt.

"The bad kind," my uncle said.

I know now it was a brown water snake, surely one of the biggest I've seen in a lifetime around the water. Belligerent, but non-poisonous, water snakes often developed viper-like bodies as they aged, turning dark-brown so their normally distinctive markings became blurred and mottled. So cursed, they suffered the misfortune of being mistaken for the cottonmouth and were persecuted. We made the same mistake, or maybe my uncle knew and embellished it for me as he did everything outdoors. Regardless, the challenge was chilling.

For the next three weeks I staged assaults with the little Remington Sportsmaster, morning and afternoon, often three and four times a day. My uncle was farming and I'd get up early to ride with him. A little after dawn he'd ease the truck to a stop on the hill above the creek and wait whilst I picked my way to the bridge, my nerves strung like banjo strings. Later, I'd sneak down from where we were working on the other side, or along the creek bank from one direction or the other, hoping to catch the big reptile unaware.

I saw him several times the first week. He'd be draped over an alder sprout along the creek or sunning on the rocks where first we'd seen him. About the time I'd spot him, he'd do as well, sliding off into the water and leaving no chance for a shot. Or I'd hear a heavy plop in the water or maybe he wouldn't be there at all, and I'd know he'd outfoxed me again.

I ended his reign one afternoon when things fell to my favor. Normally, the heavy base of crushed flint on the road made a stalk from that vantage hopeless. It would roll under your feet at the worst possible time, grating an alert. But a thundercloud the hour before had left it soaked and muffled. I tiptoed my way to the first plank of the bridge and held my breath while I studied the limbs over the creek. I made him out among the leaves after a time, first the fat, dark body and then his head. I squeezed the rifle off like I'd been taught and it was a one-shot affair. We fished him out and carried him in for all to see.

Only a week later a second snake took up residence in the same place. I wonder now if we weren't seeing two snakes all along, just never together, for they were identical in size and threat. Illogical maybe, but it was unusual for one big snake to show up so soon after the demise of another.

For more than a month this one thwarted my every attempt. I'd never hunted anything more wary, not even the gray fox that had raided granny's chickens. I got a shot one time late in the siege, but he had me so unnerved I missed. A matter of pride, it troubled me for days. Nothing worked. I contrived plan after plan and each one came undone in the execution. Then one night the name of Paul Revere came up somehow – one by land, two by sea – and in the moment I had the answer.

This time I would slip into the creek above the bridge and wade. The water approach would be unexpected. He'd be listening for the rocks to grate on the road or a bush to rustle, or watching for a movement along the bank. I'd catch him in his element. Shivering at the thought of success, I lay sleepless until morning.

The next day near noon I walked the soft new-ground below the granary to the creek bottom. The sodden earth soaked up my footfall. About a hundred yards above the bridge I slowly worked a cartridge into the chamber of the Remington and flipped the safety. Grabbing an overhanging branch, I eased myself into the water, careful to a ripple. Feeling my way through the rocks, I shuffled along to the bridge pool. Hours, it seemed, it took to get there, and my heart was pounding under the sweated cotton shirt on my chest. Inching along with frequent stops, I searched with all my might – every limb, every foot of bank. Tension tightened like you'd tickled a guitar string. Finally I reached the bridge itself and still I had seen nothing.

It was deathly quiet. I stood listening. There was only the muted gurgle of the creek.

It was then I felt it. The hot prickle of apprehension. And my eyes met his. His big head was thrust out of the water from a pocket of the bank five feet from my right foot. He had been watching me. His tongue beat a rhythmic threat. The hair rose in a bristle on my neck and I was afraid to blink. I was afraid even to breathe. My throat got dry and my eyes watered. He shifted slightly, the head swaying. Edging closer. I felt weak. I thought about help but there wasn't any. And I had another problem. I was right-handed, would have to shoot from my left side. I wasn't real good at it.

It took forever to get the rifle up, by inches, when anxiety pleaded for me to bring it up quickly, like a shotgun, and just shoot. But I did it, while we stared at each other in a time warp. The sights blurred in my left eye. I kept seeing two beads and they were dancing uncontrollably. I held as close as I could and squeezed. The water exploded with the impact of the long rifle and it took a few seconds to clear. When it did, I saw the heavy brown body oozing out of the bank toward me. A chill played the length of my spine and I jacked the bolt to throw in a fresh cartridge. Then I realized. The movement was involuntary, a death reflex. For there was a gaping white wound in his head, the blood diffusing gauzy and red into the yellow water. I had ended it.

My knees were like rubber. I was sweating and nauseous. I climbed out and collapsed to a rock, and sat for a long time looking at the big snake lying there in the creek. It was the first time in my life I had known blood-thickening fear and I would not soon forget it. It would be 47 years and a lot of miles later, when I saw my first Cape buffalo at 15 paces, that it would be repeated.

More than any other I can remember, that summer was a peerless collage of adventure, beginning to end. Would that it never had to end. But August wore into the first days of September and abruptly, we were facing school again.

We ended the season with a wienie roast. On the creek, of course, at the big pool below the Coble House. The whole family was there, family by blood or friendship. While the grown-ups built the fire and palavered, we young'ns scouted the woods for roasting sticks. The two-pronged ones were all right, but you tried for three. When marshmallow time came, you would be ahead. We caught mussels from the creek and we went swimming for the last time as free agents. Tommy's mama had to burn a leech off a delicate spot with a cigarette and the kidding he took was worse than the blood-letting. Everybody got tired after a while and settled in close to the fire. We ate and sat around and told stories way past dark, watching the coals smolder in the growing stillness. Somewhere down the creek, on the cool, clear air, a big owl whooped.

It was Sunday and there's a gnawing loneliness in a Sunday. We felt it, young and old alike, glad to be together, to stave it off for a few hours. I had to start the sixth grade the next day. We would listen to Mrs. Lancaster tell us not to talk or look out the window, to sit up straight, and to march in a straight line. While she suffered to instruct us in conduct, history and arithmetic. I thought about the big owl down the creek. I thought about the leopard frog and the shellcracker and the two big snakes at the bridge. I thought about all I had felt, and all I had done.

And I doubted there was a thing she could teach us more valuable than what we already had learned.

Chapter 7

Comin' Up With Bob

T he Lord's own symphony," Grandma Betts would say, "in the miracle of two notes."

He was the concerto of spring, the sonnet of summer, and in November when the opus fell to the vesper of a covey-call, the sonata of fall.

He was family before I ever hunted him. A brother now and then. Folks were still War-worn and Depression poor. What humble earthly possessions they enjoyed were largely Heaven-sent, the product of a God-fearing persistence and existential toil. Of the modest few things that afforded them pleasure, none was more beloved than a Bob and a covey of quail. Most everybody had one. Little homebodies that were hip-pocket kin, that eked a mutual living from the small garden plot at the stoop of the woods, that abided in the honeysuckle corner of a split-rail fence, or resided in the blackberry briers at the make of the corn rows. Unlike the field bevies that harbored in the ragweed fallow of the small, quilt-work farms, they were never hunted. Without a word of barter, it was principle, understood and respected. Old horses carried yet the scars of the Civil War, banishing ever again the discord of blood-agin' blood. He and his small tribe were family, and family was to be protected – nurtured and sheltered – held to the heart.

We'd rock on the porch in the late-afternoon, near evening, after the sun bade quitting time. There'd be a golden wash over the meadows, yellow sunflowers on the hillside that stepped to the creek, a blue haze on the cap of Burkhead Mountain. The air would be warm and liquid mellow, the breeze mostly spent, the farm shushed to quiet. Granny would be humming softly and shelling peas; granpa drawing on his pipe, mending in his lap the dilapidated harness the mules wore. I'd be sunburned from a day-long odyssey on the creek, puckered in places from giddy hours of dog-paddling the swimming hole, tuckered from the scamper of my spirit.

He'd join us about then. From the edge of the garden his little song would rise onto the prayerful respite between done-and-dusk like Gabriel's Horn, collecting each of us in the space of its travel, soliciting us one-by-one to pause and listen. Clear and promising as a church bell on a country Sunday morning, it would spend itself about the heath of home, while our souls rushed to embrace it . . . like wildwood religion. Anxiously we'd wait the moments by until it would soar again, reseeding our plain and needful world with simple peace and harmony.

"BOB-white!"

Most everybody kept a country bird dog then. A rag-tag setter or a ribby, double-nosed pointer. A Lady or a Luke, a Sally or a Ben. Rarely in a kennel, but a little more convivially than the beagles and the hounds; perhaps on an old jacket under the shade of the porch, or on a rope or a chain, by a propped-up barrel under a mulberry tree. At best, in a patched-up, makeshift run off the back of a heifer shed, that sometime before was a chicken lot. Same as not, the most and happiest of them ran free.

A few had "papers.' The majority were simply certified under the considerable auspices of a man's pride. Always the "drops," of course, the erstwhile progeny of the time Ol' Mack went a-callin' on Sam McBride's good gyp Princess, the blood-get bookmarked illegitimately between proof and prejudice, and culled to a spare survivor or two, one for a man. Brag dogs eventually, light on looks but long on bird sense, that oftentimes amounted to the better of both breeds. By the time they were three or four, many bird dogs had fared only slightly healthier than the hounds, running lean through the ribs and being snake-bit or hog-gouged one-time-or-another, carrying the sloughed hide or proud flesh to prove it.

I know now there were folks "yard training" back then, replicating into a dog's head the learning that summed to "Come," "Heel," and "Whoa." It's just that I nor any of us in Cedar Grove Community ever knew or heard anything much about it. To us it mostly amounted to hollering "Jake,' and throwing a ham-hock out the back door. If you wanted a bird dog, come October you simply hooked up a seven-month-old puppy with his mommer or popper and took him bird-huntin'. He came if he wanted to go and he stayed close if he wanted to get his mouth on a bird, and he learned to point and stand by watching the old hands go about it. What they didn't teach him, the birds, a keen hickory switch and his good instincts did, and pretty soon he was a sure-enough bird dog.

Birds were as plentiful as swallowtails on butterfly weed and if he paid proper attention, it didn't take long before they put the numbers in his head. Quail mostly walked or ran where they went then, unconditioned to the present day proclivity of flying in-and-out to their dinner, rather casually meandering from roost to breakfast, to preen and dust, to supper, and back home to bed again.

An upcoming youngster told you he had the arithmetic right when he started trailing, out of the field and off down the hollow, or across the woods, roading and stiffening as the scent got better. He might run over a bevy a time or two when he didn't get the wind right, but before long he'd stop them between run and roost, pin them for the count. I'd go with my Uncle Joel and watch the old wisdom dogs do it at deep twilight, in the greenbriers, hard by the sulfur smell of a swamp bog, with the bloated, buttery globe of a Hunter's Moon just rising, shimmering on the catch-water between the spooky black stumps of the old dead trees. About the time the owls started calling. To shoot the birds you had to bend on your knees, catch them fading against the silvery window of the sky.

There are times I miss those old dogs. I suppose by today's standards they were a motley lot, short refinement, breeding, and manners, a makeshift mix of mustard-and-mischief. But there was one thing, Mister. What they gave up in rough, they made up in ready. They were Honest-to-Betsy, God-and-good golly, old-time "bud" dawgs. Old dawgs that hunted up and "p'inted" quail. That put the "reckon" to rest and birds in the bag.

Under the Christmas tree the year of my 13th birthday were three gifts that in good part set the course of my life: a single-barrel Winchester shotgun, a box of Peters Number 8s and an Irish setter pup. The Winchester and the shells I had suspected; the pup I had not.

Maybe it was the beauty of the beast. Maybe it was Kjelgaard and the intoxicating saga of Big Red. Perhaps it was the echo of a few old-timers who remembered the red dogs from their glory days, when they were bred purely for the field, and a good one could toe scratch with the greatest of the gunning breeds.

"Best I ever had," the old hands would say, with a longing in their eyes . . . "best I ever saw."

How else might you suppose so many youngsters of the 40s and 50s came up with an Irishman as a first bird dog? Except mine was a lassie: seven weeks old, eyes baby blue, fairest I ever knew. Santa Claus had hidden her out in a blanket and a neighbor's grain bin until Christmas Eve, daddy had whisked her in under his coat after I agreed to bed, and tucked her through the wee hours into the warmth of his underarm less she should cry or whimper. It was the lone and only time he ever suffered a dog to covers.

Now here she was, Christmas lights in her eyes – baby coat the fuzzy orange of a kit fox, little pot belly pokey and pink – tiny paws hooked over the lip of a big white gift box, scrambling desperately with hind legs to push over-and-out. Around her neck was the bow from a bonnet, about her a nest of green tissue paper, and altogether she was the prettiest sight a boy could ever design to see. Dumb with wonder, I looked to my folks and back again to the pup.

"In Dublin's fair city . . . where girls are so pretty . . . I first set my eyes on sweet Mollie Malone." Mama began singing. Funny, how crazy little things like that can embellish a remembrance so beautifully for a lifetime.

Unsuccessful at escape, my little miss was wailing what-for. Hardly Christmas music. Lifting her gently from the box, I nestled her against my chest. She promptly reared in my arms, kissing me profusely in the mouth.

"Mollie wouldn't be bad," mama said.

I thought for a time, between kisses. I was infatuated with Debbie Reynolds along then, the Tammy movies.

"Tammy," I said. "It'll be Tammy."

I didn't know any more about naming field dogs then than I knew about women. Or maybe I did. But what I knew I forgot. Females do that to you.

A lovely mahogany lass my fuzzy orange pup bloomed to be. Sunlight splintered into fiery bolts of auburn when it touched her coat and her hazel eyes blazed with desire.

By the time she was 13 months, she, me and the Winchester had made the rounds of most every covey in the community. My grandpaw, several uncles and three neighbors were "complainin' the birds sho' were wild this year," but nobody could figure why. 'Cause we were reasonably discrete about the matter, not exactly sneaking around, but not announcing it neither. Knowing they'd set a foot down. Boy or no, a man's birds were like his wife; you didn't go around courting them on the side.

Truth was, we hadn't pointed many and had shot less, but there'uz no denying we'd put the fear of God into 'em. M'Lady had run through them all. But once she discovered she couldn't catch them, she'd flash-pointed a time or so, and I had borrowed the good fortune to kill a single or two for her where they got up wild.

So that one lovely afternoon in December, she stood a bit longer than she meant too on Hettie's Hill. Instinct did that to her, stoving her stiffly against the silvered ragweed edge of a ragged brown corn patch. Her eyes bugged, and her tail stopped poker-stiff. The drooping winter sun spilled in, painted the world orange and mellow, and set the resin aglow in her coat and feathers.

"Whoa," I said importantly, and crept in ahead of her, the Winchester trembling to port.

Fifteen old-timey quail clattered sky-bound against the silver weeds, leveling right and left. I can't remember time to pick a bird, but there wasn't nobody else there to be polite about, so I could shoot at will. Somehow I managed to get cocked and ahead of one. The little gun spoke and there was a tiny burst of feathers, and a set of russet wings went limp and tumbled into the stubble. About the time Tammy got her mouth on that one, a straggler sputtered up and I turned my pocket inside out, dumping three shells on the ground to the one I fumbled into the gun. But I knocked it down too, shy of the woods-line.

Not long afterward we made grandpaw's dog string.

"Sakes and Sally, boy, you done played hob on every covey in three mile. Best you and that red dog stay along with us, where we kin keep one eye on you." Grandpaw smiled when he said it.

Me and my dog smiled back.

H is name was "Shot." Hardaway Delivery's Shot to be up-town about it. That was a mouthful just to call a dog, I thought. But he was a good-looking somebody.

A strapping liver-on-white pointer, he stood high on his toes – about five hands at the shoulder – and he belonged to Mister Ralph Briles. Mister Ralph asked could he run Shot on my Uncle Sid's farm, so we met them there early one Saturday morning in October, with the painted leaves glowing behind the mist like splotches on an artist's palette.

Mister Ralph not only brought his dog, but a big, black walking horse. The gelding banged off the trailer, threw his head high and blew like a deer snorts. Then he pranced around stiff-legged about four times, with his neck and tail cocked. Danged if I would've gotten on him. But Mister Ralph tied him off and threw the saddle over him.

Uncle Sid didn't say anything about it, but Mister Ralph sure was dressed fancy. He had on his riding jodhpurs and leather knee-boots, a jacket and a jaunty felt hat. He stuck a shotgun in the saddle scabbard, and corded out his dog.

"Where do you want to start?" Uncle Sid asked, and Mister Ralph looked off about the distance, said, "Well, it's more where we hope he'll finish."

Mister Ralph steered his dog to the edge of the field, Shot straining against the lead, the veins in his neck and legs bulging like mole trails.

"Whoa," Mister Ralph said.

Shot slammed stopped like he'd hit a wall. He had this keen look in his eyes, and if somebody had struck a match I think he would have gone off like a powder keg.

Mister Ralph climbed on the horse, fingered a whistle. The gelding was dancing, leg-to-leg. Shot trembled like he was cold.

All of a sudden, Mister Ralph loosed a mighty blast on the whistle, and Shot scalded away like a cat with turpentine on his tail.

"Yeeeowwh." About the time Shot hit the first corner, Mister

Ralph squalled and lifted the hair on my head. Shot whipped left and sailed on. Uncle Sid and me jumped in the jeep and followed Mister Ralph on his horse, not hide-nor-hair of the pointer for 15minutes. He'd done run by every bird on the farm, and I thought he was gone for good. But then Uncle Sid saw a tick of white way yonder on the hill.

"Is that him on that hill?" Uncle Sid said to Mister Ralph, who was sitting kinda downcast on his horse.

"*Whoooha.*" Mister Ralph yowled, his face lit like a Christmas candle.

"Looks like he's peeing on a bush," Uncle Sid said.

"Bush, hell," Mister Ralph clamored. "He's pointed."

We chased Mister Ralph fast as we could, him galloping ahead on the horse.

Shot was standing like one of the statues I'd seen at Brookgreen Gardens the times we'd been to Myrtle Beach. Mister Ralph climbed down, jerked his shotgun out of the scabbard, walked out front of his dog and kicked the birds up. Then he did something really peculiar. Rather than shoot at them, he just stuck the barrels up and fired into the air. Shot hadn't wriggled a whisker – his tail jacked tight and his head cloud-high – watching the stragglers away.

Altogether, Uncle Sid remarked, it was the strangest thing he'd ever seen.

Strange, maybe, but it sure was pretty. I didn't know when I'd ever afford the horse, but one day I meant to have me a dog like that.

We got her about a week before I left for the Army, the first "promise and keep it" quail dog I bought on my own. Prudence said I should have waited, but I never liked the name Prudence no-how. Loretta and I were sleeping between the same sheets, about the only two we had, renting a little house in Cary, and we had scrimped for a year at the means to buy a pup. I wanted an English setter, white with blue ticks. There was a man name of Quay Johnson kept some a piece down the road, and she picked us alone from a litter of eight.

We called her "Bess."

But then I had to go off to war at a place called Fort Benning. It hurt like sulfur after sin, cause November was coming and the nights were delicious chilly, and the pea patches were yellowing in the fields. I had a new pup and I knew where at least nine coveys of birds were within a trot of the house. We were honeymoon happy – Loretta and I – and she would go training with me, and she and I and our speckled pup could have gamboled bevy-to-bevy with autumn in our nose.

Instead, I had to kiss them both goodbye one glorious day in October, climb on a bus and go off to be cussed amid some God-forsaken huddle of Quonset huts by some gimlet-assed, little Yankee sergeant from Jersey.

Bess grew up with Loretta in my stead, sharing her bed and waiting out her work day in Animal Husbandry at NC State, wreaking puppy havoc in the house and welcoming her home each night to see. Through all, Loretta loved my dog as much as she loved me.

I earned a furlough for sharp-shooting and another for surviving, and I made off home each time hard as my thumb would carry me to my wife and my dog. The fields and the birds. I wanted to hate the bureaucratic bastards that conscripted me away from them long as they did, but I guess I was a little proud I went too.

Then one day I got discharged, a First Sergeant from Sill, and was home for good. We were a family again, the three of us, and the uplands had waited, the scented bottoms and the golden fields, and the quail that homesteaded them. After a while I began to forget the spite and stand on the spirit.

"We abhorred the days you were away," Loretta said, "but never the reason you were gone."

We'd lost time. Bess had grown a Miss, a beauty in need of a ball, and I escorted her to many, near and wide. What I couldn't, the swamp birds taught her. She pointed and held the ghostliest of them for keeps one dusk, on the edge of a Johnston County bog. She turned up lost and I looked for her 20 minutes, night falling – found her buried up in reeds and greenbrier, the roosted covey wadded up before her nose under twilight. Inkspots flung briefly against the faint blue pane of the sky.

"Whoom. Whoom."

I heard the splash; didn't see the fall. Heard the crash and clatter of the water, as Bess bounded out to search. Back with the sodden cockbird, she laid it to my hand. I could hardly see the highlights in her eyes. "I'm glad you're back," they said.

She proved it many times over, the next five years. Raised me out of knee pants, and made me a bird hunter. Until one dreadful afternoon in December, on that same Johnston County farm, she fell suddenly ill. Staggered. I ran carrying her the half-mile back to the truck. Two days later, there eventuated the horrible truth of a tumor and two weeks after that she was dead.

She kept a part of me life can never give back.

From his back door, the old man had but to put a foot to the stirrup, whistle away a stout foursome of bird dogs, enjoy the bountiful venue of the little farms. Any one of which welcomed his passing, for he was kind, generous, and well-liked among the folk who lived there, delivering especially upon the eve of Christmas and the New Year gifts from his saddlebags. Or sending around a wagon of warm wishes from his cupboard.

He was about the last of his kind in our part of the country, where once there had been many, and I'd see him ride by, lift a hand. Four fleet dogs testing the fields ahead of the horse. Once, in the distance, I actually saw them stop, near a gallberry head, dead tight in the distance. First one, then another behind him, drawing up until they were stacked against the tawny autumn landscape like the ones I'd seen on the Remington calendar on the wall of the Harvest Milling Company in town. Saw the old man get down, pull his gun, walk up and take the birds – *whump . . . whump*. And one of the dogs when he released them, running out to punch the grass with his nose, gather up a bird and recover it to the old man.

How I had envied him, and dreamed endlessly of doing the same, and now finally I was. Maybe I didn't have the mansion yet on the hill, but I had the horse, a good Parker gun in the scabbard and three spanking-fine dogs. There they were, way out front – pretty as Paradise – and I no longer had to imagine. In ten more years the country would close down and my little window in time would fall shut just as his had, and I would have to motor to Georgia and Texas to find what semblance was left. But right then, I had managed the time warp.

The Swamp Fox Classic, flagship event of the Swamp Fox Sportsmen's Club of Charleston, was that year a class stake of 15 trial-seasoned youngsters, over a low-country shooting dog course that demanded nothing less than their best.

Medway was the old South, a gift to gentlemen at the grant of a king. An aura of big house and boxwoods, mists and magnolias, grace and three centuries. A place of mood and magic, a pause of wish and wonder.

It was the rhythm and stroll of a good walking horse, over an avenue 200 years to dust under the hooves of a thousand others. It was boots and chaps. Stirrups and straps. Gents and hats. Shotguns and spats. It was dog folks – gentle and gay. The stiff, sharp scent of newly crushed bay. It was dignified old live oaks, bearded, grizzled and gray. A lazy old mule wagon, creak, rattle and sway. It was the shiver in the silver of dawn, the sparkle of frost in a fresh Dixie morn.

A storybook trip through a time warp of piney woods and short-grass behind one more generation of fierce young pointing dogs, and completing it all was the reality that three of them were mine.

I was recently returned from Oklahoma, had just talked to a friend who'd hunted Iowa, Texas and Kansas. Another back from Mexico. I was parleying all this to an old South Georgia dog man, espousing the virtues of a good Texas quail year.

He listened cordially, turned his head and spat copiously. Pushed his hat back, past the reddish tan-line on his pale forehead.

"They's birds in Texas," he agreed, "but they ain't gentlemen."

"**R**ed is the rose, that in your garden grows, and fair is the lily of the Valley . . ."

Back in the kitchen Mama was singing again. Time had turned. There was the gray in her hair, like the winter on the years. The years that had finally seen me home. It was springtime, near dusk, and I sat on the back porch of the old home place. Looked and listened. There, still, by the garden was the rose; gone, the little two-noted voice that caused it so deeply to blush.

Hard for us old hands, brought up with Bob, that you have to lose so much to gain so little.

The social pundits like to crow that our standard of living is better than it's ever been. I suppose if you're content to measure it simply in dollars and dalliance, it's hard to deny. Though in more unfashionable parameters I think of Granpa and Granny – the folks back when – that toiled dawn to dusk and never had more'n a hog and a hedgerow. But in the hedgerow, thick or thin, they had a family of Bobs.

And nary a one of 'em ever knew he was poor.

Chapter 8

Never Get Above
Your Raisin'

The wagon path to the old homeplace left Highway 49 about five miles west of town. I rode with my Grandpaw and Grandma, for they usually left early and I wanted to be first there.

When Grandpaw geared the '56 Fairlane down and crawled off the hardtop, an unmistakable sense of renaissance swelled. Even the old Ford, after the monotony of the highway, seemed to welcome the personality of the country path, jouncing around happily atop its springs over the ubiquitous ruts and wallows. Immediately the familiarity of the surroundings wakened girlhood recollections in Grandma, who with twinkling eyes would recant vagrant memories.

The summer haze over the lowgrounds would rekindle the story of my great uncle Osborne who spoke with a stammer, the morning he "was layin' aside the corn rows and had to climb the mule to avoid a vicious shepherd dog with the "hydraphoby." Afterward, when he could climb down safely, he had run all the way back to the house to warn Uncle August, stuttering "A-A-ugg-ie, A-A-ugg-ie . . . g-g-it yo'r g-g-gun, 'ers a-a mad aug up de road." By the time he had spluttered it out, the dog was way gone and the mule was back to the barn.

And there just ahead, where the old roadbank turned back, where the purple violets grew in profusion: "Almost as prettily as the ones I got from a sweetheart the year I turned 14," she would say.

By early afternoon folks were arriving from near and far, mingling in welcome with child-like sincerity. Besides my grandpaw and grandma there were mothers and fathers, brothers and sisters, a plethora of aunts and uncles, a diverse assortment of cousins and a gaggle of family friends – of all ages and several generations – most intertwined with the other through a quaint multiplicity of bloodlines, traced with reliable accuracy only through the yellowed pages of the family Bible. There in the parlor, should you wish, on the walnut table that Walter Hooper built, by the wheezy old pump organ.

Soon the rocking chairs and porch swing were busy, and the air droned with the heartfelt industry of reunion. As the discourse warmed, so did the aura of comfort and security, as on a cold winter night when you snugged the quilts up tight beneath your chin and listened with cozy impunity to an angry wind gnawing at the eaves, an icy rain drumming a sound tin roof. The week had turned by, it was Sunday again and like Capastrano swallows we had all reached home.

Imprisoned by polite manners for the initial assemblage, we young'ns sat like juvenile retrieving dogs at "Stay," obedient but fidgety, chafing for the command to go. While the palaver of the adults made its normal and slothful evolution from the weather to farming to the state of affairs about town. Boredom is boundless when you're ten years old and tethered to manners like pointers to a stake-out chain, and to Aunt Viola's launch into another linear diatribe about some remote and afflicted relative in east Tennessee who suffered from a chronic mal-alignment of distal sciatica. You knew, before it could be gracefully corralled, it would have to run the gamut from diagnosis to prognosis at least twice, and threaten a rebound.

But the while it was a command performance. That is, we were commanded to listen, while precious minutes stumbled by like a horse on a hobble. While, still, the womenfolk would not loosen our reins, and we fretted increasingly against our plight, waiting for the first chance to escape. For the serendipity and fascination of country freedom was no more than a vault over the porch rail and a dash past the corner of the house.

Finally, out of desperation I suppose, the menfolk would wrestle the conversation away, and the women would trickle off to the "front room" where they could dote on femininity without interruption. Their departure would be accompanied by ardent orders, to whoever might listen, to "watch out for those young'ns," and most of the girls would be beckoned along or admonished to stay close to the house. Girls being girls, they always minded, except for Sandra Hoover and Barbara Mason, my second cousins, who forever insisted on tagging along with us boys.

Barbara was cute as a lop-eared July pup, and near as much fun, but Sandy Hoover was worse than the whooping cough. Sandy was a hard case who thought she was a boy, forever insufferable with her "I can do anything better than you" taunts, who dodged our most fevered attempts to ditch her. Even Jimmy Varner had gagged the time we buttoned her up in the corncrib and threw in a maggoty possum, and Jimmy was almost 15.

Now they sat watching us, knowing what all females know, that with the women occupied elsewhere, the responsibility for our proper comportment and general welfare had fallen to the wandering attention of the menfolk. That escape was imminent, that soon we would gamble a renewed request for liberation, carelessly attended, and that Richard McCombs, always first and bravest, would launch away over the porch rail.

To effect the actual emancipation, Rich would cajole the tribunal with something innocuous, like "Can't we go see Charlie?" Charlie was a huge, white, Belgium-mix plow horse with shaggy feet the size of dinner platters. The men diverted abstractly anyhow, usually volunteered a sympathetic verdict, with general orders to "stay out o' trouble" and "watch out for snakes." With that, Rich was off and gone, the rest of us disappearing behind him like yesterday's money. Charlie was but the 15-minute entrée to the country at large.

The fishing poles were kept in the corner of the rock chimney on the west side of the house. It took only about a 30-minute detour – from the barn to the rich black dirt of the chicken lot, there to fork up a few corpulent and juicy earthworms – to get there. By that time Uncle Wade would have slipped away, would be waiting for us, for he had learned our itinerary well. Forever young at heart, he would welcome us with a broad smile, put a finger to his lips, promise not to tell. He was one of us, basking in the frivolity and banter over the choice of poles. Who would commandeer the best demanded several minutes of ployful and sometimes heated negotiation, with Sandy forever at the center of discontent.

"Don't get in an argument now, honeys," Uncle Wade would say. "You can each take turns." Which, of course, nobody wanted to.

Typically, some spirited trading was required to reach an uncontentious resolution. The rock chimney was chinked with red clay, which over the decades had been pockmarked by the incessant drilling of bees, weakening the makeshift mortar and loosening the stones. The interstices between the inner and outer rocks were grand for secreting valuables, and each of us had a cache. A little dark hole where we hoarded a few pieces of Indian money. The boxy chunks of iron pyrite were plentiful in the new ground, if you took the time to look, and the combined treasury of it hidden in the old chimney must have threatened its very integrity. Before we left for the creek the mother lode had revolved once more between us, so that everyone was a bit poorer but a lot happier, the poles bartered to a substantiation of pride. The "money" left over, we stuck in our pockets, come time a redbreast might not muster for somebody else's catfish.

Usually, little Barbara was left without a pole, and uncle Wade along the way would "step into the woods," which was Randolph County fair warning that someone had to answer the call of nature. But we were onto him by then, never surprised when he emerged with another pole, an ash or hickory sapling.

"Here, little Bar'bry, we'll make you up a pole," he'd promise, and little Bar'bry would finally stop her balling. We thought Barbara hardly more than a chubby, little crybaby then. God, she would grow up pretty.

Limber of tip and stout of butt, uncle Wade knew just where and how to pick the best of poles, and he would rig it right there, jig-time, right out of his overall pocket. With a hank of line, a crooked hook and a corkstopper. Corkstoppers were more meticulously crafted in those days, with a body shaped like a turnip, hand-painted in alternating bands of reds, yellow and green, and with a long wooden stopper protruding for several inches each end. The stopper served to hold the line at the right depth, and provided the balance to hold the cork true. Uncle Wade always had the prettiest and the best. He'd slip it on the line, then with his jaw teeth mash on a small submarine-shaped piece of lead with little wings on the ends that crimped over the line to keep the bait down. Finally, on went the hook with a granny knot.

When he finished, it was all so doggone pretty we were jealous, cause now little Bar'bry had the best rig of all. Which she wouldn't trade for no amount of "money." Our first grasp of how quickly stock values are altered.

The fishing hole, swimming hole, bathing hole and baptismal hole were one and the same, the priority depending upon your mood, the day of the week and the urgency of your religion. A long, deep, black pool behind the ancient rock dam on Taylor's Creek, it loitered for the immensity of 80 yards between lush green banks, a half-mile from the house. It was magnetic, dark, cool and inviting in the swelter of July and August. Beneath its lazy waters was a proliferation of sunfish, chubsuckers and horny-heads, and yellow bull-cats with their spiny dorsal fins that could inflict a painful, festering puncture to a careless bare foot. All could, with reasonable persuasion, be enticed onto a hook with a boy or girl on the other end, the erstwhile pledge of which kept us occupied for hours.

One pole we always allocated to a "set." A set pole was a kind of a self-managed fishing device, which in those days was one of the few things that might have qualified as automation. When you did it up right, you could go off and be about farm chores for a spell, leave it to its own and come back d'rectly to collect a fat catfish from the end of it, gratis, for your supper. Prospects were always best when a heavy cloud had roiled the creek the night before, sending the catfish on a feeding binge.

Rigging a set pole took a bit of finesse. First you picked a promising spot over the deeper, more sluggish flow of the pool, just off the main channel. Then you jabbed a hole in the bank with the butt of the pole, jammed it in tight to stay, at an angle – just like somebody was sittin' back holding it.

"Set it plenty deep," uncle Wade would advise, "or he'll yank it out and haul it plumb off to Union Grove Bridge."

Once we got the pole set, we threaded a big bait of worms on the hook, or better yet a glob of chicken gizzards, and dropped her in. A set pole didn't use a cork, the whole proposition operating on a taut line from a tensioned pole, so that Mister Catfish would come along, all gluttonous and greedy and stick himself onto a cocked hook. Once we had it in place, we were free to worry the sunfish on a better stretch of the creek. Nobody ever stayed to watch it. The fun was in the return trip, hoping to see the pole dancing like a puppet on a paddle at the State Fair and the line turning drunken figure-eights where it met the water. That meant your catfish was latched on, waiting to be hauled ashore. It worked wonderfully well, always with a bit of intrigue.

"When you do it right," my aunt Louise would tell me, "the skies will smile and one of the trolls who makes his home in the caves and crevices of the bank, who would otherwise not give you the time of day, will be obliged to come out and watch it while you're gone."

That was the magic of the thing, the troll who attended the rig in absentia and yanked at the fish to be caught. It seemed this troll was kin to the ones who lived under the bridge between our two houses, the ones that had threatened me with their sinister presence since I was three years old. It's just that he got saddled with an obligation and like a lot of us, had to make the best of it.

You'd never see him, of course. But it was fun to try and picture him there, watching the pole, a wizened, bare-footed little fable with a wild thatch of white hair and a frazzled beard, in tattered overalls woven of spider-web threads and a poplar-blossom cap adorned by a galaxy of hitch-hiking butterflies. Puffing on a gnarled old pipe carved from a butternut root, casting improvisational glances at the sternum of a breast-pocket branch turtle for the time and whiling away the hours by counting out gold nuggets from a lady's-slipper poke.

Inevitably, we'd end up in the water, Uncle Wade included, searching out mussel shells and collecting the small, conical snail husks that adhered to the mossy under-belly of the creek rocks. The water was pleasurably cool and sometimes we'd just lay in the tail-race of the pool and let the hours wash by. After a while you got chilled, especially Barbara and Sandy, and your acorn would shrivel up – which we could never say for certain about Barbara and Sandy – and the ecstasy of it all was to crawl out on a big flat rock and bask in the sun like painted turtles on pond-side lily pads. Meanwhile, Uncle Wade would doff his great brogans, rolling his pant legs up to his knees and wading the edges like a shite-poke looking for a minnow. We would hoot and holler, kid him about his lily-white legs, which had shunned daylight for 40 years, and he'd throw back his head, laugh in that thunderous baritone and kick off a water-fight.

After mid-afternoon there'd come a hail from the house, signaling a general quarters alert for a watermelon cutting or an ice cream turning. Garnering the same reaction as the starting shot for a July Fourth horse race, it would set us off in a wild gallop for the porch, leaving poor uncle Wade behind to collect the poles. Always it was the same. Little Bar'bry would booger out about halfway, having once stepped on a dead field rat in mid-dash. Uncle Wade would gather her up as he came along and we'd get fussed out later for leaving her there.

Sandy Hoover was a different story – Stanley Lassiter's worst nemesis – who first stride to last, turned every such occasion into a flight of honor. Stanley was seven, plump and slow, meek as a mouse, but country proud. Sandy was two years older, as slender and racy as a black snake through a pea-sheller. Stanley knew if he lost he would catch hell and blazes from us boys for weeks. It was nip and tuck, settled at the wire and the biggest part of the time Sandy won. Years later, incredibly to many of us, they were married. When the race changed to a chase, I guess Sandy finally let him catch her.

By the time we made the house, the grown folks would have gathered around the melon tub, where the fat green melons floated on top of the icy water, or about the frosted wooden tubs of the ice cream freezers. We never had both at the same sitting, warned religiously by Aunt Mae that "ice cream and watermelon don't set well together."

Skeptical of anything that would handicap my stomach, I would test this adage in coming years and find it true, though not exactly in the way it was represented. It's not the alchemy of the mix that does you in. It's the magnitude of the desire. There are certain things the Good Lord put on Earth that mortal men, and particularly boys, are simply too shallow of character to handle. Womenfolk have known this for eons, though in the matter of ice cream and watermelon, the discovery may have been more recent, like say, the 15th century. Faced with the opportunity of both ice cream and watermelon at the same instant, no self-respecting male can resist gormandizing, which is a fancy word for eating yourself into a bellyache. Meanwhile, enjoying neither as much as you would had you eaten only either. The rhyme and reason of this is infallible. Imagine hoping for the Easter bunny and waiting for Santa Claus on the same day.

Mostly we had watermelon, which could be raised handily on the farm by scratching up a few hills on a gentle, south-side slope, throwing in a measure of seed saved from an especially good melon of seasons past, and spiking the bottom of the hole with a robust investment of chicken manure. The chicken manure had to be as equally ripe as the fruit you hoped to harvest, else it would "burn" the germinating plants, causing you to be, as my great Uncle Joel would literally proclaim, "shit out of luck." Ice cream, on the other hand, was less spontaneous, took store-bought fixings, and was generally reserved for the most festive of occasions. Like birthdays, out-of-town company or somebody's wedding.

Freshly retrieved from preparatory confinement in the spring box, where the mud puppies lived, the big, bottle-green melons with the black rattlesnake stripes would be toted by the men to the icy water of the chilling tub. There they would happily float for a time, alongside the frozen block you borrowed from the ice-box, soon to become tooth-numbing cold and beaded with sweat. A hearty thump on their backs would return a dull, resonant, bass echo, pronouncing them fully ripe and ready for plunder. At the first thrust of the knife, their cold green hulls would pop and split, a great round of "Hoorahs!" would climb the rafters and the feast was at hand. The two halves would fall lustily apart, revealing the glistening red flesh of their epicenters, the long rows of seeds dressed neatly about its perimeter, like ranks of soldiers in sparkling black uniforms standing review on a parade ground.

"Oooh, isn't it pretty," the womenfolk would exclaim, followed by a parlor chorus from us men and boys.

Slices apportioned by gender, soon the saltshakers were at work, patronizing the tastes of those who preferred tart embellishment, while the largess of us fell in mouth-first and au natural. There was a certain method to the madness, each participant assuming a practiced, adaptive posture convenient to the mission, a quintessential extension of personality combining an acceptable mend of utility and manners. Generally, and excepting Sandy Hoover, the women and girls would stand in the yard, taking dainty nibbles from the heart of the slice, bending from the waist to avoid dribblings on their Sunday frocks and holding the melon at arm's length meantime. The menfolk would find a straight-backed chair, or sit at the edge of the porch, hunched over their work on knee-braced elbows, spitting seeds and depending on gravity to leach away the run-off. We boys, given to utility over convention, plunged wantonly in, immobilizing the pillage in a position most vulnerable to assault, cramming our faces into the cool succulent centers.

Conversation sagged for a time as anticipation and fulfillment found common ground in a juicy urge of destiny.

When the feast subsided, it was left to us boys to gather and haul the rinds the few steps to the woods, a chore accomplished with both delight and purpose. For later, if we placed them along the edge, in the sun, we would find them swarming with wasps and bees, furnishing great sport for the BB guns. But for now, the grown folks would lapse mellow, retiring once more to a favorite chair under the shade of the porch. The stories would flow then, we knew, having transcended the vagaries of pestilence and old age, to subjects of more wordly importance to boys.

Soon uncle Sid, sensing a receptive audience, would launch into his latest fishing tale. We would crowd the steps around him, eager for every word, never noticing the glint of mischief in his eye.

"Joe, you know Robert Hussey?" Uncle Sid wanted to know. Uncle Sid's stories were always preceded by a question, which was really a statement, a declarative interrogative aimed at securing a character witness. For us boys, the story was rendered all the more important.

"Well, Robert, he went fishin' the other day in that hole west of the Brier's Chapel bridge," Uncle Sid began. "Told me he was almost there when he noticed something' quare about the crick.

"Allowed the water wadn' runnin' just right. Said . . . rather than runnin' downstream like hit ought to, hit'd take spells of runnin' back'ards."

Uncle Sid paused a minute, letting that sink in.

"Yeahh," he continued. "Robert said he got a bit uneasy there, the more he watched it. Just wadn natchr'l."

Uncle Sid turned to my Grandpaw Joe. "You know how Robert talks, Joe." My grandpaw laughed. Uncle Sid waited a few seconds, until he saw us boys fidget, impatient for the story.

"A'ter he stood there awhile," Robert said, "he noticed it had a rhythm to it. The flow there in the crick. It'd move up'ards and

62

back'ards, up'ards and back'ards. Robert said he's about to get boogered, about to leave from there."

Uncle Sid paused to watch our eyes widen.

"But then he decided he'd come that far, he just had to go a ways further, see if he could make sense of the thing. The closer he got to that big hole, he said, the more boogered he got, cause ever time it'd back up'ards, hit'd roll over big rocks there in the crick."

Now even the grown folk were riveted. Uncle Sid, sensing his advantage, pressed anew.

"Robert said he didn't really know what to do by then. What he really wanted to do, he said ag'in, was leave, but he couldn' make his feet work. Said he wadn' breathin' just like he'd like too either. Fine'lly, he said, he decided haymake or Hades, he had to know what was causin' the water to go fickle that way.

"By the time he got nearer to that big hole there above the bridge, the backwash was rootin' up sycamore trees 'long the bank . . . washin' the dirt right out from under 'em. Said he ev'n had to jump out of the way a time or two to keep from gittin' hit when they fell."

I saw a smile growin' on uncle Wade's lips. Jimmy Lassiter was latched to Uncle Sid like he'd discovered Jesus, pining for the next word.

"When he could git to a safe spot," Uncle Sid said, "he looked to'rd that hole o' water and it was all riled up like."

Uncle Sid stopped a minute, throwing in a short intermission while he made an entrepreneurial issue of digging his knife out of his pocket. He knew he had us hooked.

"What happened then?" we chimed in chorus.

"Well, he saw two big logs 'bout midways up the hole, a-straddlin' the crick. And the lower end of that big hole would go plumb dry when the water backed up and fill up ag'in when it'd run natcher'l. Robert said he'd just never seen anything to beat it in all his born days.

"Then, when he got close enough to see what wuz happenin', it all came clear.

"But he'd a-never believed hit, he said, if he hadn' seen it for hisself. One of them big logs weren't a log at all!"

Uncle Sid paused one last time, letting us ride.

"Robert said, 'No sir, the second of them logs wuz the biggest old chub bass you ever laid eyes on. Layin' in a-hind the first one, his back slap out of the water. Just idling' there, longer than I was.'"

Jimmy's eyes were about to pop out of his head.

"That bloomin' fish wuz so big, Robert claimed, that ev'r time he'd fan that big tail, the water'd go one way, and when he'd fan it back, hit'd go the other.

"So help me die," he said.

Uncle Sid finished with a sideways glance at us boys, his face a study of irrevocable fidelity to his tale.

"I'd reckon that fish is still there," he declared finally.

We looked at each other doubtfully, but it was sure enough a wondrous proposition.

One story fed another. The mainstays were fishing, gardening and religion. If someone could find a back-fence way of poking fun at the Lord while weaving in a few tomato vines, he got double credit.

"The deacons at the church decided it would be a good idea to gather the congregation and have a communal garden," my dad would declare, laying the foundation. "The preacher asked would I be willin' to prepare a plot of ground for them in the name of the Lord?

"Don't know how much the Lord'll have to do with it," I said, "but if the Ferguson cranks, we'll lay her by and then the sisters and the breth'ren can take care of the plantin' and cultivatin'."

"The preacher 'lowed as how that'd be just fine. "Come harvest time," he said, " 'ever' heart and mind will have been enriched by honest labor, ernest benevolence and the sweet, simple blessings of the Lord." He was putting an awful lot of credit on the Lord, I thought, when the ground had'n even been turned.

"Amen, preacher," I agreed, and not wantin' to be unseemly I broke an acre or two there on that gentle hillside south of Clifford Hammond's place. That's good land in there; Cliff, you know, al'ays has his garden in that rich bottom just under the hill.

"Those beefsteak tomatoes of Cliff's are about the best there is," Uncle Ed said. "Puts compote and catfish under 'em, you know?" Everybody agreed.

"Well," daddy said, barely missing a beat, "the church folks turned out and we all threw in, even the preacher, and got the congregational garden planted. Everything was goin' fine for the first month. Ever'thing was up and comin', the tomato plants were bloomin' . . . it was all folks talked about on Sunday mornings.

"Then, it turned off dry. I mean the sky dried up and cracked like red clay at the bottom of a spent mud hole. For weeks. Ther'd be a piddle of a shower now and when, but nothing' to do any good. Course, the holy garden started sufferin' there on that hill. For a while the congregation hauled water from the crick by the bucketful. But that was about like wishin' for milk under a bull, so they did the only thing left and took to prayin'. Night and day at first, then anytime between.

"All the while, Cliff was sittin' pretty there on that low ground under the hill. His sweetcorn was head-high and tasslin', and he had green "maters the size of a baseball."

By this time, even Uncle Evan, who was a trifle slow, had seized the irony of the situation and was all ears. Every ear on the porch, in fact, was pricked for the finale, wondering which side of the bed the Lord would climb out on.

"Finely," daddy said, "one day when all seemed lost . . . the garden was withering to the roots and the Lord seemed to be a-spendin' the preponderance of his time with the Methodists . . . (daddy took a few seconds to flap away a fly) ". . . the thunder rolled and the rain broke loose. Rained ever' evenin' for two weeks. And folks took to prayin' all the more. Finally, you couldn't even git in the garden for mirin' to your knees. By then the church plot was lookin' like a million dollars, tithin' had surpassed the Jugtown Revival, and Cliff's bottom looked like a Deep River floodplain."

There was a murmur of laughter. All Baptists coveted salvation.

"Well," daddy declared, "I was down there one Satiday afternoon and saw Ol' Man Cliff a-comin'. He threw up his hand, said "Howdy,' but it was plain to see he wadn' happy. I didn't let on 'cause Cliff was forever raggin' me about my spindly garden when his was ahead, but now, I knew, it was my turn.

"So there he stood. You know, Cliff's got that hang-dog, dry wit mope about him. Didn't say a word. Just stood there, rollin' his eyes toward his drowned-out, low ground. It sure did look pitiful. Finally, he turned to me with a grin hangin' off one corner of his mouth, said, "Reckon you folks could let up a mite on the prayin'?"

C ome the dog days of August every year my great Aunt Rachel would rail in from some far off place in Mississippi called Kosiosko, to make Uncle Manly's life pleasantly miserable for a month and to see the big house back to order. The best part of Aunt Rachel's arrival meant Baxter Skeen would come callin'. She and Baxter had carried on a seasonal romance for 40 years, at a smoldering temperance that defied anybody's notions of matrimony, frustrating the pee-daddle out of Aunt Rona and Aunt Mae who were nonetheless committed to the match. This should have been a signal to Baxter that Aunt Rachel meant to remain footloose and free, but Baxter was an uncommonly persistent man.

My grandpaw claimed otherwise, that maybe he was a sandwich short of a picnic.

Whatever, Aunt Rachel would indulge him at arm's length, which the family tactfully encouraged, 'cause Baxter was a cocked hammer over a full charge. When he was there he livened festivities immensely. Even the chickens quit laying.

About the best thing of all Baxter did was to haul in George Pegram and the Boys to pick and sing bluegrass under the oaks in the side yard. George and the Boys hailed from the hills, and the drums of their banjos were covered with groundhog hide, which George claimed was the very best of all for "wrestling" the music from a "banjer." He'd tell us boys how he caught and skinned them, and laid them over the drums just so, so's the sound would come out sweet and lively. George even had a live groundhog as a pet that he called Scruggs. We'd always play with Scruggs when he came.

Being boys, we were always greatly intrigued by how anybody transformed a groundhog on the hoof into a banjo drum. George would cackle, throw back his head, and with a sly grin at Uncle Wade, roar, "Why that's easy enuff . . . you jest Flat 'n Scruggs!"

Then he and the boys would tear off into a breakdown, and everybody would whoop and guffaw, crowding the band in a toe-tapping sing-a-long. The tunes would spin progressively faster, the old house would shake and shudder, and when the boys really got to cranking and shifted into The Orange Blossom Special, you expected smoke to rise from the strings.

"Throw on Rocky Top, George," somebody would holler, and the Orange Blossom would roll right on over into Rocky Top, Uncle Manly would explode into a spirited buck dance there in the path and the dust would billow. Whoops and hollers and clapping-in-time would egg him on, while Scruggs orbited the head of his banjo-case cage like a ball on a string, and George and the boys would be going so hard then it sounded like a high-ballin' freight train.

The sweat would be rolling down Uncle Manly's reddening face, his feet flinging faster and faster, taken with the feeling, until finally Aunt Rachel would have to rescue him, tow him off to fan in the shade.

When George couldn't make it, Baxter would fire up the Victrola, digging through the collection of 78s that had accumulated over the years until he found a romantic number like Rudy Vallee on *Good Evening*. And if all else failed he'd crank up Spike Jones . . . "Hail, sptttut, Hail, spttut, Spttut in Der Fuerher's face!' Any hopes he had for a secluded get-away was a pauper's wish, 'cause the sound of the Victrola was a siren song. Soon we'd all have drifted in with a request for a favorite melody, and Baxter would look like the calf that couldn't find the cow. There'd be calls for *Hello Bluebird, By The River St. Marie, Mollie Darlin'* and everybody's beloved *When You and I Were Young, Maggie*. Those days you didn't just whisk your sweetie off in the Ford on the ner-do-well. First, you were expected to earn the blessing of the tribe.

Once, after a cloud came up and ran everybody inside for a time, Baxter, always enterprising, instigated a singing around the old pump organ in the front room, coaxing Aunt Rachel to sit beside him and lead the lyrics. Twenty voices strong and four generations deep, in baritone, bass, tenor, soprano and falsetto, we shook the timbers with *Will There Be Any Stars In My Crown?, Rock of Ages, Amazing Grace* and *In The Good Old Summertime*.

With each new chord, the ancient organ would drone along like an old man – full of felicity but short of breath – humming a mellow bass. Reveling in the refrain, we would reach for each succeeding line like the higher rungs of a Heaven-bound ladder . . .

> *"Rock of Ages, cleft for me,*
> *Let me hide myself in Thee,*
> *Let the water and the blood,*
> *From Thy wounded side which flowed . . . "*

It would swell and swell, that incomparable sense of being and belonging, until it literally stirred the hackles on your neck and raised goose bumps on your forearm. It was through the assurance of the old hymns, as interminable as bloodlines – through the faith of family and friendship – the simplicity of gentle favors, and wren's nests and heart pine floors, that we all persevered. We would take it with us, beyond that hour and day, to have as we needed, to covet and ever draw upon in a troubled moment.

Once the singing petered out, us kids would break for freedom again, grabbing up the BB guns and pelting for the woods, where now the varmints would have gathered around the cloying watermelon rinds. We'd shoot the barrels hot and hope next for September.

The highlight of the summer came in September, even though the year was wearing into fall, even though school came with it, and there was a growing pall of melancholy in the air. I could see it in my grandma's eyes, even then, as a child, and didn't have to wonder why. Though later I would come to understand more deeply the austere awareness of impending mortality that came to be laid upon a man's years, I could sense it, even then. You could see it in the season as well, in the worn and age-splotched leaves of the dogwoods and sweetgums, in the way the chickens huddled ever more closely about their evening roost. We would reach then, one and all, for a last flotsam of happiness to stave the sadness.

It came in September, in the form of a century-old grape vine. It rambled atop stilted cedar legs at the crest of the hilltop above the old Sheridan Mill site, overlooking the gaily painted meadow bottoms bordering the black vein of Taylor's Creek. Hazel nut bushes grew there too, in profusion, along the northern slope of its watch and there was a small apple orchard to its east. It had the character and vitality of Methuselah, and was so earnestly southern that, in years afterward, I would come to think of it as an ageless widow of the Confederacy, bent and demented by sorrow but of infinite hope, waiting there for her man to come home. And each year in late September, upon an occasion endeared to both, she would braid her long auburn hair, put on a bright yellow dress, and set with thought and care a special table. At its centerpiece, a bottomless, china bowl of chilled scuppernong grapes.

For it was at the tag end of September that its fruit fully ripened. It stood an honest quarter-mile from the big house, and the journey there was a delightful trek through fields of nodding black-eyed Susans, down woods paths of green moss, ferns and toadstools, across lush pastures brimming with butterfly weed and laden with Devil's powder-puff.

We went there in late afternoon, under a waning sun, as the cool of the evening began to rise. In a loose procession of little order, save the frolic of our spirits. The boys and girls of us gamboled ahead, breaking trail, chasing grasshoppers, trying to be first to the next powder-puff. You could jump high and stomp on them, and they'd spew a powdery cloud of bilious purple. The grown folks would amble to-and-fro behind, admiring this and that – a head of sweet clover, a stalk of goldenrod, a tuft of thistledown – bantering back and forth. Joking and teasing, men reminisced about courting days and mule-wagon rides over that very path; the women tarried momentarily to gather wildflowers and to remember the picnics at the Big Rock, just below, at the fiord of the crick.

If the breeze was friendly you could smell the sweet musk of the ripened grapes well in advance of the vine. In all of nature, excepting perhaps the gardenia, there is no fragrance more alluring. The very gates of Heaven must be heavy with scuppernong vines.

With quickened step we would top the rise and there it beckoned, Eden itself. A hundred feet long, 60 wide, guarded by only a few, reasonably amicable yellow-jackets and an occasional green snake. No one tarried around a grape vine. Temptation was too great. You gave yourself to a scuppernong grapevine like you would give yourself to a homecoming lover, in an impassioned rush. The incomparable, sugary burst of flavor from the first grape fueled a desire so lusty that you wondered how the apple earned first dibs as the forbidden fruit.

Once you succumbed, there was no stopping. Hidden loosely among the golden leaves thatching the scaffold, boundless clusters of luscious, bronzed and freckled globes lay for the taking. Their numbers were so prolific that you were compelled bunch-to-bunch, driven to pick cluster-to-cluster, until both hands were suddenly full and you had to pause and eat, until you caught up and could go on. You ate and ate, and picked and picked, until you thought you couldn't anymore. But you did, as you would love, to a climax of breathlessness.

Uncle Manly would be in an industrious fury, picking from the top of the vine for the smaller of us, dropping into our doubled palms from his big, farmer-tanned hand another great filling. Until all had finally reached their means, and the men and boys fell to the grass to ruminate while the womenfolk picked a bucket-full more for the ice box.

Eating a "bait of grapes" is polite Dixie for rampant intemperance under a grape vine.

The sun would be surrendering to the deep-purple cloudbank on the southwestern horizon as we made our way back to the house. The legions of post-meridian shadows, which had marched so boldly across the open fields, had retreated to join the growing ranks of dusk. The meadows and the woodlands were quieting – the wood thrushes stilled – the early autumnal colors of the leaves draining away into the pallor of the rising evening. The mood was pensive. A little lonely, a little sad, a little frightened by what might lay in store on the morrow.

Closing together, our band seemed suddenly smaller, vulnerable. There was little talk, even among us kids. Midst the grownfolks, responsibility was reasserting a toehold, the burden of the obligations that would come with the dawn. Tomorrow, we would face the world once more, for yet another week. Six full days would pass before we could know this happy place again, and soon enough, winter would come.

In the gathering twilight Aunt Rachel would light the oil lamps in the front room and the soft yellow light would filter softly through the blown-glass windows, through the screened doors in shafts of faint lemon, gently illuminating the porch. We would assemble there a last time, the women embracing fondly around, the men venturing the liberty of a hand on a shoulder or a clap on the back. The girls would clasp hands and whisper 11th-hour secrets. And though us boys jostled yet, and thought mostly to our next meeting, we could sense something deeper. It was in the following week that Billy Thompson was killed in a wagon accident there on his daddy's farm and that we came to know its meaning . . . that the certainty of life was change and loss, and that Fate held its timetable. That we could never take for granted we would be there to come together again.

We would cling to the last fleeting minutes before "Goodbye" as a child clings to mother. Then one by one each family would take its leave, another set of outward-bound headlamps winding away into the night.

From the back window of a '49 Chevy someone was calling to me. It was Sandy Hoover, waving a last farewell.

I hesitated.

"Don't forget your raisin', boy," my grandpaw said.

I put up a tentative hand. "See you next Sunday, Sandy," I yelled back. I think I meant it.

S oon, everyone was gone. All but my grandpaw, grandma and me. Grandma willed it that way. There was something very special to be taken from those final isolated moments. It was like sitting past the ending of a wonderfully inspiring movie, closing your eyes and listening quietly to the after-score. Grandma would stand in silence for a time and we would respect her reverie. If you listened along with her, you could sense it too . . . the fragrant fusion of lilac, jasmine and honeysuckle that rose on the cooling air of the evening, the abbreviated rasps of the cicadas and katydids, the long, throaty yeeeaannnks of the toads, the whip-sawing of a whippoorwill, in the wood ashes, by the edge of the garden. The heartsease of your soul.

I knew in those moments, along with my grandma, as I have always known since . . . who I was and how I came to be, and where I was going, and most of all . . . where always I would return.

Sadie

Chapter 9

She was a lithe, fragile, wisp of a pointer, whose blue-black ticking hinted of Rip-Rap blood, though you were hard-put to trace it up a family tree limbed with homebreds. Her field manners and poise weren't show quality. I can't ever remember her standing one bird with another in her jaws, or retrieving by the brace. By her owner's own admission, she was just a gun dog. She came unheralded many years back to share a part of her life with my friend Bill Williams, and she was called Sadie.

Bill and I were in college at the time, a lot like brothers. But not through a fraternity. Didn't have a lot. Didn't need a lot. What one had, the other could claim.

Sadie was already on the downhill side of her prime when she partnered with Bill. And adopted me. Unassuming and devoted, she demanded nothing more than our company. Youth and yammer had departed, and energy without dividend was beneath her dignity. Times later, she'd carry it too far. We'd invite her to help drill some bird sense into a bunch of rambunctious puppies, hoping to use her steadfastness as an example. But she'd shrink like a violet. Tag along at heel, wouldn't hunt, enduring the annoyance of the puppy scamper and looking at us with wounded eyes.

Without a gun along, there wasn't profit in scouting up birds just to watch them fly off. It was a lot like her hunts — when she did hunt, when we were hunting for real. If we stopped, if only for a breather, she'd stop too. "What was good for the goose was better for the gander." She'd plop down and stretch full out, limp as a rag, eyes walled up at us to say,

"Holler when you're a mind to go."

She was ever that way. As long as you were serious and participant, her soul knew no other helmsman and she'd hunt until she couldn't. Just that we could never convince her the puppy work was serious.

The first time I saw Sadie serious was during one of the Christmas holiday hunts that became tradition with Bill and I for a number of years. That first time we headquartered on Bill's family farm in Union County, Carolina. Carolina North, but barely. The three of us stayed in a small cabin that split the difference between two ponds and a creek.

On every side lay farms cropped with soybeans, the stalks stiff with swollen pods, weathered silver and begging harvest. In the bottomlands were patches of still-standing corn, the fronds dry and drooping, brown and freckled, laden where their shoulders met the stalk with fat, left-over roasting ears. Among them creeks rambled, and scattered adjacent to the legume fields were thickets and brier heads, hiding remnants of old house places, their gardens and grounds grown up in beggar lice, ragweed, sedge, brambles, wild plum and rose. Along the irregular ribbon of edge between the croplands and thicket, by the old wagon paths and logging roads, grew borders of lespedeza, Kobe and sericea. Mounds of sawdust and boneyards from small country sawmills lay rotting here and there about the adjacent hardwoods. At their feet, by the stick-briers, the birds would rest, dust and preen, midday, before they trailed back to the fields to feed and to the fallow to roost.

You could still find them then, plentifully, the roosts that have become rarer than hen's teeth today, and for every roost there was a bevy, or bevies. For this was antediluvian, patch-work farming and classic, down-home Carolina Bobwhite country, in the days before clean farming, pine timbering, land-clearing and development, deer-hunting, predator protections and urban landholders posted the death knell for old-time, neighborly southern quail.

Few roads marred the landscape, and those that did were dirt. You could still step out the back door of the house come morning, walk all day, not cover it all in the round you could make before dark.

Lingering about a hand-hewn table smoking with bountiful blessings of bacon, eggs, and steaming coffee the first morning – while we awaited a sleepy sun to burn off the rime of silver frost that had grown during the night, and unlock the birds from the roost – Bill proposed the day's campaign.

"What say we start 'round that beanfield o' Mister Walter Allen's, just north of here," he allowed. "I got up two big bunches there the other day. Then we can catch the sawdust pile and ragweed head at the far end. That's where they'll have roosted if they haven't made the field yet, an' we might su'prise 'em between.

"Then we can hunt that little stretch of woods between there and Mister Oscar Moore's hog lot, an' after that call on the covey that makes home in that little sericea patch by the edge of his pond. He said 'come on,' Mister Oscar did, at the Harvest Milling Company Tuesday. If we don't do any good there we'll cross the road – at Percy Goins' store, we can tie the dogs to a post on the porch and have a pork 'n bean – then work the Bone-Yard woods and finish up at the old hous' place to the south. There's a big wad o' birds stays there.

"There's another old sawdust pile we can make in the Bone-Yard woods 'bout three o'clock; that wild bevy we never got close to last year might be restin' there long then with their guard down. It'll be over in the afternoon time we make the old hous' on Claude Rains' place. That little field by the old chimney's in beans again. That'll be the sunset covey. After that we can hunt back down through the bottoms along the creek, maybe pick up a wood's bevy or a single or two from one of the others comin' back.

"We'll be home to the cabin 'bout dark, and there's at least eight or ten big coveys usin' the ground we'll spend."

Lord God, Bill – wherever you are – wouldn't you live to be able to go back and do that today?

Sadie was still balled up on my hunting coat, on the end of the old couch, that morning, waiting for the word. She had her work cut out for her. She seemed to know.

We had along as well a big, rangy liver-and-white pointer dog as a bracemate – we hoped. He answered to the name of Jake – sometimes. He had a huge, loppy, ground-devouring gait, kind of a cross between the lope of an Angus herd bull and a racing camel. The epitome of style and efficiency long as he was in sight or hollering distance, he was pretentious as a whiskey drummer at an Anonymous meeting when he could out-distance surveillance. Then he put it in cruise and loped off into the next county, self-hunting as he went. Bill thought to even the odds by fixing a four-foot length of logging chain to his bumper.

Sadie was easy to mind that first day. Slow, close, careful and methodical. We hunted a lot of country during those ten-odd hours. She favored the parts that were birdy, quartering tolerably, and disregarded the rest.

She was almost too close. Rarely was she out of sight, and though she was no potterer, you had to accompany her most places you wanted to go. But whatever else she was, she was honest. If there were birds there, and you allowed her the time, she'd show them the hand on the clock. She was just bold enough to pin the coveys and was blue-speckled death on the singles.

Turned out that's about all we found that day. Singles. Time and again, in places there ought to be a covey . . . a covey with no reason to be scattered here-and-kingdom-come. Again and again Sadie pointed, we strode past, guns to port, expecting the nerve-bending bluster of a covey, only to be granted the whisper of a single. Usually a hen.

Suffering most of the day without a bevy find, we began to wonder what-for. When Bill halted suddenly and said,

"You hear anything?"

I listened hard.

"Naw."

"Well, that's what's wrong."

Bill jerked his hat off and threw it on the ground. "What we ain't hearin' that we ought to is Jake's chain. The old son-uf-a-bitch has done it again."

He'd done it so smooth we'd hardly missed him.

"Out front bustin' birds right and left, that's what he's doin'." Bill was fuming. "Leavin' us nothin' but the leftovers. I'm a-gonna traipse his hide 'til the hair slides."

I was laughing. Not at Jake. At Bill. In a minute he was laughing too.

You had to admire the old bastard. Shortly after we started hunting, Jake had gotten over a little rise ahead of us and thrown it into second. Bill had hollered until he was hoarse, naturally to no avail. Then Sadie had pointed. And then again, and we had clean forgotten the wayfaring pointer. I think his Papa might have been a sea-going man. Anyhow, Jake had managed a glorious day, hanging about a quarter-mile ahead of us, bouncing into the midst of covey after covey. The thing you had to admire most was . . . he never missed one.

Absent Jake's redoubtable services next day out, the situation improved remarkably.

The two most memorable hunts we enjoyed over Sadie came some time later. She had grown accustomed to us, we to her. She'd read the body language, know what we wanted, with nary a whistle between us. She was the easiest dog I've ever hunted over. By that time too, we respected the little gyp for what she was and had quit wishing the things she wasn't.

But we happened to be riding with Bill's cousin, Tom, Jr., one afternoon, from here to where. The hunt was done and we were jouncing along in Tom, Jr.'s old turtle-back Plymouth toward home. On a corduroy road that meandered worse than a drunken sailor. In the orange half-light of the setting sun. We were rehashing the day's business. The birds had been spooky as ghosts in a graveyard, several times sputtering up like doves at the opposite end of the fields and beating it for the bush before we even had the chance to get them pointed. Tom, Jr. had embarked on a dissertation that threatened to canvas every various and sundry condition that might make for wild birds.

"The damn cats," he said, "Old Lady Ludlow must have 25 and every damn one of 'em she lets run loose as a harlot in a haymow. Shoot 'em, I say, shoot ever' God-blessed one of 'em.

"Course it takes nine shells to kill a cat. You know that . . . ?

"And my toe's been hurtin'. Barometer's stuck. Did you see that yellow sky this mawnin'? If you did, you'd know it'uz the same as the one yesti'day mawnin' and the mawnin' before that. Too much o' the same. That's what it is. Too much o' the same.

"Birds get jumpy when the weather don't change. Scared o' their shadow. Makes the hawks move more. We need a front, ice acomin'. Put 'em on the feed.

"An' the birds is a gittin' smart. Done killed all the dum' ones. Then you got to sneak up on the ones that's left."

Sadie and Tom, Jr.'s setter, Dan, were deposited amongst the guns and oil cans and shell boxes on the rear floorboard. You could hear the setter snore. Bill was suffering the brunt of the lecture, and I was dozing between the bumps.

"WHOA!"

Tom, Jr. slammed the brakes on both the car and his essay, like he'd spied a two-bit piece in the road. Bill's head bounced off the sun visor, the dogs jumped up and Dan started growling, the hair roached on his back like he's expecting a fight. I jumped like I'd been goosed out of a nightmare.

But it was worth it. Ahead, for a few fleeting seconds, a huge bevy of birds, wings set and homing for the roost, was silhouetted against the lighter shades of the dirt road. There must have been two-dozen birds in the lot and, spellbound, we watched them bunch and then settle into a small expanse of sedge not 60 feet off the shoulder.

Bill and I were for getting out and taking them then and there.

"Hey." It was Tom, Jr.

Above his faded blue over-alls – the ones he wore to avoid the slap of the brush and the swish of the stems when he walked the woods and weeds – peering in the rear-view mirror at us over the brass-rimmed glasses he wore to see how to shoot, the ones that lent the unlikely persona of a jug-town accountant. His eyes were narrowed to a reprimand.

"In the first place," he declared, "it's past shooting time. Furthermore, I'd not like riding back to polite folk with two people spoiled by debauchery. What you'd best do is go along home, git a good night's rest, an' let those birds do the same.

"Besides, they'll sure-as-Sallie be right here first thing t'morro' mawnin'."

Bill looked at me doubtfully.

I didn't sleep too well that night, plagued by perpetual flurries of quail that sailed across the road to the front of me, settling into a few square yards of broomsedge so conveniently all's you had to do was climb out, saunter over and gather a neat three or four on the rise. Didn't even need a dog, though a point and back would gussy up the proceedings. Me, of course, as the principal player in the final scene, the one where I broke open my Parker – while the dogs collected the downed birds – to blow the smoke from the barrels.

Shortly after first light Bill and I were on the way to the little broomsedge field, avoiding the dubious services of Tom, Jr., who had farming to attend. Bill eased the car to a halt and cut the engine. We grabbed our guns, let the doors-to quietly, slipped a blue Peters shell in each barrel, then Bill opened the back door to let Sadie out. She never even made it out of the car. Half in-and-out, she froze, galvanized by bird-scent. There she stood, suspended between the floorboard and the dirt, stiffly pointing. Square in the middle of the road. It was lovely, lovely . . . like you knew already where the pot of gold was, but now appeared the rainbow. Then her tail trembled, just at the tip, to tell us she wouldn't yet declare it done. Slinking out of the car, she roaded a feet yards – weaving – up the shoulder and into the sedge. Then her back caved and she stiffened for keeps, her black nose lifted to the dawning breeze.

"All right, boys. Have at 'em."

Bill and I looked at each other, grinning like the cat that would have the canary. Bill fanned right, me left.

We had taken but a few steps into the sedge when the birds jumped. Lifting in a beautifully symmetrical rise. Just like they had all night before, half peeling Bill's way and half mine. For a split-second it seemed all were suspended in time, sketched in charcoal against the pale gray of dawn. The effect of all those wings was stupendous. Then inertia caught again like somebody had popped the clutch, and each dusky silhouette hurled on, rolling left and right, scattering and beating for the woods.

I swung through a cock crossing left, pulled, overtook another fleeing the corner of my eye, low and straightaway, held under . . . pulled again. When I turned to Bill, I had not heard the shots, but he was breaking his Sterlingworth, extracting two spent shells. All we could do was stare at each other, for what seemed a minute, eyes locked in disbelief. Neither of us had cut a feather.

Sadie had marked the flight. She turned, looked at us – like a sane man might wonder at a simpleton – trotted out of the field, off the shoulder and into the road, climbed back up into the car and redeposited herself on the floorboard.

I didn't hear her sigh, but then I didn't have to.

There was another day in the second month of a new year, with a happier ending. It was winter at its ebb, the sky gray and ropy at the hem, the sun veiled and pale. The fields and woods lay somber and still. The north wind was blustery and cold.

Bill and I stood shivering under a lone persimmon tree, collars turned up, backs hunched to the blow. Watching from a comfortable distance as Sadie worked a laid-out weed field, the tall ash-stained stalks tossed by the wind. You could see the run of the gusts across the field, rolling over the heads of the weeds, like a wave curling upon an ocean. The morning had been fruitless, the gusts incessant. We were discussing our luck.

"Damn a north wind." Bill was fed up

"And the man that brought it," I agreed.

Bill looked at me like I was crazy. "What in hell makes a fool stumble out of bed anyway, and venture his better sense on a day he's not likely to do any good and damn-well knows it?" He pulled his cap down lower over his ears.

"Not talkin' about nobody we know?" I guessed.

"We haven't seen a bird all day," he said.

I took a deep breath, exhaled, nodded. "You'd not think it," I observed after a moment, looking at Sadie.

The little pointer was busy, fringing the weed strip with patent thoroughness. She was hunting as if she believed in the place.

"We best get out here and show some interest," I said, "if we want to keep her on the payroll."

"I gotta admit," Bill said after a whit of introspect, "this is probably the best chance we've seen."

The thick stand of weeds was understoried with lespedeza, its edges speckled by scattered and shriveled soybeans. The vines were poor, volunteered of seed disked the year before, but on the stalks dangled a few lumpy, silvered pods. The thatch and forage could offer comfort and convenience to a reticent bevy on a day mean as this.

First evidence it did was the telltale fragrance upon an under-lying current. It caught the little gyp and whipped her sideways, into a flash point. Then she eased. Her petite head lifted pertly, her tail beating a tattoo against the dry weeds. Into the bowels of the gray weed stubble she minced, following her nose. She was winding, the birds at a ways. Bill and I hurried in behind, guns to port. Ten yards, 20. The alert bitch lost the fickle spoor, corrected – bobbing, quartering, weaving – slow and sure. Discovered it again. Slammed stopped, pointed. Broke, slipped another ten yards, stiffened again. The blood rush of our heartbeats was thumping in our ears.

Sadie stood another moment, one forefoot cocked as if she were afraid to set it down. The birds were running. Hoofing it like a trotting horse. Now she broke again, stalking them like a cat by the scent, rush and stiffen, rush and stiffen. My God, it was lovely. Thirty yards more, the black-and-white bitch threading the silver weeds – coursing, tacking and halting. Then *blam* – as if she'd jammed into a wall – her muzzle jerked down and left, her body locked in a half-crouch and her blood-lashed flanks quivering, as her tail stiffened in one last slow motion to 9:30.

We took a step beyond her and the earth shattered, in a sputtering thunder, as three-dozen wings battled upward to escape the rattling prison of the weeds. Eighteen birds reached the sky in a chaotic clamor, each beating into a fury of flight as they split, leveled or banked, and scorched for safety.

Whoom. Bill. A bird crumpled left front.

Whoom. The right barrel of my Parker found a straightaway cock, shot and down, then the left crossed to a rolling hen, nudging past – *Whoom* – her wings blown limp and cartwheeling. The smell of powder, drifting feathers, on the cold gray air.

Bill, *Whoom* . . . *Whoom*, a bird faltering, dropping into the top of the gums at wood's edge, the other lying under a shower of breast feathers, never escaping the field.

On my side – a late bird staggered up, reversed and blew back over my shoulder, racing away. I crammed one shell into the right barrel of the open gun, forgot the left, threw the gun up. Whoom. The bird shuddered, flew on. Bill's gun was up to cover, but abruptly its flight stammered to a crazed fury and the tiny body lost its purchase on the air, tumbling in a flurry of useless wingbeats to the ground.

Folly bowed to Faith. The little bitch had won the day. There were seven birds on the ground.

Sadie made quick work of six. Out and back. Pride and perfection. But Bill's last proved a problem. It fell deep into a massive expanse of honeysuckle at the edge of the woods, the kind underpinned with brush and guarded by brier, that you kind of totter around on like a waterbed. Except that it sticks and scratches.

"Dead, Sadie. Dead bird."

The little dog took Bill's orders and with utter determination fought her way into the tangle. Floundering, choking, garroted by the vines, she wallowed her way through. Disappearing completely, she battled her way through to the ground. Snuffling desperately, she worked to nose out the hidden bird. It was the Devil's mischief, but on she struggled. She'd seen the bird fall, knew it was Bill's.

"Dead, girl. Dead bird. Find 'im," he pleaded.

Fifteen minutes she labored, until she was weak and hassling. And bleeding frightfully, her tongue torn by the briers. By then the bird in the bag didn't really mean a whit in a whirlwind. What mattered was her courage. Beneath our breath, we pleaded with Fate.

Another five minutes drew by. The little dog was all but done in. Still, she would not relent. She fell through another hole in the honeysuckle, crashed awkwardly to the ground beneath. Righting herself, on she searched, snuffling and hassling, with hardly the strength to pull herself back up and out.

"Go in after her, Bill. Ask her out," I said. "It's enough." I knew he was about to.

"Sadi . . . " He was calling her name, when she emerged from the far end of the tumble. At first, it appeared she was done.

We should have known better. Straightaway she trotted on wobbly legs to Bill, attempting as often she did to rear to his chest. He caught her as she failed and lifted her upright. Her hazel eyes were soft and proud, and in her mouth was the errant bird. It was a cock, handsome and bright, blood-flecked but hardly a feather mussed. I'll not forget that moment between Bill and Sadie, the glaze of completion that glimmered in their eyes.

I t was near dusk, the little pointer had hunted all the live-long day, and was totally exhausted. It was a far piece back to the cabin, but we carried her all the way, Bill and I. Turn upon turn. It was very much our honor.

Though the sun was beaming beautifully, it was a dark, dark day when a year later – just before the next bird season – Bill told me that Sadie had a tumor deep in her breast. The vets tried to save her, but the surgery exposed the malignant truth – and at my friend's behest – she was ushered quietly on to the Thereafter. A lot of us traveled with her.

Some ten years afterward Bill lost his dad to the same cruel fate. Beyond the depths of the sorrow the day of his funeral, my mind kept turning back to Sadie, because she and Mister Earl Williams had a lot to do with staunching me and Bill up on bird hunting. She was never a show dog. But she never gave cause to hold it against her. She knew her place in life, and to it was honest unto death.

The same could be said of the man.

Chapter 10

H. S. Tilley, Fishing Boats

His business card read simply, "H.S. Tilley, Fishing Boats." The "H" stood for Hiram and the S remains a mystery.

He was a gentle and magnanimous sort, roughly as wide as he was high, with laughing eyes over a bulbous red nose and mischievous smile. He loved spring mornings at the bare birth of day, slab-sided crappie, bream-on-the-bed, a fly rod, pickled eggs, stiff coffee, bad jokes and good women, not necessarily in that order.

In the early 60s, about the measure of his age, he stabled a small flotilla of rental craft on the fringe of Lake Wheeler, close by NC State University, where a couple of bass-crazy college kids bivouacked between fishing offensives. He was as constant as the constellations, content with what he was, and never pretending differently. As regularly as restitution, he donned a gray jacket over a week's worth of green work pants, packed his jaw with a copious lump of Red

Man, and coaxed his crotchety old Cadillac the six miles down Penny Road from home to public service. He opened for trade about a month before the redwing blackbirds took up housekeeping in the cattails, charged by the hour at a simple rate, and discounted for penniless matriculates.

An hour before the sun yawned, the county said he was to open the padlock to Penny Hill. We never caught him at it. Usually first to arrive, we would find the chain obligingly limp, the path open and inviting. Bill would urge the drowsy Falcon up the slight grade, its headlights would stab off into oblivion for a time, and when they leveled out again you could see luminal wisps in the darkness below, where splinters of light crept past the cracks in his six-by-twice shanty.

His was a rightful place of business, roosting on the lee side of the hill, toe-nailed into the slope at the halfway point so it wouldn't tumble into the maw of the cove below. Burnished to silver, weathered and wrinkled clapboards left to question a faint hint of whitewash. A gathering of crappie poles was lashed to its brow, bait buckets, boat cushions and a cast net hung properly under its eaves, and on its sliver of porch rested a 50-gallon barrel brimming with paddles. On a hammered-up cross-board perched a two-lunger Evinrude and a stripped-down Wizzard. About and below, a dozen boats loitered lakeside, bailed and clean, begging customers.

A prop-up awning declared it open for commerce, hanging at full integrity like a droopy eyelid on a hung-over bank teller. Against the cold mornings of early spring, with its eyelid battened down, it provided a reasonable semblance of consolation. If you parked your rods and tackle boxes against the neighboring pin-oak and slipped in sideways, it would snugly hold three.

I remember it particularly in March, in a raw, blustery fore-dawn, when the air was icy and numbing, the stars were a secret and whitecaps foamed the banks. Sleepy still, Bill and I would trip down the hill, fumble for the wooden latch, and nudge open the door. Inside, the little shanty would be yellow and cozy – the gas heater hissing, wind rattling the tin roof – as volleys of sleet began to pepper its flanks.

He'd be waiting for us, three tins of coffee steaming an invitation on the makeshift counter.

"Mawnin'. . . mawnin'," he'd croak, raspy as sandpaper on snake hide.

Wailing gusts would shiver the underpinnings and ice would chatter against the thin walls like spent shot pellets.

"Blowin' three spades o' hell," he'd observe mordantly, massaging our impending misery. His mouth would be screwed into a wry, challenging grin. "You boys best stay by the fire."

Idle prattle, dredged from the banked fires of his own youth. A wish bettered by wisdom, still yearning. We would never have let him down.

Fortified with coffee and palaver, we'd stumble out into first light, slap the five-horse Johnson on the transom while the old man held the boat, and brave the bluster.

"You boys ease back "bout qua'ta tuh nine," he'd advise. "We'll have a little bre'kfast."

We'd shove off into the wild gray day, turtled into our coats, and steer for the open water where the whitecaps spumed. Past the shelter of the cove, the wind would stiff-arm the boat, stalling it like a punch-drunk fighter. The motor would groan and squat, laboring the bow slowly into the wind, and the sudden force and sting of the blow would numb our faces like the whipping lash of a rebounding limb. Spray drove over the bow in pelting, soaking sheets, while we clung to the gunwales and held for the deep, windblown banks where the pre-spawn, lunker females first gathered to pilfer the waylain baitfish. One of us fought the wind while the other knocked the ice out of the guides, and laid a jointed Creek Chub Pikie or Heddon Vamp hard against the banks, until the brutal surge of a heavy bass rendered it all worthwhile.

Flushed with windburn and exhilaration, we would return at the appointed hour, stone-cold outside, heart-warm inside, to show him the fish and tender the tale. You could see the pride rising, and it was all for us.

"Reckon you boys earned salvation," he'd declare doubtfully, "c'mon, "fore it's ruint."

Together, we'd retreat into the tiny shanty again, into an enfolding blanket of steeping Java, sweltering smokehouse sausage, smoldering grits cratered with molten butter, and skillet-simmered eggs. On a two-by-six atop a minnow bucket, tendrils of vapor would waft above a cake tin of cat's-head biscuits and standing by in reserve would be a steaming bowl of catfish or Brunswick stew.

Through the years he had accessioned to memory a dubious repertoire of richly tinctured and ribaldly humorous stories, in sum no more than a half-dozen, which he raucously regurgitated to season the occasion. He would delight in dredging one up as he offered a pickled pig's foot or whilst we coaxed the catsup onto the scrambled eggs. There was never a confiding "Did I tell you about . . . " He'd simply roll it out through a mischievous smirk and the stage was set by the familiarity of the oratory. The most infamous concerned a train-bound chap who stumbled sleep-drunk into the bathroom next morning and mistook his wife's used sanitary napkin for a misplaced wad of chewing tobacco. Bill and I would wince and shake our heads with mock disgust, while he shook, cackled and wheezed.

Hiram Tilley was a simple man in a simple world, and if you came up around creek banks, millponds and boathouses like I did, before we all got sophisticated, I imagine you have one like him. He was a little crude, a lot honest, infinitely benevolent, inalienably trustworthy, and largely the reason that fishing is so quintessentially human. He's both the measure of our angling miles and the distance back to home. He's the foundation upon which we built the house.

I miss him and his world.

Chapter 11

Believing in Samuel Tisdale

O ccasionally life goes too well. It is then that I worry most.

For yesterday's insight promises that it will turn back upon itself, returning tomorrow trouble or sorrow in exchange for the euphoria of today. So, more often lately, I spend the quiet hours that frame either side of midnight in the small log structure a few hundred feet from the big house . . . the one mandated into being during the opening years of my 40s. I like the imperturbable lay of its dove-tailed corners under moonlight and, especially, the cadence of its heartbeat when rain visits, spattering on its tin lid like an old friend patters across the back porch and taps on the screen door. Inside, I contemplate the shrinking dimensions of time and space that bracket my mortality. It happens best there, in the company of the things I love most.

Tonight, Meg and the Parker 16 share my reverie. Sometimes I bring the big rifles, pull down Jack O'Connor's *Rifle Book* or Ruark's

Use Enough Gun, and think about bear and elk and buffalo in far places. Sometimes, it's the long twelve-bores, copper-coated fours, and _Gunning the Atlantic Flyway._ But tonight my mood wanders the uplands closer to home and glides on short, blunt wings toward a roosting spot in broomsedge. I want to rest a while somewhere close to where I started. Rein up a bit, offer a humble word of gratitude and regain my worldly footing. Tonight I will be thankful for the liquid reflections of adoration in the setter's hazel eyes – and hope that I have earned them.

The Parker came along as the bridge to the promised land, on the heels of Bess, my first bird dog. Loretta and I were young and in love, about the extent of our resources. The $40 for Bess wrung us out pretty good. Opportunity rarely checks ahead to see if you're in your best clothes. When I accompanied my Aunt Louise that day to meet Murray Hoover, it found my wherewithal a bit shabby. Murray was legendary in our rural community, always in association with accomplished dogs and vintage doubles. By the time our meeting made its way to his gun cabinet, I was a feather in the wind. Inside were four gorgeous Meriden guns, standing elegantly on their barrels like soldiers on-toe for inspection, all richly burled buttstocks, fine shoulders and latch forelocks.

I listened and drooled as the old man paid his respects to each in turn. There were a couple of D-Grade twelves, a C twenty and the relatively plebeian Vulcan sixteen. When he reached the latter, he ceremoniously broke open the breech and handed it to me. It felt like the rites of Passover, the moment when the minister offers you the symbolic wafer from a silver plate, while a prism of color streams in over your shoulder through a stained glass window adorned with the crucifixion. I accepted it devoutly and was taken immediately with its spiritual transformation in my hands. The case colors were a memory, the checkering at its waist no longer chaste, the bluing cloudy, but it was all Parker Bros., from the finely spun circumference of the muzzle walls to the dog and woodcock in the hard-rubber buttplate.

"Your aunt tells me you want a Parker," he remarked, rather casually.

"Yes, sir."

"Well, you might like that one. I've carried it since I was about your age. The others are mostly for show."

For a disbelieving instant I thought it was to be a gift. In fact, it was. The rate at which it was tendered was defrayed by a prescience

I could not share, and unknowingly, I had prepaid the balance with my unequivocal love for the woods and waters since boyhood. In less than two years, Murray Hoover would be gone, having chosen that day to place in trust with me the embodiment of his existence.

As elated as I was then, I remember a last, covetous glance at the grade guns. *They will come,* I promised myself silently. And they have. Yet, it is the venerable sixteen that nurtures my bird hunter's heart. Forty-two years of quail, grouse, woodcock, snipe, dove, chukar and pheasant, generations of setters and retrievers, sunrises and sunsets, miles and memories . . . special days with special friends . . . have endeared it beyond anyone's comprehension save my own. Wrested away by theft, given for lost, returned miraculously two long years later, it seems endowed with a life of its own, one meant to share a destiny with mine, a continuity within the echelons of time, which started with an old man's behest and encapsulates the limits of human immortality. I have taken great care to preserve it in the condition it came to me. Absent the slightest tangible blemish beyond that of rightful engagement, yet encrusted with treasured associations, it enshrines the deepest passions of my life, as it did his. It came with an invitation. I think he knew I would accept it with sincerity.

About me, the flicker of firelight continues to pull from the shelf of my sporting life other volumes similarly dear. My first Randall knife, companion on many an excursion since the mid-60s. The .300 Weatherby that hasn't quite made it to the Alaskan Peninsula yet, but still longs to go. A first edition copy of Buckingham and Brown's National Field Trial Champions, with the stirring period accounts of Sioux, Geneva and Gladstone that impelled me into class pointing dogs and 20 years of impassioned field-trialing. The diminutive brass reel with the bone handle and the secret past, which has come to symbolize the magnetic intrigue of all my angling endeavors. It bears the inscription: *Samuel Tisdale, 1843.* Is our association also one of destiny?

I think more now about how deeply a part of me these things have become, how solidly they anchor my wellbeing, and most of all, what will happen to them when I'm gone. Will someone cherish them as I have, or will they be scattered among strangers as impersonally as flotsam from a foreign sea?

"They can never mean to someone else what they mean to you," my wife admonishes, "Enjoy them now as completely as you can. We control little enough while we're here, nothing when we're gone."

In my heart I know that, predominantly, she is right. Nevertheless, it is a premise I shun. However uncertain, I prefer to believe in Murray Hoover and the Parker – and *Samuel Tisdale.*

I will do what I can. The recipients of those things most closely attendant to my soul will not be determined by blood alone. There must be more. There must be a passion for secret places, an inherent wildness, an abandonment for the outdoors.

I want to know a boy who has an endless fascination with frogs and snakes and turtles, water and trees, shoots a BB gun and watches for the puppy in tow when they cross the blacktop; a girl who catches lightning bugs on a summer evening, who wades barefooted in the creek, threads oozing earthworms on a sharp bream hook and attaches her dreams to butterfly wings. I want to see a swelling idealism given most often and most completely to the incomparable adventures beyond walls, life without boundaries, the sensuality of the seasons, the need for brotherhood with wild creatures. I want to know a young man or woman who, by all indications, will come to appreciate a sportsman's affinity to trappings of affiliation, the timeless beauty of tradition, the trust in the eyes of a hunting dog and the serenity of solitude.

I will instill this when I can, for the opportunities are not the same as when I was a child. Mostly, though, it must arise independently, of the spirit.

Where I find this, I will apportion my modest share of the sporting legacy, and extend with immense gratification the same invitation that was passed to me.

Chapter 12

In Our Time

I n my day," the old man said, "there were times . . .

"Times that were, times to be, times can never be again."

There was a suddenness of light in his eyes, almost as lightning blinks, and sobriety on his face. It took me by surprise. Rarely, for months I was told, had he been lucid. For the long and mindless minutes I had feared, I had sat awkwardly while he seemed transposed of notice. Wishing I were elsewhere. On a northern bench of the Burkhead Mountains in January maybe, with snow falling on spruce and the world at a hush, not even the bark of a crow . . . or the bench of a homemade wooden skiff on the Uwharrie in June, under the baste of the sun and a run of white bass. Somewhere he would have been.

The memory of him would be more comfortable there. I had known that. But there was all this between us that I did not wish buried unended. So I had come.

Now I wondered, hoped, as he seemed to be watching, if he knew me. Knew that he was, would forever be, so deeply a part of me. But he did not speak again and in the uneasy silence I listened to the rhythmic beep of the vital functions monitor, and the echo from another next door. Thought lightly of his only previous confinement, a few years before when he was trapped under similar circumstances but greater faith.

"It's their mating call," he had observed. We had laughed, friends and family, orderlies and nurses alike.

Only this old man, I had mused, this old man that had smelled most often like leaf mold and hound dog, sassafras and crushed cedar.

I gazed about the limits of the small room. It was close and airless. Inert. Far from the travel of the wind and the rustle of the oak leaves as it passed. The scream of a hawk. The plaintive pleading of disordered quail at gray dusk. He had known them all. Still the silence persisted. I thought maybe to leave.

The lightning blinked again.

"My Uncle Jesse, down by the Little River, near the mill my daddy built," he said, "taught me how to hunt and fish. Showed me the woods, the water. When I was a boy.

"How to trap a varmint, set a pole . . . twist loose a squirrel."

I acknowledged with encouraging words. He seemed not to hear. His blue eyes were cloudy, almost expressionless. Like a pale cold sky in winter.

"Crazy over it, I was," he said.

The nurse came in. Glanced at him appraisingly. Rearranged the bedding.

"He's like this mostly," she offered. "I'm sorry you came all this way."

I smiled and shrugged. She left.

Uncle Jesse. So it has been for the more fortunate of us, I thought. Someone older and wise, with the smell of the woods about him, who looked softly into our eager young faces and discovered his own reflection. Someone with smiling eyes and outstretched hands, who lifted us to a knee, and squeezed at the bend of our leg like a mule bites. Until we wriggled and grinned. Someone infinitely patient and wise, who cared enough to give us back his years, who told us about the haints in the hollow and the catamounts on the ridge, and the nerve-splitting scream of a red fox in a lonesome winter night. Who taught us how to bring up a shotgun and knock down supper, to tickle a bullfrog into a frying pan with a snitch of red cloth, and sniff out a bream bed on the first full moon in May. Until my teens, when this old man had come along, it had been an uncle of my own.

His voice again.

"Pushed it I did. In my time. Never let no grass grow un'er me. Night 'er day. Al'ays a-goin. Me and Woolever, an' Thornburg, 'n' Lowdermilk."

A moment's hesitation. A shiver that could have been a chuckle.

"Hard on the old woman. Always off a-critterin' som'ers, me and the dogs.

"Good . . . it was."

He left off then. Let his head gently back to the pillow. Rested.

I remembered them. Woolever and Lowdermilk. Thornburg. The bunch of them. But it was the old man that lit the fire under them. They trailed after him, like the lead dog in a pack. Course he was younger then, in his salad days. Fore he went to seed. Cut a pretty big circle, he did, for those days, most of three counties. Trapping, hunting, fishing. The best, he was, and folks knew it. Never let go. Canniest buck in the woods, wiliest mink on the branch, slickest old tom in the timber. Wouldn't cotton to less. Never quit with less. Took me under his wing about then. Guess you had somebody like that. Showed you the wonder and the wander, and the grit to go it with.

So that in our time we have pushed it too, even unto the corners of the Earth. Thrown ourselves agin and agin against something wild and wise, as he taught us to do, and it might have been Mozambique, Montana or Mongolia, but the difference is little more than scale and dimension. Nothing more than a sign of the times. The snows of the Burkheads have become the winters of the Rockies and the little runs of white bass on the Uwharrie have become the rush of silvered salmon in Alaska. And we have spent of ourselves nothing short of our best, as relentlessly as the breakers against the rugged cliffs of the Hebrides. Because he made us as stubborn of will as he was.

Except that somewhere far and away, farther than his dreams – on a mountain on another continent – we stopped long enough to thank him for it. For the ticket there. For something he kindled in a little piece of woods behind his house, a lick and a spit from home.

Consciousness flickered. An ungathered whisper. He had spoken again. He had not moved, seemed weaker. But he had spoken again.

His lips moved, but the words were as short as his breath, and I leaned closer to catch them.

"You were there, Boy. A part of me."

And in that moment I knew. And there was all that was left to say to him. But when I could manage, he had retreated again, beyond my reach. Or so it seemed, and in his time, those were the last tangible words he left to me. Departing the tiny room, I stepped from the dimly lit corridors into the clarity of day.

I had been too long. Too long in coming home. Years had passed. Times that were, times to be, times that could never be again.

Hard on him, me off a-critterin' a world away.

But I like to think he found the pride in it too.

Chapter 13

For Pete's Sake

(*Author's Note:* Lorene Wood Klepacki, a.k.a "Pete," was a dear and lifelong friend, my mentor in childhood, and through the rarest of privileges after 40-odd years of absence, my closest ally and confidant in maturity. Independent, zany, eccentric and fun-loving, with the spirit and passion to go with it, she embellished many lives, mine most especially. She was widely traveled, loved fine art, music, artifacts, antiques and literature.

We could talk about anything, and did – never a secret between us. Clyde Wood, her Dad, whom some of you may remember in fictional context from Jenny Willow, was a renowned 19th-/20th-century sportsman who instilled those same traditional values in his daughter.

I sat on his knee as a boy while he related the grandest of hunting stories. Pete spoke of him constantly, and this tale from the winter of his years – slightly fictionalized – was among her most treasured memories.)

I n a chilled November night, the big house lay quiet. Still, save the pops and crackles of its bones, and the ticking of the mantel clock. The fire lay gasping in desperate flickers from dying coals, and in the ebb and flow of its feeble light I sat studying the man I had known since my first breath. He was painfully different now, more mortal . . . the toll of the years clearly etched into his brow, into the corners of his mouth and eyes, and in the droopy, yellowing edges of his mustache . . . compelling yet, but suddenly vulnerable. It hardly seemed possible. Somehow the years between us had dwindled.

I was his only child. I climbed trees, whittled sticks, wrestled and fought with the boys. It was partly circumstantial. Partly it was me. I craved adventure and there wasn't much of that around the kitchen. Mama worried herself sick over the prospects I would grow up wild and unruly.

"For Pete sakes, Henry," she'd say, "that girl's been off with the Harris boys again. Lord knows where! Folk's will think we don't care. Don't you worry about her reputation?"

Papa knew I had the wanderlust in me. Came naturally. He was a will-o'-the-wisp, forever off on some odyssey most folks thought strange. He refused to engage the question openly, and to lighten the tension and tease mama, he started calling me "Pete." He had been more than my father. He had been my friend.

Papa was a hunter. He shared it with me, all the trappings and traditions. I came to love it almost as much as he.

By the time I was 12, I was well-blooded. I could carry a fairly decent bird hunt to completion, judge where a rabbit would sideslip the beagles, and talk the spurs off a careless gobbler. Papa and I would haunt the oak and hickory ridges on still sunny mornings prospecting for squirrels. He'd walk and I'd watch for a tick of movement or a bump that looked suspicious. Then I'd walk and he'd look. I shivered alongside him in pit blinds on the Pamlico and on stilts over Currituck. We were a team.

I tried hard to make sure Papa was never sorry I wasn't a boy. Some nights I would fall into bed and sob into the pillow with the sheer exertion of it. In spite if it all, there were times I fell short. The intense reckoning of those occasions was inescapable, and I would think, *If I had been a boy, I could have done that.* He took my shortcomings well. Still, there was an allowance of sorts, a certain, unspoken tolerance between us that forestalled the equanimity I had longed for all my life.

At 14 I had gained more of the independence I had yearned for.

Other girls my age were into homecrafts; I was still in the woods wandering for excitement. Papa had turned the kennels over to me, and on opening day of the hunting season that year he gave me a shotgun.

"For keeping the dogs in fettle," he said.

It was a Specialty grade Smith, an exquisite little 20 gauge, and it came up just right because Papa had the stock dimensions built to mine. I may not have looked any different on the outside that day, but I changed a lot on the inside.

He began hunting with me in earnest then. It was wonderful, and I felt the closest to him I ever had. It was so exciting! One afternoon we'd hunt quail, jacksnipe or turkey, the next, rabbits, squirrels or ducks. But it was more than just the hunting. It was the sharing. Often, we'd pull up and simply sit by a creek or under a tree on top of a hill, and he'd share thoughts of life and living, of striving and struggling. Of what he wanted me to see and feel in the world, the things he didn't want me to miss.

Even so, there remained places I couldn't go. As unpredictably and spontaneously as a summer thunderstorm, he would simply disappear for a week, and return as matter-of-factly as Sunday religion. Sometimes, like the falling barometer, I could sense its coming and would beg to go. Now that we were practically inseparable, I was sure he would finally take me. But he wouldn't. A day or two would lapse, then first light the following morning his chair at the breakfast table would be empty and the vacancies in the kennel would complete the story.

In a few days more we'd get a card from the Dakotas or the Mississippi delta or some other foreign location. Mama would read it to me and I would strain for his promise of return.

It was a little thing I guess. I really should have been satisfied. But when you're young and tender and really, really love someone, distance of any kind is an untenable anomaly.

Papa and I remained forever close, but there was always that final, small measure of insecurity. I wondered again, often, would it be different were I a boy.

Meanwhile, the miles and years turned by . . . so very quickly. One day I left for school, and suddenly, I had a life of my own. After college, I landed a job as an art buyer for a San Francisco gallery. Soon I was traveling to exotic places, doing exotic things. There was Paris and Rome, the Serengeti and the Alps. I met David and, for the first time in my life, fell in love with someone other than Papa. Mama no longer had to worry about what I had done as a girl. We make our way in life as we are, not as we were.

I never forsook my roots. With David, I hunted most of North America, Africa and parts of Europe. I was proud of that.

I was so caught up in matters of my own that I hadn't been home in years. It hurt papa I know. And now that I was finally here, I was paying for it. Papa was no longer the young and virile figure of my memory. He looked tired and gray. But he was still hunting and fishing. That hadn't changed. I was just back from a buying trip in Scotland, and he had engaged me for an hour on driven grouse. There was a semblance of old times that was good for us both. We had talked until we grew weary, then retreated to our thoughts.

Now I had been nudged back to the present by the broken cadence of his gentle snoring. It was hard for me to look at him, and hard not too. He was failing so, hounded by emphysema. I kept studying his face, trying to picture him as a young man again, the one I had worshipped as a child. How far we both had come. How would I manage when he was gone?

He seemed to sense my gaze and stirred slightly in his chair. "Awake, papa?" I asked softly.

"Uummhm. Gone awhile, huh?" he said groggily.

He slowly pulled himself to his feet and punched the fire to life. The shadows danced on the walls.

"We'd better be off to bed, Pete. It's early-up come day."

"Think I'll sit a bit longer, Papa. I don't think I could sleep."

His hand brushed my shoulder as he passed. There was a soft swish as he left the room, and the sweet stench of old man and tobacco smoke.

"Night, Papa," I whispered. I was glad he could not see the tears.

I glanced at the hands of the mantel clock once more. It was already Thanksgiving Day. I thought about that for a long while.

We returned thanks that year on a quail hunt at the Stidwell farm, where it all had started. It had been the first place he had taken me as a girl.

We hunted from the jeep with the pointers, dogs that could whittle the long beanfields down to size. Papa carried three braces of dogs, all finished to perfection. We spelled them in hourly rotations. And did they find the birds. We shot only the coveys, no thought or need for the singles. I shot the old Smith and papa shot the Perazzi, his "Sunday gun."

I was determined to make papa proud that day, to give him something to hold on to in the difficult days to come. Sometimes when you try so hard to do something special and so much depends on it, it doesn't happen. That day, it did. I doubled on the first two rises and had few misses for the day. Evening was close when Jake and Sandy stood the last bevy.

Minutes before we had watched the demise of the sun. Momentarily, it had rested, bloodshot and spent, in the limbs of a lone persimmon tree. Then, slowly and peacefully, it was interred in the softening blue loam of the horizon. There was more than a casual symbolism, and for a fleeting moment I had a deep feeling of loneliness. I had turned to be sure papa was still beside me.

We walked to the dogs in the gathering dusk, papa and I, wanting to freeze the moment in time. Then the birds were up and away. I swung past a fast-crossing Bob, watching him fold crisply at the shot, then recovered in time to stop another as it topped the treeline. I took a single step to regain my balance, and a lay bird bounced up from my feet so closely I could feel the rush of air from its wings. And I was spinning as I thumbed in a shell, and then the gun was up somehow and the bird dropped in a shower of feathers before it could reach the woods.

A few seconds passed before I realized papa had not shot. He had not intended to. He stood watching me, beaming.

"By God, Pete, I must have done something right," he exclaimed, ruddy with excitement. "That was damn fine shooting."

For those few seconds, all was right in the world. In the arena of his choosing, I had proven myself an equal. In the span of a fleeting minute, the years and distance between us had closed.

I left again the next day. But not all of me. There was an untoward holdover in Dallas, and the flight back to the West Coast was extended. It mattered little; my mind was still in Duplin County.

We had sat on a hill, papa and I, on a day late in September many years before, a mossy knoll that spilled into a laughing meadow. The meadow was gaily painted with black-eyed Susans and a small creek chortled happily along its belly, the highlights on the water dancing like refracted light in cut crystal. Among the thick, green ferns were leaves of gold from the sycamores and there were mare's tails in the forever blue sky.

At the end of a long silence, Papa had turned to look at me.

"What is it, Papa," I had asked.

"Pete, you know that little liver pointer, Breeze, you like so much?"

"Yes, Papa."

"What makes her so special?"

"I just like to watch her, Papa. She always runs happy and she's the first to birdy places. She finds more birds than the other dogs. She's just exciting!"

You've got a good eye, girl," papa had teased.

He had turned to me and caught my hand. "Breeze is special, Pete," he said, "because she puts her absolute all into everything she does. You can breed dogs for generations, good dogs, and maybe one in a hundred puppies turn out that way.

"Pursue life with a passion, Pete," papa had said. "Put everything you have into it. Never settle for less from yourself. There's so much to see and feel. One lifetime won't be enough."

All my life I have taken that to heart. It was his greatest lesson and it would be his greatest legacy.

Lulled by the drumming of the plane, I looked out the cabin window to the earth far below. It crept by at a deceptive pace in great multi-colored patches and rectangles, tearing me mile-by-mile far away from him again. I could imagine him hurting now as I had hurt on the occasions he had left me as a girl, to pursue his own passions. Yet, it was what he willed me to do. What was inexplicable then was understandable now.

I must get back soon, I admonished myself. Almost immediately, I wondered if I would.

So very often, human aspirations have lonely destinations. Yet it was in me. There was much left to finish, seasons to go. And I was a grown woman long since, and no longer the girl. When it all ended, would there be someone who cared, someone like myself with papa, who would ultimately understand that there were simply places that I, alone, had to go. I hoped so.

The blare of the cabin speaker broke my reverie, announcing the impending arrival.

I fastened my seatbelt and began to mentally make ready for the landing.

Settling against the seat, contemplating my itinerary, I smiled inwardly. I was my father's daughter, even more than I had known.

Chapter 14

Legend's Legacy

For every season of love, there is a season of pain. It was the cost of caring for someone. But now it was spent, and in the afterglow of the hunt we sat quietly, watching the blood-orange fires on the horizon incinerate the remnants of the withering sun. Melancholy was stealing up the hillside. After so many afternoons of so many years, its probing inquisition had become a rightful homage to the quest, a tithing of the soul within a sanctuary of bittersweet clarity. I even encouraged it now, pledging the closing half-hour of certain days to its arrival and demanding the same of my company. On certain days fate graced the seven decades of my sporting life with another tender favor, pressing for a proper thanks. Today was such a day.

Keegan had come home. And he had been a long time away.

So long, in fact, I could read in the lines of his weathered face the shrinking limits of my own mortality. Such a twist on what had seemed patent reality those 40-odd years ago, when first I encountered a fledgling youngster who harbored an entreating passion for wild things. In the extended season we were inseparable, I had walked far more confidently in the role of mentor and he could readily have been my son. As must be, I suppose, he had drifted away to blaze his own course, and our reunions had grown ever more infrequent. Now he was grandly accomplished, perhaps more than I, even in the realm of my highest attainments. For all that, I could not bring myself to resentment nor was he given to arrogance or braggery. Despite the parting and absence, the affinity that had prospered from our first meeting remained vibrant. And on this day he had returned to me, all that I had given, and far more, at a time I needed it most.

Although I had not grasped its depth, there was a thing of importance between us that had to play out in its own measure. So often, one must reconcile a matter for himself before it may proceed to resolution with another. So it was with Keegan. It started with a deer hunt.

I

T*here was still a lot of boy in the man,* I was thinking to myself that afternoon as I watched Keegan into his stand.

Even though he was 20, even though he had a full-time wife and job. He was still struggling with the transition.

Maybe I was pushing him too hard; I was prone to intensity. Maybe I was a little less understanding than I should be when his attention lapsed, as so often it did.

But I wanted him to learn the gratification and self-respect of a difficult thing carried to its end, so I prodded him toward the big deer when he still delighted in the pursuit of the does and the fork-horns. The discipline and deprivation of trophy hunting did not wear so easy, though at heart he yearned to master it. He looked to me for that, for the way there. And I, in turn, was trying as earnestly for him to see that I could not do that, that it lay only within him . . . that you had to give more if you wanted to go higher. Likewise, he struggled with the boundaries of daily living, with work and family, still given to whims of flight and fancy in the face of responsibility. For that I had similar concern, but the same design, drawing on his devotion to the hunt and trusting that mastery in the one would carry to the other. I had seen it happen before, in another kid I knew pretty well one time.

We hunted that afternoon hardly a 150 yards apart, on opposite sides of a small glade of bottomland hardwood girdled by deep thickets and cut-over. I sat its creekside perimeter, Keegan the ridge at its crown. The rub-line we would sentry was staggering, six- and eight-inch cedars, mutilated trunk to waistline by deep gouges, rakes and gores, scattered like survey flagging along a trail that wandered within a few yards of each stand. The pre-rut was in swing and the dominant bucks were beginning to roam, looking for the first receptive does. Odds were good that the perpetrator of the big sign would walk before dark, and that one of us would see him.

Keegan had earned the right. In recent weeks he had re-embraced the trophy ethic with remarkable commitment, willing himself from friends and pass-times into the isolation of self-discipline. It was he who had found this place, returning from his scouting foray breathless and exhilarated over the heavy rubs, effusive with enthusiasm and over-confident with youth. On his own he had chosen the two stand sites, and chosen well, and with faintly shrouded pride had invited me along to occupy one of them. It was the gratifying burst of initiative I had awaited. I encouraged it, hoping it would be rewarded.

Long, diagonal shafts of sunlight cut through the thinning woodland canopy in stairsteps of temperate color, banding the floor of the glade with midnight shadow. The contrast was beautifully disconcerting. Through such a flush of hue and texture, a mature whitetail might ghost unobserved, camouflaged by prismatic delusion. I guarded against the possibility, until the sun was overtaken by the distant cloudbank that presaged the approaching weather front, and the light was leavened into a premature dusk. In the ensuing netherworld, the big owls commenced their clandestine murmuring, pleading the ascent of twilight. It hastened in an untimely rush, along with a foreboding supposition that the few minutes of faith that remained would transpire emptily.

In a telepathic instant I was drawn to movement. He materialized almost as an illusion, in the dreamy cloak of gloom which had gathered at the fringes of vision. Melting into obscurity then reappearing, he glided almost imperceptibly along the rub-line path, the long tines of his antlers bone-white against the shadows. He was well past me now. Somehow, he had managed it. I could still shoot, but then I had never intended to. I mused in admiration at his cunning and watched him by as he picked his way toward Keegan's ridge.

Silence stalled like a misintended promise. Five minutes. Ten. The whisper of the water as it cobbled through the creek rocks grew to a meddlesome clamor, the impatient beating of my heart a throbbing irritation. The buck had to be close by Keegan now. Any second the roar of the shot would shatter the sweltering suspense into fragments of relief. But time dripped by in an unknown dimension. And on I was left to strain against the deafening stillness.

In a dazed instant the wait was ended, cleaved with the precision of an ax blow. From the surreal half-light of the ridge arose an alien sound . . . bizarre, eerie, humanesque . . . and apprehension choked my throat like a hangman's noose. It surged and fell, a double-noted guttural gasping punctuated by asthmatic desperation. It was bewildering, unnerving. I could not place it with any wild creature, yet there was an unmistakable wildness about it. Alarmed, I started to call out to Keegan, but resisted, fearing that I would spoil the moment he had aspired to for so long. The buck had to be near him. What the strange noises were, I did not know, but I believed that Keegan would have called out had there been trouble.

But what if he couldn't? My mind played Devil's advocate. *What if he somehow had become entangled and was hanging by . . .* I cut the thought short, not wanting to press the point. Holding my breath, I listened with all my might.

The uncanny chorus persisted. Anxious now, I would delay no longer. I loosened the waist belt and started to rise. As abruptly as it began, it ended. In the same instant, a burst of fear burned through my insides. Its impact was immobilizing. *What if I had made the wrong decision. What if I had waited too long!* I fought with that for five minutes more before I could bring myself to move again.

Night was falling. Move, Alva! I clambered down the tree and forced myself toward the ridge. It was dark and quiet there, dark and quiet everywhere. Quiet except for the rustle of the leaves under my feet, which fanned the terror in my chest.

The sudden stab of light from Keegan's flashlight brought inconceivable relief. He was waiting under his tree in no apparent distress, though perhaps a bit more impassively than normal.

"Are you okay?" I said.

"I'm fine." His tone was frivolous. The concern in my voice clearly reflected on his face, but the veneer of surprise seemed a trifle shallow. So I asked again.

"You sure you're okay?" I spoke a little too impetuously. My heart still raced with the after-shock.

"I'm fine," he declared," Are you?" The defensive inflection in his voice signaled irritation.

"Yes," I said. "What on Hell's hearth were those God-forsaken noises up here?"

"What noises?"

His response was so unexpected it took my breath.

"You didn't hear them?" I shot back in disbelief.

"I heard some owls," he continued.

"This wasn't owls," I vowed.

"What did it sound like?" he asked.

"Like some pitiful creature on its last breath. Like somebody strangling. It scared hell out o' me. I thought you might have gotten tangled in your safety belt or somethin'. I started to holler at you several times, but was afraid I was over-reacting and would mess up your hunt. I dreaded comin' up here, even, didn't know what I would find."

Keegan could tell now that I was seriously alarmed.

"Good Lord!" he exclaimed. "I swear, I didn't hear a thing."

I heard him, but I was still reeling with disbelief. There was no way Keegan could have missed those sounds. They had emanated from somewhere close by. It would have been impossible for him to miss them. Nobody could block something that weird, and I certainly had not been hallucinating. There was something artificial about Keegan's composure, but I could not put my finger on it, and would press no further. I returned instead to the hunt.

"Did you see that buck?"

"No buck. Two does fed in right under me. I cou'dn't see 'em. It's tight in here. But I could hear 'em eating acorns. I heard another deer come out of the bottom about 15 minutes before dark and ease up the hill. The beat was heavy and steady. I figured that was him. Whatever it was got within 20 yards, but I couldn't see it."

"It was him," I said. "He milled around in the back of the bottom and then headed straight for you. He was big. Real big. I was waiting for your shot. When it didn't come, I was worried he'd hit our ground trial and backtracked. But I never saw him again. And then those God-awful noises started."

"He did hit our track," Keegan shot back, seizing perhaps a bit too readily on my second-hand explanation. "When he got to where we came in, he locked up like a bird dog. After a minute or so he shot across it on a dead run. I could hear 'im, but I couldn't see 'im."

"Too bad, cause he was the right thing," I said, and let it die. I turned and started out, toying the while with the incongruities of Keegan's account, which I was at a loss to explain. Keegan himself had scant else to say and our conversation lapsed into remission, absent the ardent reconnoitering normally given to a day afield. Remote and absorbed, he appeared besieged with dilemma of his own, heightening the mystery.

I slept fitfully that evening. My mind churned with the enigma of the hunt, and I could not leave it, chewing on its extremities as a dog worries a bone. First the noise and then the buck. He didn't hear the one nor see the other. Yet, the ghastly sounds had arisen from the very ridge he had occupied, and the buck had walked a collision path with his stand. We had taken infinite care to route our ground trail so that it would not be detected until well after a deer was in rifle range. A buck directly on top of it, as Keegan had related, would have been standing less than 15 yards away. Point blank! Also, the timing bothered me. Keegan said the heavy deer approached about fifteen minutes before dark. I had seen him earlier than that, and it should have taken scarce minutes for him to slip within view of Keegan's stand . . . about the same interval that had passed from the time I saw him to the advent of the strange sounds. It made no sense.

I dozed in and out of the puzzle like a ship falling and rising amidst the swells of a turbulent sea. And then, within minutes of dawn, the answer erupted in resounding revelation. Keegan had encountered the buck. There was no other plausible explanation. No doubt the deer had approached with painful leisure, as he had while I watched him through the glade. The tension had built until it had become unbearable, and when he finally emerged, the visual impact of heavy antlers and supreme confidence was overwhelming. Keegan had been stricken with the "fever" and what it could do to a man was disconcerting.

It was clear now that he had frozen on the trigger. The buck had walked on unscathed. I could see it happening. Feel it transpire. The tightening in the chest, the flush of heat, the elevated heartbeat, frantically muddled signals between the brain and the muscular system, the screaming supplication for the moment of release. The grotesque noises were the aftermath. Keegan had hyperventilated, gasping for breath until he was exhausted. "Coming off the mountain," the old folks called it. I had been there; knew it well. Small wonder Keegan had not seemed himself.

Empathy welled. Another fly in the ointment. Another impediment to overcome. Just when there seemed to be progress. But I would say nothing. I thought about that for a long time. The lasting lessons of life are self-taught. Particularly this one.

I soon had cause to question that decision. For Keegan, the confrontation with the buck had been curiously profound. It tripped something deep inside, a thing dark and fiendish. Had I gauged it better, I would have tried to intervene. He began to change and I began to lose him. And then it was too late.

Afterward with Keegan, the hunt became a misdirected obsession, to be wielded as an instrument of reprisal. The game I taught him to respect, he pursued as the object of rancor. It was obvious to me that he had sworn with scarlet vengeance never again to yield to emotion nor to be humiliated by intimidation. I tried without avail to interject some levity into that oath. But his vehemence was malignant. It consumed him and all that I stood for, so quickly that I was taken unaware.

It would be many years before Keegan could live up to that dubious standard, for his passion for possession was deeper than he fathomed and its unbridled rage more than his self-confidence could withstand. He threw himself at the hunt with rash and angered determination until there was little else in his life. For a time, deer became the singular force in his existence, and great bucks the epicenter of his purpose. Again and again he succumbed to the same uncontrollable rush of anxiety, braced himself sternly against the temptation of discouragement, and renewed his challenge anew.

He did not tell me this, of course, but he did not have to. I could read it in the frustration of his striving. Day and dark meshed into a syncopated battle plan. Every available daylight hour was devoted to the woods and every night to conjectures of tactic and strategy. When the hours weren't available, he stole them, from Kathy and from his work, and paid for it with worthless covenants. And then came a day when the first buck fell. And another and another until they were deprived of individuality and became mere numbers in a vindictive coup.

For a time it seemed his agenda for retribution had finally been fulfilled, but by then the greater demagogue of self-grandeur was affixed. It drove him into a company of men I scorned, who measured the value of wildness solely by the sum of the figures tallied into a scoring sheet, and he was propelled by the arithmetic stamina of one kill to the next, an impassive faction in an exponential equation. He took the first book deer from our county, and unsatisfied with the others that followed, he pursued with wanton absorption the demise of the state record until that too he possessed.

He called me with the news, the first time in many months. His message was more proclamation than conversation.

"He was a 190s-class typical," he said. "I had seen him under the headlights about a month before." He spoke with a taxonomic worldliness unfamiliar to me. My best measure of a buck was pretty earthy, little more than the yardstick of personal experience. Until recently, and otherwise only because of Keegan's notoriety, Boone and Crockett might have been a jug-town hardware store.

"He never knew what hit him," Keegan declared. "He was working an early scrape-line; I got there first and walloped him. He had a 23-inch spread and wrist-thick beams." I think he thought I would be impressed. I was . . . with the deer. For Keegan, I could not say as much. The texture of his words was rankling, and there was a coarseness to his demeanor, even a well-disguised insolence. It throttled the enthusiasm I would have lavished on the occasion. I'm sure he sensed it.

"It's a fine deer, Keegan, a fine deer," I replied, finishing with an edge I couldn't resist. "Take some time to appreciate him. That deer's probably five or six years along. They don't ever come easy unless they're off their guard. He was probably carried away with something other than you that day."

"He was definitely hot," Keegan admitted.

I heard little from him after that. There were never hard words between us, only buried regrets that neither of us could disinter, and for many years the distance between us would grow. His life proceeded within its own sphere and I was largely forgotten, at least it seemed, though he had hardly known butt from muzzle when first he came to me. People who go places often forget where they started. Perhaps it was as well. With Keegan, the line between quest and conquest had blurred to indistinction and pushed the boundaries of fair chase. The respect I had worked so hard to instill had disintegrated. Maybe I was the one who had failed.

Maybe I was feeling secondary. Things no longer came so easy. I had taken good deer, not book deer. Maybe a piece of it was envy. Maybe I wanted to know how it felt to be young and on fire with desire again. I still did alright in the woods, and I probably had more respect from peers than I realized. I had been there, several times over. But I was not the man I was. My hearing was gone in one ear and dampered in the other, and what sounded like here was there. My vision was failing; where there was one I often saw two, and even though the muscles were still hard underneath, the skin over my gut sagged and shingled in a way it had never before.

There were days now, more than before, when I could no longer live up to my own standards. That was the worst of it, for my ability to excel at what I perceived to be exceptional had always been the bellwether of my being. I had always been hard on myself that way. Getting older was an expense only younger men could afford. For me, the cost was becoming much too high.

For months the circumference of my existence shrank and I fought a deepening depression. I became phlegmatic, in and out of myself like a light bulb loose in its socket. It reduced me to the places I loved and depended upon most: the solitude and serenity of the woodlands, the soothing explications and ceaseless ambition of the streams. Gradually I found the way forward again.

As my world closed, Keegan's only grew the larger. The allure of giant antlers and celebrity drew him first to Texas, then Montana, Ohio, Iowa and Illinois, the Provinces . . . anywhere huge whitetails were in the offing. There was family money to provide the means. A. K. Jeffreys and Trident Securities, Intl., were big names in overseas properties and development. The old man viewed his son's nomadic mania for guns and hunting at worst a hereditary aberration and at best an excusable rite of passage. It made good dinner party conversation when the politics was comfortable. Keegan's name was redoubtably displayed on the corporate marquee as VP for Intergovernmental Relations, and the latest performance audit had the company prodigiously into the black and clamoring for international investments. It was easy enough to float a few trips here and there, with an occasional eye toward a lucrative write-off.

Keegan had never worried for money. Perhaps that was a part of the problem.

The family wealth bought the best rifles, the best outfitters, the best everything. It bought several more eminent entries in Boone & Crockett, but it was not enough. Even the glamour of world-class deer staled, and his insatiable lust for adventure and conquest fell next to the cosmopolitan enchantment of large and dangerous game. For Keegan, North America would prove only a tease. After a turn or two at the great bears of Alaska and the ice cap, he succumbed unequivocally to the siren song of Africa. His hunting itinerary became a whirlwind of exotic destinations, always as far and foreign as the stars to me, as familiar to him as back-porch memories: Tanzania for buffalo and lion, Botswana for elephant, rhino in Bophuthatswana, leopard in Zimbabwe. Undeterred by civil intrigue and political turmoil, he finagled and hunted his way through Angola, Uganda and Mozambique, and on to Zambia, Senegal, Ethiopia and the Sudan. Evermore, the animals kept falling until I wondered if anyone even kept score anymore.

Out of sheer loneliness, Kathy accompanied him on some of the earlier safaris and found the experience far more beguiling than she had imagined, until the brutal inertia of Keegan's compulsion killed it for her, as apathetically as it killed the last lion or buffalo. I'd run into her now and then, and she'd relate the circumference and drama of their latest exploits. We grew closer and she started calling me, occasionally at first and then more frequently, talking in an arc of tangents until invariably she settled to Keegan. Because I understood, I suppose, as much as anyone could. She was hanging on, and the only thing that kept them together, if together was a proper word for their distant and tenuous union, was a son, Orrin. Orrin himself was a gift of the hunt, conceived somewhere in the struggle between love and obsession.

"It happened either in a quick, grimy grind in the back of the lorry while our hunter was out checking some rotten leopard bait or a hot, sweaty pop on top of the chop box while the boys hacked some poor antelope apart," she told me, laughing and tossing that dazzling length of auburn hair, highlights firing through it like resin ignited in heartpine kindling.

In the same instant she caught herself, thinking that she must have embarrassed or offended me. But I was grinning.

"I guess you can bleed romance into that somehow," I mused, causing her to laugh again.

Thereafter, a comfortable assurance opened between us and deepened the bonds of our friendship. I even confided to her some of my own discomforts. Mostly, I was there to listen and lighten the burden. She and the boy were my only link to Keegan in those years. And I missed him even while I recognized his passage as a natural order of living. I was hurt by his apparent indifference, and even more by his seeming departure from the things I had tried to teach. He had meant much to me. I knew that once you leave something behind, it's rarely that you can return. It was a repetitive lesson of life, made none the easier by its familiarity. So I held on to as much as I could, through Kathy and Orrin. And the years kept trickling by.

Orrin was ten, coming eleven, when Kathy came to me with a request I might have anticipated, but somehow had not. You ask yourself, sometimes, how you can be blind to things so obvious.

"Alva, I would like for you to take Orrin along sometime, to the woods I mean. Maybe let him tag along with you hunting or fishing. A boy needs that. Would you?"

Our eyes met, and there was sincerity in hers and reservation in mine.

"Kathy, I'm pleased that you would think enough of me to ask, but I'm not sure I'm comfortable with it, to be honest," I replied. "Orrin is a fine boy, and there's no better upbringing for a boy than the outdoors, but that privilege belongs to Keegan. I'm afraid he would resent my interference and there's already enough distance between us, without inviting more.

"Besides, I don't seem to have done all that well with Keegan," I said. "He loved it and we were closer than father and son for a long time, and yet, somewhere along the way, I let it get out of hand."

Kathy skewered me with an unreceptive stare. "What happened with Keegan happened because of Keegan," she admonished. "The demons he carries around are his own. I should know that better than anyone. I love Keegan for his passion and intensity. I always have. I've been hurt by it more times than I want to remember.

"But I think maybe he has too, despite his damned insensitivity. One day he'll need a healing place and some day, if we last long enough, maybe he'll realize it's been here all along."

The tears welled and they were not all hers.

"As far as any right Keegan has to Orrin, or his well-being," she continued, "it's been fairly well left to me!"

"But Keegan is home some," I said. "He takes an interest in Orrin when he's there, doesn't he?"

"Home?" she returned incredulously. "Home to Keegan, Alva, is wherever he happens to be between today and tomorrow . . . it has more to do with time than place. It's just a whistle-stop, until the next round in that endless, breathless contest he's laid out for himself. He passes through, so preoccupied he scarcely notices either of us. He just goes through the motions."

She was crying openly now, grimacing against the sting of the words. Though less obviously, so was I. The words were similar to those I had heard from Loraine not so long ago in regard to my daughter, Melissa and, once again, I was drawn up hard against them.

"Do you know, for all his almighty profession of love for the wild, he has yet to take his own son for even a simple walk in the woods? It would thrill Orrin beyond belief, but it never happens. Between The Safari Club, Rowland Ward and a token stint at the office, Keegan hardly acknowledges him."

"It'll come, Kathy. It seems hopeless, I know, but it'll come. One day he'll realize . . ."

"And what's Orrin to do in the meanwhile?" she interrupted in a swell of despondency, pleading to me with her eyes. "He sees all these wondrous animals on the wall and hears all the grand stories his daddy tells when we have friends over. And the closest he ever comes to the reality is 30 minutes of Nova on PBS.

"He'll be 13 in little more than two years, Alva; I don't want him hanging out in some upscale mall with a gaggle of potty preppies and a joint of marijuana in his back pocket!"

"I'll think about it, Kathy," I said quietly, taking her hand for a moment as I turned to leave.

Days later I was still impaled on the dilemma. It was sobering . . . the thought of taking another boy under wing. Sooner or later the price would be a season of pain. It had happened with Keegan and it would happen with Orrin, perhaps differently, but it would happen, and that was the way of things. No man leaves his own footprints in life trodding the path of another. Yet the notion was compelling.

What was the line? I could have missed the pain, but I'd have had to miss the dance." I hadn't been granted a grandson. It wasn't to be. But now that time was shrinking, I was being offered something close. And a second chance.

I walked to the gun cabinet, unlocked the door, reached for the little Remington Sportsmaster inside. I worked the bolt to make sure the chamber was clear and the magazine was empty, and let it take me away, across the years. The mended scars of ancient scratches wandered in light-khaki legions over its age-darkened walnut stock and there were quarrelsome nicks in the brown metal of the barrel. But its imperfections were honest and I had put many of them there when my Uncle Jacob had first taken me to the woods. Keegan had added his share when I took him. I eased a drop of Hoppes into the action, slid a few .22 long rifles into the tube and jacked the cartridges through the chamber and onto the table. It was still reasonably smooth, the bullets fed cleanly, and the extractor was hanging on. I guess it could stand one more boy.

"Take your time now Orrin and s-q-u-e-e-z-e," I whispered to the 11-year-old drawing a bead on his first squirrel, which was frozen halfway up a shagbark hickory among leaves golden with October sunfall. Even with its forearm resting on a sapling, the muzzle of the little .22 wobbled like a fawn on new-found legs.

"Take a breath, Orrin, let a little out and hold it."

The boy was struggling, with the gun and with himself and with the over-powering exhilaration that had come tumbling down in a heady swill through patrimonial bloodlines to capture his fiber and his being, and awake him to what he was and was to be. I could feel it in the squince of his face and the tremble in his fingers, and feel its kinship in my insides. My nose was burning and my vision was beginning to blur, and all the beautiful melodies of all the beautiful seasons were gathered into a prideful essence, and I too was a young hunter again, to the core, as my uncle had taught me to be. I had created the moment as he had created mine, and now Orrin would recreate the memory.

The crack of the .22 split the prolonged tension like a comma of relief in an extended sentence, and just left of its target the tiny bullet splattered shards of bark against the leaves and whined away into oblivion. The squirrel side-slipped around the tree and renewed its hope of obscurity.

"It's alright, Orrin, try him again; you've still got a shot. Take your time and make it count."

The boy settled into the stock once more, the fledgling beard on his face downy in the sunlight, a full-grown determination pursing the corners of his mouth. I watched him pilot the bead into its harbor at the bottom of the notched sight and navigate the barrel into alignment. I studied his small body as it fought the instability of its labored breathing and began to win, began to relax, and his finger as it slowly tightened to the trigger. The sensation was strangely soothing, the feeling you get watching your portrait unfold on an artist's sketchpad. I was seeing myself, through my uncle's eyes, 60-odd years ago.

There was another diminutive crack and a hollow pop, and the squirrel dropped limply into the arms of gravity, bouncing and somersaulting its way through the intervening limbs and plummeting to the ground. About the same moment Orrin was shaking off the binding shackles of disbelief, split-seconds before he vaulted into unbridled exuberance.

"I got 'im! I got 'im!" He was jumping up and down in cadence with his excitement. "I got 'im! I got 'im!" he repeated deliriously.

"Yes, Orrin, you sure did." I was laughing outside, smiling within. "You made a great shot!"

His face was flushed and his lip was quivering and he was making little whimpering sounds in his throat like a disoriented puppy. He scarcely heard me, but he saw my lips move and knew their meaning. And then the tears flowed, tears of relief and attainment, joy and fright.

My nose was burning again. I was wondering what I had done to deserve this, what I had done to deserve so many exquisite gifts in my years outdoors. Each time the effect was the same, so utterly humbling, so fulfilling, so consummate, that for a time it seemed whatever remained of life could only be desultory. It hit me now, on the threshold of my seventies, as it had never before. I almost wished the option would be called, in that moment.

There was no time to contemplate the matter. Orrin was off in a dash for the stricken squirrel.

"Whoa, boy!" I hollered, "throw the safety on that gun."

"I have," he said with pained inflection, turning and pausing, whining and prancing from one foot to the other like a fiery young pointer marking flight at the end of a check cord.

"Never run with a loaded gun, Orrin," I scolded. "You could fall and shoot yourself or ram the barrel in the dirt and have it blow up in your face next time you pull the trigger."

He looked at me pitifully, and answered with a terse, but obedient, "Yes sir." His dampened look wrung me out. Hell, he was a boy who'd just killed his first squirrel, the round in the chamber was spent and the damned safety was on. It was no time for the curb bit. I might be old now, but I wasn't born that way.

"Hell, boy," I smiled, "find your squirrel," and broke into a jog beside him.

The squirrel was balled into the yellow leaves at the base of the hickory, a large boar with a beautiful gray coat sparkling with silver guard-hairs and a full, bushy tail that looked as if it had been washed and blown dry. The bullet had taken him just behind one ear. There was a dark, ugly, matted spot there and bright red splashes of fresh blood on the leaves. Beauty and death. How many times had I suffered the agony of its message and the piercing introspective of its refrain.

It hit Orrin hard. He stood there, silent for a long minute, staring and biting his lower lip. The rifle listed limply in one hand. A wet drop of remorse thumped the leaves, then another and another. I let it be. I knew what he was feeling and I wanted to encourage it. This world was crammed full of people, hunters and otherwise, heartless to life. Orrin, I was determined, would not be one of them. The foremost doctrine of a hunter must be respect for the hunted. It is the only way he can justify the merits of his existence.

Orrin turned to me with misty, sickened eyes. "I don't think I want to do this again, Mister Alva," he said. I laid a light hand on his shoulder.

"You will, Orrin. Not again today, or tomorrow, or maybe even the day after that. That's as should be. But you will."

I picked the squirrel up by a hind leg with one hand and laid it gently in the other. A tiny shaft of sunlight found its way through the leaf canopy and burnished the gray-brown jacket and brilliant white underbelly to a velvety sheen. He was still soft and warm. I stroked and smoothed the hair with the back of two fingers, and teased the buoyant tail plumage. After a time Orrin reached out gingerly and did the same.

"We won't dwell on it right now, Orrin," I said, ". . . his dying. It's right to feel it and to think about it, but right now we're going to take him home and skin him out and afterwards I'll show you how to dry and work the skin, so you can hang it up or cover a knife sheath with it or something. Meantime, we'll look up Miss Loraine and get her to fry him up all nice and brown for our supper, and when we sit down to the table we'll think mostly about gentle October afternoons and hickory leaves the color of cured tobacco, and return a word of thanks for your squirrel and the privilege of being there together."

I stood and started for the truck. After a few steps, Orrin stopped me.

"Can I please carry him?" he said.

"Yes, Orrin, you surely can."

Ahead, somehow, the path blurred, and once more there was that stinging sensation climbing the bridge of my nose.

Orrin was good for me. He was a sensitive lad, much more than his dad had been. I realized that now, through the strength of the contrast. Kathy's influence, I guessed. But he had the passion too, and the grit to go with it. And with his came back some of mine, some of the old zest. We bought ourselves a couple of bird dog pups, whoa broke 'em, and started troubling the local bobwhites again. We got a hound or two and chased the coons out of the roasting ears, punished ourselves in the cold, steely bluster of the Pamlico for redheads, bluebills and cans, and rose up before day in the gladdening of Spring to call on the turkeys.

After Keegan, I had let myself become old and tired. Might have remained that way. It would have been simple enough. I had lived through several generations of dogs now and with the loss of each I had buried a bit of myself. I was forced to think in disbelief more often than I should about the passing of friends and hunting companions, and how it was that I was still here. I had watched day-by-day as woods and waters I loved were despoiled by the alien agenda of an endless proliferation of humanity. Many of the things that had anchored my life had been lost and soon enough what few were left would be threatened. I hadn't to look far for despair.

Orrin had saved me from myself, at least in the hours we shared. It wasn't like it was in my day and could never be again, but it was good. In the boy burned the man, at least one more time.

In the special moments Orrin and I enjoyed together, I thought often of Keegan, and occasionally had that guilty feeling again that I was robbing him of something rightfully his. But it was hard to feel too terribly about it. Keegan was still the proverbial will-o'-the-wisp, bantering about the continents in banal disregard for anything aside himself. On the rare occasions he found his way home, it was always the same. Once the laundry was done and the bags repacked, it was off again to the next incursion. He had come far. He owned several of the most magnificent heads in the record books, had won all the international SCI awards, the Weatherby Award, and was well known to the world's sporting elite who settled for nothing less than the pinnacle of aspiration.

But the celebrity came at a price he could ill afford. Orrin barely knew him, resented his absence and indifference, perhaps irreparably. Kathy, too, had reached the end of her patience and was but an attorney's visit from filing for divorce. I looked for something I could do, for the sake of them all, but could find no clear or rightful way to intervene. Because I could not totally condemn Keegan. It would have been easy, but it would not have been honest.

We are all driven in our season. The obsessions of my own were not nearly so far flung, but little less remote to those whose task it became to love me. To condemn Keegan I would have had to exonerate myself, and I was not free to do that. Try as I might I could never reclaim some of the things I had lost with Loraine and Melissa. Funny the things you never see so clearly as when someone else holds the mirror in front of your face. Yet to live life free of regret is to live someone else's idea of what life should be and to bury the passion that gives breath to dreams.

Life is a market place in which desires are purchased with emotion. We solicit, sell and barter at every corner, learning that to have one thing we must usually sacrifice another, and struggling in somber, rational moments with what might have been a more favorable rate of exchange.

How swiftly and irreproachably, now, Orrin's season was approaching. From the first day, almost six years before, that I had taken him to the woods and invested a portion of my heart, I had dreaded it. Now, here he was on the eve of 17, and only a few chapters of geometry from high school graduation. He was becoming more independent, of which I was acutely conscious, given the insistent anguish of Keegan's passage. Already he was beginning to drift from me, spending more time with peers and particularly with Haley, his girl.

Of course, it was summertime, the turkey season was two months gone, and the fishing had been slow because of all the rain and high water. And he and Haley did drop by in the jeep ever so often. Still, it was changing. I could sense its momentum and it scared me. It wasn't Orrin I worried about; I was confident of him. He had a clear head on his shoulders, a genuine concern for the feelings of others, and a penchant for forethought. Though his passion would burn brightly, it would be less damaging to bystanders. Nevertheless, there would be the distance of circumstance, and the ache of increasing absence, and I knew how it would affect me. It was me I worried over.

I was coming 80. Could it really be? It was hard enough to believe, let alone accept. But the numbers didn't lie and neither did the image in the looking glass. Ruark's book, *The Old Man and the Boy*, had always been a favorite. When first I read it, I was the Boy. Now I was the Old Man, twice over. It was hard to think of myself that way. And I knew how the book ended. I didn't want to be old and I didn't want to feel old or think old; I didn't want people allowing for me, or worse, pitying me. I was striving mightily to stave off the drag of the years, but it was becoming ever more difficult.

Try as I might, there was a spasm of despair in the morning of each new day, like a stitch in a cold muscle, which had to be warmed away before I became useful. Orrin had been my foremost defense for a crucial while, and the thought of his impending absence brought a surging prescience of loneliness and vulnerability.

I hated the damned creeping feeling of vulnerability. It had first seeped into my 50s, arriving in chilly zephyrs that brought unwelcome shivers of apprehension, shaking my self-confidence. Each gust whispered an unnerving intimation, reminding me that I wasn't as good as I used to be. It shook me to the core. I had been fiercely proud and self-reliant all my life. But there was a substance to it I could not deny, something different, strange and fearful. Harboring an encounter that would come in a weak moment, an encounter so formidable that for the first time in my life I might not cope. In my 60s, its ambiguous threat hung overhead for days at a time, like a dread disease devising the incapacitation that would overrun my ability to resist. Now, it visited regularly and pressed boldly, a predator ever more certain of its prey. And always closely behind were the scavengers.

Without Orrin, I wasn't at all sure I could beat it back another time. I had given in to it in the depression of Keegan's leaving. I didn't want to again. I knew too well its listlessness, a self-induced coma from which I might not awake. I could lean on Loraine, thank God, in those embarrassing moments I felt like a helpless child. When I needed to cringe from the world against the softness of a woman's breast. But more than that, I needed someone to keep me going as a man.

I had to hoist myself up by the gallowses. Orrin and I still had time together and I would savor each minute and squander none. All my life I had lived for today. I would not forget that now. Tomorrow is a wish without a warranty. How painfully cloudless that becomes the older you get.

August was hard upon the heels of September when Kathy called. The evening had grown weary and I was dozing under the book that had collapsed to my chest. When I picked up the phone and recognized her voice, I was reminded that I had heard from neither she nor Orrin in over a month.

"Keegan's home, Alva," she said, her tone taut and drawn, as if she were hesitant to release the words less the message should be voided.

I was silent for a moment, grasping for the subtlety that seemed to validate something hopeful in her disclosure. Maybe I was imagining it.

"I guess the obvious question is, how long?" I replied.

"Six weeks and five days, so far."

"You may have to change the sheets this time," I said laconically.

"Already have. They're still dirty on just one side, in case you're wondering," she returned.

"I wasn't. Didn't figure anything had changed *that* quickly," I said.

"Actually it has," she declared. "He's been genuinely tender and sensitive for the first time in two years. He kissed me at the door when he arrived. Took me totally by surprise.

"I had made up my mind to ask him to leave for good the next time I saw him.

"There was something of warmth and sincerity in his eyes I haven't seen in a long, long time. And he has tried to talk to Orrin more honestly than ever, though Orrin won't open to him. He seems to be trying. It's weakened my defenses. Enough for second thoughts. I'm mad at myself for it on one hand, and hopeful on the other."

"Better go slow, Kathy. I wouldn't read too much into it too soon," I cautioned.

"I'm not. I've been through too much hurt for that. But I honestly believe it may be different this time, Alva. He's different. Something's shaken him.

"Remember, I told you once that one day he would need a healing place. I think that day may finally have come."

I pondered her remarks for several moments. People in love want to believe, and I knew she still loved him in spite of all. Belief can be blind. But men do change, particularly in their middle years.

"Time'll tell," I said, leaning on the timeless cliché.

"You don't think so?" she asked.

"Don't think what?"

"That he's changed?"

"I don't know, Kathy. Keegan's an iffy assessment at best. I learned that the hard way, too, you know. I'll simply hope for your sake, and Orrin's, that it's true."

"Thanks," she said, frightened again.

She lapsed into a long period of silence, and in it I could sense the depth of her need. Neither of us was sure where next to go.

"Kathy, if you sense a change, I'm sure there is one. Let's hope it lasts.

"I do know this much. When a man sees 50 on the horizon, it scares hell out of him. All he sees is an hourglass with more sand at the bottom than at the top, kinda the shape his body's comin' to be and next, all the things he's neglected or hasn't done. He either wants to slow down or speed up, or do the one when he ought to be doing the other.

"Meanwhile, he gets a lot less sure of himself, like an old hound that remembers he's supposed to hunt, but can't get past a cold track. After a spell, he gets it all sorted by, usually in the right direction.

"Keegan's done and been more than most men ever will. Maybe you're right. Maybe he's finally realized what he's left along the way and it's shaken him."

There was still silence at the other end of the phone. Not exactly silence, either. She was crying.

"Call me, Kathy, anytime. I won't drop by; I don't feel comfortable with that. But call me. And send Orrin around." I depressed the button on the receiver and the headset went dead in my hand. I held it for several minutes before I thought to put it down.

Trrue to himself, Orrin did not forsake me. He cut his own path and tithed in his own church, but he did not forget me. He'd call or drop by on the spur of the moment, less than before, of course, but reliably, to check if I could try the quail on the morrow or go see if the woodcock were in the Stidwell bottom, or to simply walk and talk and look for arrowheads in fields washed naked by winter rains and March winds.

Nothing got in the way of my going. I made certain of that, for the time was important to us both, I who frugally spent and coveted each day against a rapidly dwindling balance, and he who must determine within so meager a daily allotment and such an expansive array of youthful priorities, where an occasion with Alva Treadlock might be fitted. I was thankful that I remained on the list. We worked hard against the time we had and what was neglected by occurrence was attended by affection. Still, it hurt terribly, as I knew it would, to see him grow away and take with him days I could never hope to have again.

For a while, in a mellow moment I would find a way to inquire about his mother and dad. He would talk freely and affably about his mother, but the subject of his father was a closed matter. Each time it was the same. His face would harden and he would look at me with a question in his eyes that ran close to an accusation of betrayal. That I could not stand; resolution of the impasse between he and his dad would not come at the cost of our own. I would not allow it. I could not bear it. I quickly backed away, and then laid it aside altogether. I had spent as much of myself at present as I could.

Yet I wanted to help and knew the extremity of the need. In the eight months that had passed since Keegan's return, Kathy was calling now and then, optimistic one time, distraught the next. I had heard nothing from Keegan. That he was still home and seemingly making the attempt was incredulous really after all the years on the fly. It was as if he had recalled something of pressing importance he had long overlooked and finally having done so, was overwrought to attend it. Typically, he was straining at it too hard. But I was beginning to concede there might be hope. Between he and Kathy, from a distance, there appeared to be a modicum of reconciliation. It might prosper, but for Orrin.

With Orrin, there remained much discord. He resisted Keegan's every overture and likewise spurned his mother's efforts to mediate. He wore his resentment like a plate of armor, and wielded his anger as a divisive sword. It was splitting Kathy apart, trying to minister to both and sustain allegiance to each. And it all depended on Kathy. Yet even while apart, they clung to her. She fought mightily, their lifeboat in a stormy sea, throwing herself against the heaving swells of strife and distortion, striving to hold together long enough for all to pull at once.

How desperately she labored to mend a badly broken dream, to put together again something that in its short season of happiness had created the driving force of her life. For every man lost to disenchantment, there is a woman left to believe.

She needed me. I knew that. Now, if never again. Had it not been for her, there wouldn't have been Orrin. Perhaps I should try. Maybe I owed her that. No doubt I owed her that. But did I have to lose myself in the process. If I lost Orrin, I would lose myself. There was a real danger of that. Did I owe her, or anyone, that?

What was my role to be? Mentor to father and son, and in the twilight of my life caught up in the chasm between them. What fine quirk of destiny had brought that around? Estranged to one and saddled with an obligation that could threaten my relationship with the other, I wrestled with the way ahead. Finding the answer in the one place we all still had in common, would ever have in common, in the place it had all started.

Bock . . . *Bock!* . . . *"Bock!* . . . *Bock!* In the lee of a soft run of yelps, the sharp retort of the gobbler rang through the Spring woods in electrifying, staccato syllables, emanating from the hillside no more than 80 yards to our fore. To the uninitiated, it would have sounded deceptively familiar, like someone pounding an inch-thick stake into hardpan with a claw hammer.

Orrin whirled to look at me, his face screwed to a question mark.

"Bird!" I confirmed in a whisper. "Close."

Tugging up face nets and jerking on gloves, we dropped to the ground by the largest trees available, backs pressed hard against their trunks. Dead still we sat, doing our best to melt into the greening woodscape as the pounding inquest of the aroused bird rose and fell on the neighboring headland, and then faded into the first light of a fresh April morning. Against the acceding silence played the melodious flute and woodwind notes of nearby songbirds, and on the distance floated the raspy bark of a crow. Minutes drained past, laminated in suspense. It was time. Against the prickling uncertainty, Orrin plied the age-old invitation.

Yooelp . . . *yoelp* . . . *yoelp* . . . *yoelp,* ever so softly, in a tender suggestion. The inflection was perfect, the cadence virtual.

Nothing for minutes. Had he quit us? Apprehension hung like a guillotine.

Gobble-obble-obble! In a sudden, stabbing proclamation, he hurled his intentions into our face. It stung through the tension like a backhanded slap.

Gobble-obble-obble . . . *Gobble-obble-obble.* Somewhere near his original position and moving left across the swell, he periodically beseeched the insolent hen on the adjoining rise to put a move on. He was ready.

Yoelp . . .. *yoelp* . . . *yoelp.*

Gobble-obble-obble. He was riled but reluctant. *Gobble-obble-obble.* He continued to pace the hillside, refusing to budge. It wasn't his place, he argued.

Orrin waited past the point of politeness, edging him on, making him sweat.

Gobble-obble-obble. Still hung up on the hill, he cajoled constantly. I could see him in my mind's eye, pompous and red, swollen and spread, pirouetting and humming.

A half-hour hour into the duel we were at a standoff and progressively his ardor was waning. Time for a trump card. I awaited the next move in a neutral corner, enjoying the drama of the challenge.

W-h-i-n-e, cluck! w-h-i-n-e, Orrin pulled the siren's song from my ancient box call. Nicely done, Orrin, I thought proudly. Very nicely done.

Gobble-obble-obble. Gobble-obble-obble! It got his goat. *Gobble-obble-obble!* His rejoinder was closer now. Then the woods fell silent again. Minutes trickled by. He was on the way.

Presently I caught the patriot colors of his snake-like head weaving through the trees, closing. I saw Orrin stiffen, settle into the readied gun on his knees. Forty yards, in and out of a half-strut, then 30, the bird was drifting left. Orrin held his composure, maneuvering his gun over and around an intervening sapling when an obliging tree obscured the movement.

The blast of the shotgun thundered the climax. Orrin's shot took the big gobbler squarely in the head and a scant two hours into opening morning, the dominant tom flopped against the pine needles under the natal rays of the sun. Iridescent bursts of copper, rose, black and green flashed against the morning sun.

Orrin was up and running, dodging the sharp shin spurs and grabbing the bird by its feet, lifting it high above the ground. He stood braced against 19 pounds of pandemonium, the heavy wings buffeting his body and legs in powerful throes, fanning exhilaration into exultation, the stiffened primary feathers reverberating at each beat with the thump of a shaken bedsheet. The boy's face was to the clean, blue sky and there was a jubilant prayer in his eyes.

I watched it all transpire, thinking, somewhere along the way this time I had done something right.

Finally, the great wings weakened and fell limp and Orrin, likewise drained from exertion and emotion, laid the turkey to earth and collapsed beside it. He was flushed about as red as the gobbler and his hands still trembled. I lowered myself against a neighboring sweetgum and we sat reverently, drinking it in.

Orrin reached out and smoothed the rich plumage, caressing the glistening green breast feathers with his fingertips.

"Could it have happened more perfectly?" he said.

"No," I said.

"I wish I could put him back now."

"I know."

Long shafts of saffron filtered through the pale, newborn leaves of the oaks, hanging in shimmering, pollen-impregnated suspension between the pines. Here and there, at their tips, the woodland was splotched with gentle anomalies of sunlight and shadow. Within an adjoining hollow, a wood thrush anointed the morning with lyrical secrets.

If the moment would ever be right, it was now.

"Thirty-three years ago, Orrin, I watched your father take his first turkey on this same ridge." My throat was so constricted with anxiety I almost choked on the last few words and wished at once I could retract them.

Orrin shifted his feet and looked at me. His eyes were dark and penetrating, but free of accusation.

"I can almost understand it, right now," he ventured, tears welling.

"How he's off and gone the way he is. If I could feel like this, on and on, I'd as soon never go back either. At least I tell myself that."

"I don't think he can feel it any longer, Orrin," I said, in a partial flush of relief. I had dreaded this unbelievably, but someone higher seemed to be taking a hand. "I know he did once. We shared it together, like you and me.

"I think maybe he lost the feeling a long time ago. There's a fine line between passion and obsession. Sometimes when you push something too hard, you end up robbing yourself of that and everything else too. Maybe that's part of the reason he's back. There's an honesty in hunting. It catches up with you sooner or later, in a lot o' ways.

"He loves it, same as you and I. But something went awry. How, I'm not sure. It started with deer. I'm maybe as much to blame as anyone."

"What do you mean," Orrin asked.

"I wasn't a whole lot different from Keegan myself, Orrin, when I was younger. It just played out closer to home. I've realized that more and more as I've grown older. I pushed it and I hurt people too. People I loved.

"I pushed Keegan, probably way more than I should've, away from the real reason we were there. I didn't mean too. I didn't think he was that close to the edge. But I was wrong."

"I don't believe that," he said.

"It's true."

"I could never hurt the people who love and trust me the way my father has," Orrin declared with a hard edge of anger.

"No . . . you couldn't, Orrin. You're a different person."

"I hate him for it! I always will. He's hurt my mother terrible. I've heard her crying in bed night after night for years. I've seen him turn away from her as coldly as he would eject a spent shell. Now he thinks he can just come home and take up like he never left," he declared.

"He keeps trying to make amends, get me to cotton to him. Like I'm so damn naive I can't see through it all. He doesn't care a thing about me. He hasn't for all the years. Why would he now?"

There was a long pause while both of us repaid the emotional debt. Overhead a hawk screamed. A stiff breeze had arisen with the ascending sun, jostling the leaves and exposing their white underbellies like petticoats beneath a compromised hemline.

"Hate's a long, lonely highway, Orrin. You'll find you can stand only so much of it. It hurts you more than it does anybody else.

"You end up burying it because the person or thing it's directed at is just not that damned important in the bigger scheme of things, or you find a way to forgive. When it's somebody you love, it's much better to forgive."

"I'm not so sure of that," he said.

"You will be, when it happens. You've got to decide how important your dad is."

"It's not gonna happen!" he exclaimed in anger. "Not with me and Keegan."

"You might remind yourself that your dad and Keegan are one and the same."

He threw me a sour look.

"I'd give it some thought. Your mother's trying, Orrin. If you believe in your mother, give it some thought. She needs you."

He looked at me with piercing eyes again, and now there was an indictment, the hollow resentment of stubbornness brought face-to-face with a moment of truth. It played hard against the trust between us, then trickled away, and I knew in the moment that we had weathered it.

"Yesterday's gone, Orrin," I said. "Tomorrow's to come. Never forget, it's not that certain. Even for you. More so your mother and dad. When you get to be my age, each one's a blessing.

"Your dad's tryin' to get back. By all counts he's serious about it this time. We spend half our life going and half coming back. Sometimes it's a lot easier to go than it is to get back. And a lot of people never have the courage to try.

"Keegan's searching for where he started. You might give him credit for that . . . help him find it again, in a way your mother can't. If nothin' else, do it for her, give it a chance.

"Look around, Orrin; you've got a chance to share somethin' you couldn't before. No matter how encumbered it seems, it'll never come this freely again."

We sat on in silence for the next quarter-hour, listening to the wind play the trees, sorting out thoughts. Then Orrin arose, lifted the turkey to his shoulder and turned to me.

"You ready?"

I nodded.

The words had been spoken.

We went fishing, the three of us, the following Monday. Orrin and Haley showed up in his jeep, 30 minutes past daybreak, with the boat humping the trailer every time it hit one of the potholes in the driveway.

"Get your pole, Old Man," Orrin chided. "The croppie are bitin'."

It didn't take but a minute. Haley jumped into the back with the minnow bucket and gave me the shotgun seat. She had on a white sports bra and yellow shorts, and was as deeply russet as a buckeye. How I loved the nut-brown women.

I tossed her a grin, and looked at Orrin. "If I was younger, boy, you could have the crappie and Haley and I would go sportin'."

She laughed gleefully. "I'd go, too," she teased, punching Orrin in the back.

My old hat blew off when Orrin hit third gear. Last time I saw it, it was being devoured by a Kenworth.

"Hell with it," I hollered, so I could hear myself. "Let's go fishin'!"

Blackberry winter came and went, July sweated into August and the oppressive swelter of the dog-days' humidity loitered like a summer cold. The afternoon had been galling. Comin' sunset, Loraine and I had invested a scant 30 minutes in the garden, and were drenched in 20. We gave it up and pottered back up the path at dusk for a light supper of biscuits and buttermilk. Nightfall had set in, and there was a whippoorwill in the orchard that sounded like he could use a jumpstart. Raine was humming along in the rocking chair, shelling peas.

I had the shotguns out for inspection, three Parkers and a Lefever, scattered about the kitchen table in assorted pieces, searching for the slightest taint of corrosion. Muster was complete and I was applying a fresh coat of 3-in-1 when I caught the sweep of headlights across the back yard and the whisper of a car engine at the side of the house.

Loraine flipped the post light switch, eased to the window and peered outside.

"Kathy," she announced.

I listened with amusement at the muffled babble of the two women as they exchanged pleasantries at the door. Same drift as always. Hello took a dissertation. Mostly because of Raine, who steered it into an inventory of births, community ailments and obituaries, which is about the last thing most younger folks want to hear. They sit through it politely, nodding and smiling, while they endure the 50 lashes. I guess all old women have to carry on that way, as natural as breathing it seems. After they got hung up on the side porch, I figured Kathy needed an out.

"Evenin', Katherine," I called briskly. "Hope you're bringin' some relief with you."

The diatribe withered and Kathy trooped into the room, that gorgeous sweep of auburn hair done up neatly in a mid-back braid. It made her school-girlish.

"Fraid not. There's some heat lightnin' in the distance that's not gonna amount to anything. "Bout the best I can do. How ya doin'?"

"Well, I'm still here."

"You figurin' on goin' somewhere," she baited, pulling a smile from Raine, who had gathered herself back into her rocking chair and had her hands busily into the basket of peas again.

"Ummmn! . . . no time soon, I hope. Care to sit?"

"Can't stay," she apologized, pulling up a cane bottom. "I've been meaning to get over now for a while."

"You seem happy," I said. "Glad for that."

"I am, Alva, happiest in a long time."

"You deserve it."

"I guess. I had about forgotten what it was like."

"I think I owe a good bit of it to you. That's why I'm here.

"Orrin told me you talked to him about Keegan," she said. "I don't know what you said to him, but I want to thank you for it. It's made a difference.

"He and Keegan are talking, I mean really talking; they've even been fishin' together a time or two."

"Yes, Orrin's told me."

"I hear them talkin' now about huntin' this fall and my heart chimes. It's been good for Keegan and me too. We're actually beginning to feel something with each other again."

She paused for a moment, and grinned. "The sheets are dirty both sides now. What'cha think of that?"

I saw Raine bury deeper into the peas and accelerate her rocking.

"Scandalous," I kidded.

She laughed, tossing her auburn hair.

"Keegan hasn't mentioned once the possibility of going away again. I know it'll come sooner or later. It's in him too deeply. But this time I think it will be different, Alva. I think he's found something he won't want to lose again."

"Maybe so, Kathy. I hope." I was wondering if he had ever thought that way about me, or ever would.

"We both hope so, Kathy," Loraine said sincerely.

"Thank you."

I was preoccupied with my former thought. The words about finding something you don't want to lose had struck hard.

Kathy detected my momentary distraction. "You're still skeptical, aren't you?" she asked.

"A little. Less than I was a few months ago," I said honestly.

She studied my face for several seconds, then leaning across the table, she placed her hand on mine. "Thank you, Alva. Thank you for everything," she said.

"No kiss?" I said, looking disappointed. She leaned across again and pecked me on the cheek.

We saw her to the door and safely to the car. Raine put a brown grocery bag full of summer squash in her arms as she left. I stood on the porch, after Raine went inside, watching the car lights wander down the winding drive to the hardtop and vanish into the night. Into the void rushed a loneliness, like floodwater overriding a floodgate into a sheltered inlet. I could not stem it. Though I tried to restrain it as I had grown accustomed, I could not. It swept aside my last defenses, and in its wake welled sentiments of abandonment and longing. I was glad for Kathy and Orrin, and sad for me, and could not help it. Now, it seemed, as the others were finding their way back, I was left the searcher. Looking for something loved and lost, something that might never be found in the time that remained.

I turned to go inside. Through the window I could see Raine stirring in the kitchen. I had been comin' home from somewhere or the other for 60 years and the most comforting sight of all as I made the porch was Raine stirring around in the soft light of a warm kitchen. When she was younger, the backlighting always put an alluring glimmer in her long brown hair. Supper had waited on a low burner many a night when I was a younger man. Now her hair was silver and coarse, and no longer fell in the long fine tresses about her shoulders. I watched her for several minutes.

"Thank God, Raine, there's still you," I whispered. It would be a long night, and I was feeling weak.

II

Three weeks later, every roadside ditch, meadow and field border was painted with a gay profusion of tick-seed sunflowers, goldenrod and black-eyed Susans, brightening the countryside and inviting picnics. You couldn't help but be happy. It was all quite deceiving, of course, beauty bent on betrayal. Come November and bird season, the dried stalks of the sunflowers would become a nettlesome nuisance, their small, sharply pronged black seeds brushing off onto your pant legs and boot socks in throngs and clinging with dogged, scratchy insistence while you transported them from here to there. Finally, they would become so worrisome you were forced to stop and pick them loose one by one, throwing them to the ground in disgust and thereby assuring their proliferation another year, which was the whole purpose to begin with.

But now their ubiquitous flowers stood sweet and innocent on verdant green stalks, bowing their pretty yellow faces before the sun like curtsying maidens in white sunbonnets. Legions of Monarch butterflies fluttered among the lacy white heads of the milkweed, climbing tittering spirals into a fleecy blue sky. In the deep, shadowy woods'-bottoms, the creeks idled along gin clear and cool, as frugally as if betrothed to eternity. It was hot yet, but there was a welcome feeling of change in the air. No matter the calendar, it felt like the beginnings of fall. Anyone born to the South could have told you in a reckoning it was September again.

Orrin was off bowhunting somewhere, Raine was at the house canning beans and I was left to my own. I was lazy as the afternoon, would rather have been on a creek bank with a cut pole and a can of worms, for I was in that mood. I thought about it pretty heavy and almost mustered the gumption, but somewhere between might and manage I got waylaid in the garden.

It wasn't intentional, just a case of tortured sensibilities. I was rummaging around in the crib, looking for a worm can, and the crib happened to be next to the garden. About the time I found a Maxwell tin and was ready to leave, I made the mistake of glancing at the late squash, and the choice plant of the bunch was sprawled flat on the ground, terminally wilted. It looked so damned pitiful I couldn't walk away.

The vine borers had done their evil work, drilling into the leaf stems and encircling their tender walls until they were cut cleanly through and had collapsed helplessly to the ground, leaving the center of the plant exposed to the scalding sun. They, along with hoards of fruit-sucking beetles, had grasped the advantage now that the plants were weakened and almost spent. Every hill in the row was infested. The tomatoes were similarly under siege and short a rapid counter-attack, hopes for a late harvest would be futile. Remembering that I like fried squash about as well as I like fried bream, I cursed a mite, put the fishing trip in my back pocket and went instead for the Sevin dust.

Soon I was lost to my task, muttering in and out of the rows and dispensing insecticide with diabolical relish. It took the better part of a hour to powder the bugs into remission while sustaining a collateral battle with the sheep flies, and long before I gained the upper hand I was drenched with sweat. I was down on both knees with my cap off, wiping my brow with a shirtsleeve, when suddenly I was overcome by the strange, unnerving awareness of something or someone close by. I froze, dropping my arm slowly to my lap, listening. On cue, some inexplicable bidding seized my faculties and snapped them hard left. In the same instant I jumped, shot through with the same startling voltage you get when you blunder into a roosted bevy of quail in pitch dark.

There was a man standing there. It was Keegan!

At least it favored Keegan. The features were his, but they were no longer the boyish ones I had known. His face was lean and seasoned, and the years had chiseled deep diagonal, lines into his cheeks, and had begun to loosen the skin under his chin. There was a considerable wash of gray at his temples and gray in his mustache, and a tired, almost penitent look to his stance. It was perturbing really, that in his person was accentuated the rapidly approaching limits of my own mortality.

"Sorry if I startled you, Alva," he said. "Loraine said you'd probably be here."

"Turned out that way, it seems," I replied.

"You're well?" he asked, belying the rush of emotion inside.

"Still about," I said, managing a grin.

It seemed so little to say to someone special you had not seen or heard from in so long, but anything more was stymied by time and distance, the erosion of the amity we once had shared so freely.

"You?"

"Okay," he said.

There was an awkward, extruded pause, neither of us knowing how to proceed. Our conversation stalled like a vehicle under the restraint of an emergency brake. Beyond hello, what the hell could I say? What could I allow myself to say? What I felt? That was not easy. You can only say what you feel if you sense a reciprocity in the one to whom you are confiding. It had been a long, long time, and Keegan's way and absence had so many times seemed a betrayal to all we had known. Not a single day had passed that I had not thought of him, sometimes with pleasure, sometimes with pain. I was lost to know where it balanced. When I was honest with myself, mostly I missed him . . . very intensely in the times I wandered the wild places that had been important to us. At heart, I could not deny it. The bond between us was strained, but not broken, could never be. Least with me. Despite the consternation, I was very glad to see him.

"I never meant for this time to pass between us, Alva," he said, his voice trailing.

"Hasn't been so much the time, Keegan, as the distance," I said.

"I know," he said.

"Thought I might hear from you now and then," I said.

"I was lost for a long time, Alva."

"Maybe, Keegan, it was not so much where you were lost as what you lost." I spoke on compulsion again, not only for me, but for Kathy and Orrin.

He stood silent for a time, as if he wanted to open a door and let me in, but was hesitant to know how.

Then he looked at me with a muster of pride and sincerity. "Thank you for what you have done with Orrin. He said you encouraged him

"It was a natural thing. I'm the better for it," I said, fighting aside the greater things I wanted to say.

"I think I can remember when you felt that way about me, as well," Keegan said. "I hope I haven't lost that too."

He turned and started away. I wanted to say something, but couldn't. I wanted to stop him, but didn't.

For days I chastised myself for that afternoon with Keegan, for letting it slip away without saying the things I truly wanted to say. It plagued me like a haunted dream. It was absurd, after the hundreds of times I had wished for the opportunity to see him again, hoping that fate would somehow bring us together just once more, and that in some way we might regain a portion of what we once had known. At the moment I had been fighting the years of resentment and had not done well with it. I had wanted to punish him, to return some of the hurt. I had spoken to him through Orrin's anger and Kathy's pain, but most of all, through my own. It was a thing that had to be removed, like a splinter from a festering sore, before there could be healing. It was a step backwards, before I could again expect to advance.

I did not condone many of the things Keegan had done, but I could not condemn him for them either. My heart would not let me. He had meant too much to me. It was not so much a matter of understanding, or even forgiving; it was a matter of believing. I had been around long enough to know how very long you must sometimes believe in something, to endure all the outwardly impossible things that must transpire for it to happen, and to trust that sometimes, somehow, it will. If you place limits on faith, you circumvent hope. Hopelessness is a living death. Deep down, though he had disappointed me, I had never lost faith in Keegan . . . nor hope.

Now he had returned to me, of his own volition, and I had bluntly turned him away. He had beaten back a lot of pride to come after so long and so far. I knew a bit about that. When a man trades pride for humility, it is only because he longs for something greater, something missing, something closer to his soul. Keegan was a man of passion and extreme self-confidence. He would not have come had he not wanted, and needed, to come. I took heart in that. But he would not come again. I had given him too little in the exchange. If I had the chance again, if I wanted the chance again, I would have to make it. Now it was my turn.

III

Easing slowly out of bed, I left the soft assurance of Raine's breathing, gathered my clothes from the side chair and made my way into the hall. I pulled the bedroom door to, switched on the landing light, and dressed. It was the 25th day of September, the morning of my 80th birthday. In the fore of an approaching cold front, the rain had visited most of the night, whispering a gentle supplication from the roof and gossiping from the eaves in thoughtful, intimate whispers of years past, of my boyhood and of people gone. It had stolen away far too soon, like an old friend who must leave while the conversation is still warm. Gusting northwest winds had arrived thereafter, bullying the trees, wringing miniature downpours from the leaves, signaling the passage of the front. Behind them, the first good push of cool Canadian air would build in. Orrin would be by a bit before noon and we would go dove hunting. It would be a delightful day.

I tipped down the stairs to the side door as the wall clock registered a single stroke. Half-past-five. Slipping the lock, I stepped across the porch and let myself outside, into the face of a stiff west breeze. The air was alive and bracing, billowing into your spirit the lilt of a mid-river baptismal. It was still dark, but the sky had cleared. Beyond the brilliant flirtation of the stars, you could see forever, and the yard was bathed with a faint aura of white light from a quarter-moon.

It had taken two weeks of indecision to come to a means that might bridge the gnawing chasm between Keegan and myself. Then, a few days more for this occasion.

I stepped back inside and felt my way to the study, turned on a single lamp, and sat down before the heavy mahogany desk. On its top lay the workings of the past evening: a pair of scissors, the brown paper bag I had begun cutting for wrapping paper, an old Peters' shotshell box and a photo. The picture was a small, black-and-white snapshot of a man and a boy. Slightly yellowed, tattered at the edges and worn thin, there were tiny white creases in its once shiny surface where the backing showed through. In the more than 37 years since it was taken, it had never made it to the photo album. It had resided more accessibly in my desk drawer, from whence I had retrieved and held it many times.

Despite its depreciation, its image was clear. The man was in his prime, robust and muscular, with full, dark hair and mustache, under a cocked Borsalino, a hunting vest and a pair of field chaps. Quite self-assured, he would have been, given to wildness. The boy was about 16, slender and bare-headed, cradling a shotgun over one arm and exhibiting a grin as broad as Georgia. He was proud of who and where he was. On their flanks were a tri-colored setter and a rip-rap pointer, obviously capable, for hanging between them all on a peg was a game strap laden with quail. On back of the picture I had scrawled three lines: *Keegan, Meg, and Joe, bird hunt, the Lewallen farm, December 28, 1956.* The gent in the fedora, if you looked hard and twice, was me.

We had pointed nine coveys of birds that morning. Snow was due in the afternoon and you could feel it on the moist, chilly air and read it into the slick, gray sky. It was deathly quiet with a faint southerly breeze, just enough to keep the scent adrift. There were 12 bevies on our docket; 11 were home. Two got up wild and we pointed the rest. Meg and Joe were impeccable, trading finds and posting honor almost equally, so many times it became a matter of perpetual splendor. At every field-side and woodland pantry the birds were stirring, loosely scattered and feeding. In laid-out pea patches and spent tobacco beds, amongst the silvered pods along the beanfield edges, under ragweed over summer wheat stubble, in fallow fence corners amid the beggar lice, secreted into scrub lespedeza patches and ensconced in gallberry heads, they were foraging and reluctant to leave the larder.

Laying to point as if contained beneath a blanket, they staggered up before the gun in polite, laggardly clusters, always a straggler or two in gratuity. After the fourth bevy, we had quit the singles; there was simply no need. At the time I had known only two other such days so flawless in my entire hunting life, and have known only one other since. To Keegan, who had shot quail but relatively few times, it was a maiden lesson in the ecstasy of perfection.

We shot the last covey about the time the midday siren went off at the Coleridge fire station. The birds blew out of a ground-tight lespedeza strip, exactly as the dogs said they would. Joe took one slight step at flight and stood on his toes, marking the birds away, and Meg, backing at ten yards, swelled up where she was to honor the gun. I was shot out, at Keegan's side only to try and keep the birds honest. I flared left and inward, pressing the issue. It happened immaculately. Save a tardy, splintering pair, the entire bevy hooked right, to Keegan's side. He was shooting an A.H. Fox 16, light and fast, that he had used since he was 12. It was "his" gun by then, and though my gun shelf offered a pleasing choice, he would carry nothing else.

I watched the little gun jump into his shoulder as he planted a forward foot and leaned into the rise, his fluid swing starboard, the pull and follow-through, his unhesitant recovery, and the punch of the charge against his shoulder as he triggered the second barrel. Breaking into a puff of feathers against its own frontward momentum, the first bird fell in the field and the second collapsed into the branches of a persimmon tree at wood's edge. A drift of pinfeathers sifted by on the chill gray air, as the dogs dashed to divide the retrieve.

Keegan had looked at me then, in a manner I could never forget. He was ebullient and his eyes were wet with excitement and joy. But there was something else there too, something unexpected, which had meant far more to me. There was gratitude. It was why I could still believe.

I had smiled, placed a hand on his young shoulder.

"There'll be a few other days like this in your lifetime, Keegan," I had said to him. "If I'm not there, think about me."

He had nodded, blinking the tears from his eyes, understanding.

We picked up the two blue Peters hulls and carried them home for the special shelf in the study we had set aside for such things. It was a shrine to our most cherished adventures. Some things in it were mine, some were Keegan's and some were ours. The ones we shared were most exalted. On each hull I scribbled: _Keegan's double, comin' snow,_ and the date. Into each Keegan had slipped a small, checkered breast feather.

Of all the happenings Keegan and I had cause to celebrate, this was one of less than a half-dozen recorded to film. Raine had snapped the picture as the first snowflake fell, crowning a priceless day.

I picked up the scissors, finished cutting the brown paper bag to size and opened the flaps on the shell box. Pushing the chair from the desk, I walked to the bookcase and stopped before the center shelf. Between a wingbone call and a .35 Remington case, inside a worn and blackened dog collar, rested the two Peters hulls. I reached for them gingerly, with two hands, wishing to disturb nothing else. Two clean rings remained in the dust where they came away. Returning to the desk, I sat for long, reflective minutes, studying both the cases and the recollection. Reliving it would have been my idea of Heaven.

Inverting the shell in my right hand, I shook it slightly. Out sifted the tiny, barred breast feather, along with a sneeze of dust, its first resurrection in more than a quarter-century. I was shaken, again, by the distance and years. Not today, Old Man, not today. I entombed the feather once more, trusting that the other was intact. Wrapping the cases in separate sheets of white tissue paper I had found in Raine's ribbon box, I covered the ends tightly so their contents could not escape. From the desk drawer I retrieved a small notepad and tore away a sheet. Pausing, I considered myself a few seconds longer, and then reached for the old Sheaffer pen in the center drawer.

On the sheet of notepaper I wrote a simple message: If I'm not there, think about me.

I folded the note once, dropped it to the bottom of the shell box, and placed the wrapped hulls on top. I closed it then, wrapped it in the grocery bag paper, and taped it securely. On the face of the small package I scrawled an address: *Mr. Keegan Jeffreys, 337 Carriage Rd.* Finally, I tied it up in white twine. I'd deposit it in the mailbox after breakfast. Jim Lowdermilk would be along about ten with the morning's delivery and he would pick it up and see it safely to the post office.

I sat back in my old, creaky chair and relaxed, collecting my emotions and suddenly remembering. Eighty years today, huh? Well, it had been a hell of a long ride for such a short trip.

I got up and stretched. Raine was around and about in the kitchen. I could smell percolating coffee, new biscuits and ripening sausage.

There was a new pair of bibbed hunting coveralls on my end of the breakfast table under a birthday card and a big red bow. The fabric was the latest brushed cotton stuff with a nap like thistledown. I pinned Raine against the kitchen counter, kissed her deeply on the mouth, softly cupped her buttock with my spare hand, and mouthed my way down to the swell of her breasts in a mock frenzy before she beat me off. She backed away, flushed and grinning.

"Who're you kiddin'," she sputtered, laughing the while.

"I'm old, not dead," I countered.

Breakfast was cold when we got back. But the microwave took care of that and I was warm anyhow. Raine was floating around the table in a flight of exuberance, carrying on like a mockingbird in a pokeberry torpor. At that moment Rhett Butler didn't have a damn thing on me and I was feeling pretty good. Melissa and Dan came over mid-morning, bearing a hug, a bottle of Korbel and a case of

Winchester AAs. Kathy dropped by about 11:00 with a w
fifth of Wild Turkey, just before Orrin got there with a b
Morseth knife.

The doves flew relentless sorties over the sunflowers long after
Orrin and I had finished our 12-bird limits, and Wren, Orrin's
Springer, had worn herself happy. Under the sheltering limbs of
a big white oak, we traded easy observations on blissful thoughts
until almost sunset, sippin' cold lemonade that Kathy had sent and
watching the birds feed in and out of the field. Orrin dropped me at
the house as the day closed down, and when I walked into the kitchen
the first thing I saw was a punkin' pie cooling on the huntboard. It
was two months until Thanksgiving, but there it was, still a-steaming.
About then Raine traipsed in.

"You're pretty good to have around, old woman," I said, drinking
in another long helping of the cloying aroma.

"There's a bread pudding, too," she cooed.

I hung my cap on the door peg, stood the Parker in the corner
and eased to the table, primly set. There were two crystal stem glasses
at its center, a single, lighted candle and a bottle of our homemade
scuppernong wine. We made a new batch every year, putting the
grapes up about the first day of fall and taking the young wine off
on New Year's Eve, to toast another year. It doubled for other special
occasions over the months. I lifted the bottle and glanced of idle
curiosity at the year marked on its bottom: 1976. One of our best.
The grapes had been sweet that year.

Raine joined me, filling a portion of each glass with liquid antiquity
and handing me one. We savored the rich bouquet for a few seconds,
gently touched the glasses together and talked to one another with our
eyes. The flicker of the tiny candle flame danced in the crystal, softly
ignited the amber of the wine and reflected from her eyes. Dainty
wisps of white hair fell alluringly onto her forehead, as they had all
the many years ago when first we had met, and they were yet golden
brown. I could feel it swell, that old enchantment. I took her glass and
put it down on the table with my own and pulled her closely against
me, so very thankful she was still mine.

She leaned into me and whispered into my ear.

"I love you, Alva; please don't think of leaving anytime soon."

There was a trace of trepidation in her tone. I hugged her more
tightly and kissed her on the cheek.

"Never would be too soon," I said.

"You've been there . . ." I told her, "all these years. When I've needed you most, you've been there. You anchor my life. You always have.

"You always will."

We talked well through supper and on into the evening, visiting places we hadn't been in a long time, places that belonged only to us. It all seemed the dream it was. We retired blissfully, newly in love again, after 59 years.

But then came the insistent inquisition of darkness and it pressed me mercilessly. I lay awake in the infinite honesty of the final minutes preceding midnight, stricken with a needling apprehension. It had caught up with me . . . the uneasiness. I had done well, to hold it at length through the day. But now I could no longer elude it. I was thinking of the promise I had made to Raine, wondering if it was given with more assurance than I could warranty.

A few nights later Keegan called.

Raine handed me the phone, and there was a brevity of silence at the other end before he spoke. His voice was thick and we talked for only a minute or two. At his first word, I knew he had received my small offering.

"You kept them all this time," he said, "through it all."

"Little things from happy places," I replied.

There was another silence.

"Alva . . . the four of us are going to the mountain Sunday to sight in the rifles, maybe pack a picnic . . . just get out. Would you and Loraine come along?"

The twinge of apprehension twisting my stomach from the time I had taken the phone was subsiding, giving to gratitude. It would be what I had hoped for, a start back. I cupped the mouthpiece with my hand, relaying the invitation to Raine. She smiled, nodding "Yes." There was a gleam of thankfulness in her eyes, as well.

"Yes, Keegan, we'd like that."

"Good . . . we'll be by for you. About one?"

"One's fine." Raine was waving for my attention, reminding me to ask.

"What can we bring?" I asked.

"Bring your rifle," Keegan retorted. I grinned, knowing he was doing the same. It was an omen.

There was a last, uneasy interlude. I was about to say something when finally he spoke again.

"You'll always be there, Alva," he said, struggling with the words. I think he wanted to say more, but it was not the time nor place. For me either.

As I put the phone down, Raine speared me with a questioning look and an obligatory observation. She was already working herself up over what to bring.

"What did he say," she inquired.

"Bring a rifle."

"What!" she said.

"He *said*, bring a rifle."

"Men!" she huffed, hurling an inculpate stare at me as she made for the kitchen.

The following Sunday was one of those God-gifted, glorious October days when a numbing chill puts your breath on the air, sends chimneys of mist towering into the sky above every secluded creek and hollow, and reinvigorates your will to live. I was up to greet it, walking a winding path through wood and field as a sleepy sun began to poke a bloodshot eye above the eastern horizon. The dawning temperature stood at a fraction of its midday height, and the need for a light jacket was a homespun blessing, after the endless swelter of summer. As daylight swelled, newborn beams of sunshine stretched across the dusky landscape, gently anointing the tops of the tallest trees on the opposite hillside, softly awakening the warm hues of autumn. A band of crows swept by in a raucous rally, agile essays of obsidian written against a robin's egg sky. Staggered tribes of larks lifted from the shadows of their roosting hermitage in the tawny broomsedge and banked uniformly away in small squadrons of umber and gold. Across shimmering meadows laden with dew and spackled with shadow, each of a thousand tiny spiderwebs captured an infantile sunbeam, transforming its fragile arbor into a glimmering, milky galaxy in a vast terrestrial universe. The breaking morning was infinitely beautiful.

My step was light and the path fell away easily. I floated along with the ambiance of the morning in time with Creation and was reborn a part of it. I stopped here and there in the warming caress of the rising sun to lean on a post and do nothing more than bask like a lizard on a split-rail fence. My mind wandered comfortably with my mood, uncluttered with minutia and open to fascination. The world was full of it, the least as important as the greatest, if only you allowed yourself to look. To feel young you had to let yourself act young, and give yourself things to look forward to. I had something to look forward to. I felt like a child again, at home. Tomorrow might be a different story; tomorrow the melancholy might rise again, but today I was happy.

I piddled around the countryside until late morning, before deciding I needed to check back on the house. Raine was humming around on the front porch with the broom, frisking away the maple leaves that had blown under the eaves. They were vivid red against the gray floor, and I kind of hated to see them go. Left to my own, I would have leave them lay until December.

"Gorgeous morning," she declared.

"Truly," I said.

"We're ready." A large, oak-split basket was brimming on the side table, beside a pumpkin and a shock of Indian corn, covered with a gaily crocheted throw of navy blue and cardinal red. Picture perfect.

"Pretty," I remarked as I opened the screen and went inside. I grabbed up a Winesap as I passed the kitchen table and made my way to the study, stopping before the cherry gun cabinet and studying its contents as I worked on the apple. After a few bites I laid the core aside, unlocked and opened the glass door. I'd take the .270 Winchester today and the Weatherby .257 Melissa and Dan had given me. I scrutinized each and then cased them. The Weatherby was a Lazermark, a pretty little piece of modern-day laser fabrication with typical California styling and a 2.5 x 10 Swarovski scope. The recoil was negligible, which made it a joy to shoot, but I still leaned toward the European lines of the pre-war Model 70.

I sorted through the ammo stores and found plenty of each. I dropped two boxes into a canvas bag, started to push the door to and hesitated. The little Remington Sportsmaster begged my attention. It sat humbly in the back of the cabinet, heretofore subordinated from view by its larger brothers. On impulse I pulled it out and slipped it into a soft case, then set it down beside the big rifles. Throwing several boxes of .22s into the kitty, I was satisfied.

I was a bit nervous and fidgety by noon and, moreover, angered by my unsuccessful attempts to avoid it. Apprehension churned at the pit of my stomach, pushing its way into my throat and lodging there. Would after-life with Keegan be forever this way? Would we never again know the complete ease and abandon that once we had? Perhaps not. If so, it would have to spring from a different footing. I would have to meet him as a man, a man of considerable stature, and not as the boy I knew and mentored. I might be years his senior, but I was no longer miles his better. Though that was inanely obvious, I was having a harder time with it than I should, and it perplexed me that I could not determine why. It was certainly not a question of dominion or rivalry.

Maybe it was just another, sadder form of the same old vulnerability; maybe it was that, the closer I got to Eden, the greater I yearned to be a boy again, and it was harder to achieve that in the company of a man than in the company of a boy. And I had run out of boys. It was the kind of convoluted reasoning I had been reduced too these days. The greater likelihood was simply that I was about to be in the presence again, after so long, of someone I deeply cared for, that years and the river had stolen from me, and that the outcome of our meeting was more crucial than anyone could know.

They came along shortly after one – Keegan, Kathy, Orrin and Haley – in a long blue Chevy Suburban. The highlights of the dimpling sun played through the trees and onto and off the mirror finish of the vehicle as it proceeded up the path to the side porch. Raine and I were sitting there, waiting and watching. Sweatshirted and jeaned, Kathy, Haley and Orrin all spilled out one side, Kathy spurting exuberantly to whoever was listening, and Haley lunging gleefully to escape Orrin's grasp. Young love was wonderful. Keegan climbed out the off door, smiling. It was good to see them together, and happy.

"Hello the house," Kathy chirped.

"Hello yourself."

Raine and I met them halfway up the path, and exchanged hugs with the girls. Orrin slapped me lightly on the shoulder, and bubbled a one-line account of the black racer they'd seen cross the road so fast his body had seemed a chromatic illusion in the surface of the blacktop. It pleased me that he still got excited over such a small enticement as a snake sighting. Keegan was up by then. His face was soft and he extended a hand. Our grip was warm and firm.

"It's a rare day, Alva," he observed, looking about him.

"Truly it is," I said.

We stalled at that for the moment. Fortunately, Haley blurted something that broke the awkwardness. Then we were quickly busy, gathering the trappings.

Keegan relieved Raine of the oak lunch basket, and made his way to the truck, while I grabbed up the guns. When he opened the rear hatch, it was already gorged with gun cases and picnic fixings. With a little rearranging we found room for ours. I saw Keegan glance with particular interest at the soft case as I placed it among the others. I wondered if there was a telepathic connection.

"An old friend, I believe," I said casually.

"Really?"

It was a lightly attended question and I let it lapse for the time, partly from reticence and partly for intrigue.

Orrin and Haley piled into the third seat, I helped Raine into the second and we were off. Kathy and Raine coasted into distaff pleasantries, Haley and Orrin exchanged whispered nothings, and Keegan and I were spared the clumsiness of immediate conversation. It was a small, circumstantial favor, well received. I did not do well with small talk. If there was something that would better the moment, then I said it. Otherwise, I tried not to denigrate silence. I knew too little, as yet, of what I should say to Keegan anyhow.

The hum of the tires on the road and the passing scenery lulled me into meditation and, abruptly, I was taken with irony. The reversal was replete. In the summer and autumn of my life I had spent myself on two boys, and now they sat as men on either side of me, each having taken in his way what I had given and having nurtured it far past what it could have been on its own . . . two generations of Jeffreys and a third already a gleam in Orrin's eye. There was a time when I had more of them than their own fathers, and they would have accepted from me any truth I suffered to offer.

There was a time when both had stood in awe of me and were eager to follow my beck and call, a time when we were bound inseparably by adventurous abandon. There was a day when I was confident at showing them the paths I had trod before them and a day they had thrilled at the chance to follow. And now that I had reached winter and spent ever more time looking back, I could see just how far they had come.

Each was superbly accomplished afield and afloat, confident with

themselves to be so and respected for it by their peers. And here I
sat, to myself at least, in awe of that. Here I sat the beneficiary of
their sharing and happy to follow. Here I was, feeling a little meek, a
little inadequate even. Perhaps for no reason, but still. And had they
not, with excusable exceptions, taken what I had given and done with
it exactly as I would have wanted. I was a little ill-at-ease, but it was
nothing that was going to hurt me. Mainly I was proud. Like a Lazy
Susan, the table had turned. It was all rather marvelous really.

What were their thoughts of me now? There remained an
affinity, which seemed genuine, but what was it made of? Tolerance?
Gratitude? Obligation? I hoped respect was still a part of it.

Burkhead Mountain was one of Alfred Jeffrey's many foothill
holdings. I knew it well, as did Raine. I had wandered its entirety
when I was a lad, and Raine and I had gone there often during our
courting days. Old John Burkhead was a kindly man, and all he asked
of life was a gun, a dog, a two-room shack and an existence free
of people he didn't invite. He had gained his extensive holding as a
family inheritance, had money in the bank and, by repute, had never
made a withdrawal. He scratched out a hardscrabble garden each year
in the stony soil of a southern exposure, trapped, hunted and fished,
gathered roots and herbs, bartered for the bare necessities, and sold
wild honey and hides to pay the taxes. He had a woman once. You'd
see them walking along the shoulder of the road, to and from the
mountain. He led and she followed, obediently by all appearances, by a
habitual distance of several yards. But he outlived her and died intestate,
and Alfred Jeffreys had later procured the property at public auction.

Sometime after the old man expired, a pair of hikers found his
bones, scattered about the shack and yard by scavengers. That would
have been fine by John; he scattered a bunch of theirs. The Sheriff
and county coroner were summoned and they simply gathered up and
buried what they could. Folks say you can still hear the old man hawk
his dogs from the mountain top about false dawn on a clear, quiet,
moonless night. Old John was a strange sort by some folks' measure,
but to live and die and never have to leave the place you love never
seemed too odd to me.

The mountain had not lost its charm in the years since the
old man's demise. The vast acreage on its southern and western
perimeters was now federal wilderness area, and there were state game
lands to the north and east. It soldiered the Uhwarrie River, and the

isolation of its rocky balds and escarpments continued a delightful escape from civilization. On it were pockets of magnificently mature white oak, hickory, maple, poplar, beech and pine, high above the lush bottomland vegetation draping the river and bordering strategic thickets regenerated from selective cut-overs of latter-growth timber. Sprinklings of laurel clung to the slopes, subsisting in relative obscurity until their delicate pink blooms gave them notoriety in late spring and summer. In fall the hardwoods were spectacular, pulsating with crimson and gold within the perpetual rhythm of sunlight and shadow.

The mountain itself, along with its spacious apron, encompassed more than 4,200 acres. There were only two means of ingress, that belonged, respectively, to the state or the Jeffreys. It was rich with game, with wildlife in general, sequestered as it was, and a place of serenity and loveliness.

In a primordial epoch the elements had loosened an immense outcropping of granite on the western slope of the mountain. In the aftertime the bedrock had relinquished its purchase and the entire formation had succumbed to gravity, toppling to the river and partially interceding its flow with one knobby protrusion. At its tip, the rock had sheared and a great slab lay abreast and above the current, a broad, flat table around which the water laughed and tumbled as it rollicked like a somersaulting child to regain its forward momentum. There was a serpentine walkway of smaller stones, which led there in progressive steps from the riverbank, across a lucent, eddied pool jeweled with fallen leaves of red and gold. At the inception of the walkway was a lowland glade, feathered with lush, green fern and sprinkled with toadstools. Giant white sycamores towered overhead, bending far over the river in an attempt to touch their equals on the far shore. Along the adjacent hillside, buckeyes grew in abundance and in October opened their leathery seed heads to tender to receptive dreamers the homey charma of their mahogany fruits.

Little had changed in the centuries since the rock had yielded and to the Indians, this must have been a place of special magic. When the river was low, you could sometimes find pieces of figured pottery on the sandbars. Occasionally, ceremonial spearpoints of flint and quartz revealed themselves in the glade, and once Orrin and I had found a pipestem and a fragment of its bowl embedded in the clay of an undercut bank. Many a primitive hunter must have come here to assuage the spirit of his quarry and many a brown maiden must have sat on the rocks, combing out her long black hair and speaking beneath the breath of the water her heart's wish.

On the great table of rock we spread our picnic and lazed in the reflected warmth of the mid-afternoon sun, while we ate and talked among ourselves about simple, happy things that belonged only to the moment . . . the cloudless perfection of the sky, the sparkle of sunlight on the river, the joy of being alive. Around our granite island the water swirled ceaselessly, lending a constant illusion of motion and weightlessness, a feeling that we were being whisked along in an extrinsic dimension.

Leaves sifted down on a light westerly breeze, idling and tumbling slowly to the water, painting pirouetting impressions of yellow and vermilion against undertones of blue. We lay on our backs after a while, watching them down, caught up in the drama of their destiny and the strength of their message. Beauty and death again . . . to all things a season.

Orrin and Haley slipped away presently to be alone. Raine gave me a tender, heedful look, and I surrendered as I had the first time, reaching for her hand and thinking nostalgically and somewhat enviously of what it was like to be so young and newly in love. It was the same with us upon a time, at this very place. I was enchanted with every turn of the earth, as long as Raine was in it.

I had skipped stones for her across the quiet pools and we had sat shoulder to shoulder on a hot day with our bare feet in the water while I carved for her a miniature waterwheel with my pocket knife. We had set it awhir in the tailrace of a Lilliputian rapids, interlocking paddles of ash on a dogwood spindle, and it sang like our heartstrings. I had pushed her backwards to the water and she had not resisted and I had kissed her long and deep as the cold water rushed over our bodies. Afterwards, we had stripped to little less than modesty, and dried our clothes in the warmth of the sun on this very rock, and I had marveled at the curve of her neck and the swell of her breasts and the longing in her eyes. The woods and the waters had closed about us, guarded our privacy and locked away our secret for all eternity.

I glanced at Kathy and Keegan. She was sitting within his interlocked arms, looking over the river, her back against his chest. The glow was there. Which is most lasting, the pain or the pleasure? One pushes us away, the other pulls us back. They were together again. What more was there to say?

We walked along the riverbank, the four of us, in hand with Nature. Frost had not yet ravaged the wildflowers. Scattered, extravagant clusters of spotted touch-me-not still bloomed in freckled orange pendants, each tiny flower like a swollen drop of sourwood honey. Daisy-pedaled puffs of sneezeweed hid in bashful, sunlit pockets among the ferns; aptly named, its flowers could be gathered and dried into a primitive and potent form of snuff.

In the sand at water's edge were the meanderings of the forest creatures: tracks of coon, bobcat, muskrat, otter and mink, and on the soft bench of earth between the river and the mountain, deer had walked and played. A redtail hawk screamed his hunting cry to the wind, gliding and banking in concentric circles high above the tallest trees, on wings as white as canvas. Ahead a squirrel scurried for cover, scampering the length of a fallen log, vaulting to a nearby gum and flicking into a den hole. In a moment the tip of his nose reemerged to angrily bark his contempt. On a stump were pulpy remnants of red seed clusters from the dogwood, where he had feasted but a few minutes before.

Deep within the forest a wood hen asserted its presence in repetitive shrieks, its probing inquisition into a hollow trunk reverberating soundly between-times. Splashes of chalk painted the leaves and damp black earth under a run of saplings; a few feet more and the twittering culprit sprang to air, lifting its plump body and hairpin bill through the intervening limbs and over the covert only to flitter down again a few yards farther. Everywhere about us life resounded with the rhythm of the season.

By mid-afternoon we had drifted our way back to the Suburban, meeting Orrin and Haley along the way. We hauled out the guns and a portable shooting bench, a spotting glass and lawn chairs for the ladies. There was a 200-yard fringe of flat ground between the mountain and the river, some 60 yards wide; against a hillside at its far end we erected a grided, bull's-eye target. On the tailgate of the truck we assembled a small arsenal. Keegan laid out a custom .300 Win. Mag. and a Ruger No. 1 in .280 Rem., Orrin his Sako .243 and Remington 7mm Mag., alongside my Winchester and Weatherby. It seemed almost irreverent to disturb the tranquillity of our surroundings, but gun season would be in shortly and the rifles badly needed a test run.

We exchanged turns, Keegan, Orrin and I, firing three-shot groups until each piece was tuned to minute-of-angle or better. It was good to feel the jolt of the rifle against your shoulder again, to smell the freshly burned powder on the afternoon air, and to absorb the heavy, instantaneous thud of the muzzle-blast against the mountain before it resonated down the long riverbottom. There was a time when I could print a three-shot group and have each hole touching the other. I still did pretty well, but my eyes were no longer what they used to be. I watched Keegan and Orrin lay them in with the big magnums round after round and started feeling a little inadequate again.

Finally, I asked Orrin to polish out both rifles for me. He especially liked the .257 and ended up finishing one box, and half the other. When he had, it was grouping far more accurately than I, personally, could hope to shoot it. All the better. It would be his before long anyhow.

Kathy took a turn at the .243 and the .280, and there was little doubt of her familiarity with either weapon. She was good, very good. But then Keegan had taught her, and I had taught Keegan. It was a thimble of salve for abraded masculine pride.

Orrin put Haley on the .243 then, her first go at a centerfire rifle.

"What do I do, Orrin," she whimpered innocently. Orrin hovered over her like a hummingbird in a petunia garden. Kathy and Raine exchanged artful grins, thinking Keegan nor I were looking.

"Okay, Haley, pull it tight into your shoulder, like this. Snug your cheek to the stock and relax." Every instruction came with a tug or a touch.

She looked up from the stock with soft, liquid eyes. "Do I just pull the trigger?"

"Don't just pull it; squeeze it gently," Orrin counseled cheekside.

The gun went off. The bullet printed five inches high. The second was six clicks left.

"OOoohhh," she said.

"Try again," Orrin encouraged.

She did. For some time. Her groups remained ragged, but her aim was dead on. She may not have mastered the rifle yet, but she had Orrin well within in her sights.

Funny thing . . . how men love to escort women through little wondrous adventures of apprehension, believing all the while they are the ones doing the navigating. I had seen the same thing with foxes once. The male led the female high above a creek, up a precipitous incline to a pinnacle of rock. There was another rock rising from the far bank, with an anxious gap between. The male had leapt it easily and then turned to coax the vixen. She hesitated a proper moment and then made the jump. The next time, as the male bunched for the jump, she masterfully cleared both him and the rift. When next I went there, they had a den on the hillside. I imagined the same thing would happen to Orrin soon.

When Haley had finished with Orrin, we wiped down and cased the guns, and picked up the spent brass. When things were in order, I retrieved the soft case from the back of the Suburban.

"I wondered how long you were going to make me wait," Keegan said. I looked at him whimsically. "An old friend, huh?" he said.

I unbuttoned the flap and slipped the little Sportsmaster from the case. Along with it came a flood of nostalgia.

Keegan's face lightened. "I have wondered occasionally if you still had it."

"A lot of things might leave," I said, "but not this."

I handed it to him. He turned it in his hands and brushed a palm across the flat of the buttstock. "God, Alva, it's been 40 years," he exclaimed.

"Forty-one," I corrected. "You were hard on the black snakes then."

"And everything else," he laughed. "This is the gun I learned to shoot with, Kathy, the first I gun I ever shot. I killed my first squirrel with it."

"Yes," I agreed wistfully.

"And I mine," Orrin added.

"And I mine," I repeated, "70 years ago."

There was a moment of deference as our eyes met and bonded. What passed between us was more than amazement. It was an accord of passage that could perhaps only be understood by men, bound up in the imperative link between yesterday and tomorrow. A boy must become a man in the presence of men, and tomorrow is possible only because of yesterday. What a man did yesterday in the presence of men defines who and what he is, and binds up his confidence. A man needs yesterday to brave tomorrow.

Along the same path, in different generations, each of us had made our way. Each of us had become a man because of a man. All were enshrined in the .22 Remington: the man, the rite and the reason. For me, it was all that remained of the man who had meant more to me than any other, the tangible epitome of the man whose memory, even yet, assured my daily passage from yesterday to tomorrow. For Keegan and Orrin, I realized from the look in their eyes it was the same, except that it was not yet a memorial. It was an affirmation I sorely needed.

"Seventy years and three boys," Keegan observed respectfully, handing the rifle to Orrin.

"It's survived a lot," he added. "See that long gash near the bolt handle? It got that when I slipped and fell in the creek hunting snakes.

"Remember those two big water snakes that always hung out as a pair at the Grady Place bridge, Alva?"

"Oh, I remember 'em," I said. "That's where you stayed for two summers. I'd drop you off in the morning and collect you at the end of the day. Couldn't even get you up for dinner."

"I got the last one that second summer. Then I wished I hadn't. It was never quite the same there again. There was nothing to look forward to like before."

"Anticipation is mostly the best of it," I said.

Orrin turned the barrel away, raising the little gun to his shoulder and sighting down the riverbottom. "Well, most of that 70 years is between you two graybeards," he asserted, "just like most of its scars. I took pretty good care of it."

"How 'bout that chip behind the trigger guard," I said. "Who did that?"

"Happened when some old man dropped it on the gearshift," he chided, somewhat accurately, but also forgetting that particular injury had occurred when he had banged it against the lantern runnin' for a treed coon one night.

I stepped to my cartridge bag, grabbed up four boxes of .22s and pushed them into Orrin's stomach.

"Respect your elders, boy, and show us how you shoot."

He laughed. "You two old mossbacks ain't nursing any rash ideas about whipping me I hope."

"Name your poison, boy," Keegan challenged.

"Pine cones at 50 paces," Orrin returned. I knew I was in trouble. At fine shooting, my eyes ran out at about 30.

"Couldn't we . . . " I started.

"Fifty paces . . . them's my terms," Orrin reiterated.

"Gather 'em up," Keegan said.

Orrin retired to the woods with two grocery bags and a pine cone requisition while Keegan paced off 50 steps and dragged up a dead log to mark the line. Soon Orrin was back with both bags full. He laid out 15 cones atop the log and stashed the bags behind it. Meanwhile, I was figuring some kind of edge.

Kathy, Raine and Haley pulled their chairs closer to the shooting bench now that the big noise had subsided, assembling in a garrulous gallery.

"You women got to be quiet now," Keegan admonished. "This is serious business. Young Orrin is about to be chastised for his insolence."

"I got a good idea who's about to be chastised," Kathy said.

"Pride before honesty," Orrin declared, gesturing first rights to Keegan.

Keegan mimicked a wounded grin, picked up the Remington and offered it to me.

I raised both arms, palms forward in refusal. "I'm holding myself in reserve," I said, "just in case you two get over your head."

Behind me, Raine snorted.

Keegan opened the tubular magazine, dropped cartridges in until it would hold no more and pushed the rod home. Dropping to the bench, he pulled the rest into place and relaxed into the rifle. He breathed deeply and exhaled slightly, aligning and steadying the iron sights until they were faithful to their target. I could scarcely discern the trigger squeeze. It was all in a seamless motion, so facile and fluid as to be habitual. I could immediately grasp the hundreds of times he had done it in the past 30 years, in all the many places. There was an inoffensive, searing crack as the tiny bullet fled the barrel and down-range the left-most cone shattered into bits above the log. As perfectly, he ran a string of nine more before his concentration lightened and he passed the gun with a smile to Orrin.

Orrin was subtly though visibly impressed. I don't know what he had expected, but if he was surprised, I was not.

To his credit, he collected himself, and I saw not the slightest wobble in the muzzle when the trigger traveled the first time. The fated cone ricocheted wildly off the log with the impact of the bullet. The final four followed suit. Orrin cleared the gun and Keegan went to replenish the target. When he came back, Orrin reeled off five more hits.

He handed the rifle to Keegan, without emotion. His mouth was pursed and set with determination. I could see something developing I didn't like.

"Good shooting, Orrin," Keegan observed. Then he split ten more cones almost as impassionately as a drowsy checkout clerk gives change for a dollar.

Orrin replaced the cones and reached for the rifle. He took his time and all 15 cones, and never broke a smile, even when Haley bid her admiration.

The score stood at 27-27 when the cones ran short and Kathy and Haley were sent for more. The match had become far too serious and I was growing more uncomfortable. I could sense the malice rising in Orrin and it was not a healthy thing after so much progress. Keegan seemed to have forgotten the greater purpose also. He had discarded the mitigating banter and engaged an imperturbable, proficient rote. He was in no way rancorous; he was just Keegan.

"You boys need some relief," I said, trying to levy the tension. "Maybe I ought to step in a while and put some comedy in this convention."

"Not yet, Alva," Orrin said. I settled back, noting the tight lines in Kathy's face.

Keegan had run 49 straight when Orrin finally missed at 47. After so many perfunctory hits, it seemed almost a delusion to see the cone still resting there after the shot. It might have been better had Keegan chosen to miss first, but it was simply not within him to do so. Orrin was embarrassed and sullen, enough that even Haley hesitated, uncertain of whether to approach him.

It was Keegan who restored well-being. He rose from his chair and went to Orrin, absent any superfluous gesture that would have been untrue to the moment.

"You're good, son, very good," he said, from the heart.

Orrin looked at him without compromise, fighting back the emotion, trying to remain the man.

"I wanted to beat you," he declared, frustration flashing through his eyes. "I thought I could."

"I know," Keegan said. "You will soon enough. I can see that. Meanwhile, I guess it's kind of important to me to hang on as long as I can. Maybe you understand that. If not now, someday sooner than you can possibly realize, you will."

The words cut me to the quick. They were not mine, but they were awfully familiar.

Orrin's lips worked with unspoken anguish for a moment, and then the dam broke and the tears fell, and father and son embraced. Whatever distance remained between them had closed.

In respective degrees, we were all shaken for a time. Conversation was sparse and circumspect, and it took several minutes for affairs to return to normal. Then Haley stood and moved close by Orrin's side, entwining his arm within hers. She abided there patiently, with wisdom enough not to speak, until Orrin had recovered. Haley was a girl worth the journey.

A sudden, stiff breeze broke the malaise, enlisting the swelling, late-afternoon chill as an ally and bringing a shower of leaves swirling past. Raine and Kathy took it as a cue, stirring about to collect and organize the picnic leavings, initiating preparations for departure. The sun was drooping low in the southwest, resting temporarily in the uppermost fork of a sycamore tree, above the muted purple crest of a neighboring mountain. Below, the darkening ribbon of the river was draped in shadow. The day was waning. Kathy slipped by Keegan, who was picking up .22 hulls, to whisper something in his ear and brush an appreciative kiss by his cheek. I retrieved the little Remington and occupied myself with cleaning and casing it, thinking the while of how I would make the difficult decision to whom I would entrust it, Orrin or Keegan.

When I looked up, Orrin was standing there, a bright, new aluminum Americase under his arm. Haley was close behind him, with Keegan, Kathy and Raine alongside. All were smiling as if they knew something I didn't. Orrin swung the gun case up into both hands and held it out to me. I looked at him with a question.

"Yours," he said.

I accepted the case gingerly and placed it on the shooting table. My hands were trembling, not solely of age. Tripping the latches, I carefully opened the cover, and was astounded. On a carpet of velvet cloth lay the most exquisite long gun I had ever seen. There in special order splendor was an absolutely gorgeous sporting rifle by Dakota Arms in .25-06, crowned with a Leupold 4 x 12. The wood was presentation grade maple, richly butternut and shot through with wafting feathers of darker caramel. The artesian blue of its slender barrel was fathomless. The stock waist and forearm were adorned with debonair splashes of fleur-de-lis, and within the borders defined by their flourishes the checkering fields were so finely and virtuously cut that each small diamond resounded with fidelity. Along the receiver, floorplate and breech arose tasteful accents of rose scroll, artfully betrothed to the symmetry of their purpose. Inlaid in the buttstock was an oval of German silver, with an inscription:

Presented to
ALVA AADLEY TREADLOCK
on the occasion of his eightieth birthday
by
Keegan & Orrin Jeffreys

I was shaking by then. I raised my eyes to look at them and tried to talk. But I was dumbfounded and speechless. Raine was smiling for me. She had known.

"Happy birthday, Alva," Keegan offered. "I'm sorry it's late."

I lifted the rifle from its case then, raised it to my shoulder and sighted at something imaginary in the distance. I couldn't see, of course, because my eyes were welling, but it fell in beautifully.

I looked at Keegan and then Orrin, and still I could say nothing.

They made it easy for me. Moving close by my side, Keegan left and Orrin right, they framed me for posterity. I returned the rifle to its bed of velvet, Haley faced the opened case forward to complete the composition and Kathy caught the picture. In it, I stand about as limply as an overworked dishrag in a sidewalk soup kitchen. The rifle alone was grand, but the grandest gift of all was the reunion. To have both Orrin and Keegan at my side after so long completely dismantled me. It was another smattering of reality that could only seem a dream and I was detained in the interstice between the two. I wasn't at all sure I ever wanted to return. An essential part of me had been restored and I was as close to whole as I had been in many years.

"There are some blessings in this life a man can never really deserve," I said to them, "so there must be some reason for them he was never meant to understand."

"I've asked myself, many times, how I came to have the two of you . . . how it was that forty years ago, a boy happened along with a puppy and a BB gun. I had never seen him before and yet from the first minute he was familiar. It was as if he grew out of me. He liked the woods and wild things. So did I. Lord God . . . look where it has led."

"I think it led where you led, Alva," Keegan said after a moment, his voice breaking.

I considered that momentarily, pondering the extent of its truth. I knew he was thinking of the good times, but I was thinking of the whole.

"We're the ones to be thankful," Orrin affirmed.

Kathy came forward to hug me, as did Haley. Raine, last and sweetest, kissed me on the cheek and said the rest with those deep, wet, brown eyes. As quickly as I could I broke away for a few minutes, to be alone and gain some semblance of composure.

When I returned, the sun was touching the rim of the mountain. Haley and Orrin had gone for one last tryst with the great rock, and Raine and Kathy were predisposed with packing. Keegan was sitting alone by the riverbank, elbows on his knees, holding council with the river. As unobtrusively as possible I joined him. He glanced around, informed by the slight rustle of the leaves. I stood beside him in silence, watching the dark water fade by. A leaf drifted abreast, powered solely by the current, the wind drained from its upswept sail. It wandered with the watercourse like a small Viking ship. With its passing I was given to surmise what Keegan was thinking, wondering if there was wanderlust in it. He had too much passion to forsake it indefinitely. It must be intense by now, with the months that had passed.

"It's been a good day, Alva," he said, his gaze over the river unbroken.

"Very good," I replied.

"Same old story," I said, "the happiest times of your life are the shortest."

"Wish I could stop the train," he said. "It's been pretty good lately."

"It can scare you," I returned, "when things go too well."

"Never lasts . . . not that perfectly."

"But don't worry, it takes a lot to shake the things that are really important. They become too much a part of you."

"I hope so. It's taken miles and years, but I believe I know now . . . what's most important.

"Guess I knew all along, really. I didn't do a very good job with it. But one thing had to play out before another. I don't think it could have ever been any other way with me."

"Has it . . . played out?" I asked.

He turned to look at me. There was a tempered hurt in his eyes. "No," he said.

"No," he repeated more softly, looking away again. "It still pulls at me. Every day."

"It's in you, Keegan; it will always be," I said to him. "You can force yourself away from most anything but your heart. Some day, one way or another, you'll have to go back and retrieve the part of yourself you left behind."

"The damned thing is, you can never really go back," he said. "Not in the same way."

"No, never in the same way," I agreed. "There's always a price. It's always the one thing to play against another.

"But sometimes, if you really want to, you can get back enough to be whole again. Sometimes grace allows you that.

"When it's somebody you're trying to get back to, mostly it's getting past the uncertainty that it's mutual. When it's some thing, it's usually that you wore yourself out on it the first time, and no matter how hard you try, you know you can never do it as well again.

"Or else it's finding the balance between the some thing and the some body.

"In the end, it's a matter of distance, I guess. You've got to keep enough distance to be rational, but stay close enough to feel the enchantment. I think, Keegan, maybe it's a matter of learning how to love something without killing it.

"That's never easy . . . maybe impossible . . . for some people the first time. The old thing about love being lovelier the second time around may hit pretty close to home.

"You've made it back to Kathy and Orrin, and I'll be honest with you, I never thought it could happen. All I can say is how happy Raine and I are that it has."

"It hasn't been easy for me," he said.

"No doubt," I said.

Keegan pulled himself away from the river and turned to me again.

"You were the bridge, Alva . . . you and Raine. You were always so sure of yourself in every thing we did. It always seemed so easy for you. You always seemed so comfortable with who you were and where you were.

"And every evenin' when the sun fell, you went home to Raine. Sixty years together now, the two of you, and it's always seemed so right. When things were hardest, I kept thinking about that."

"It hasn't always been quite that certain or blissful, Keegan," I confided. "I can assure you the biggest strain on it was me. There were a lot of evenin's then I never made it home.'

"But you lasted," he said.

"Yes, we have lasted. It's been good."

"I've always loved Kathy, Alva. I lost sight of it for a long time and took it for granted a long time more, but I never stopped. Then I started thinking about her more and more, and how it would be without her.

"I'd think and dream bizarre things. One night I even dreamed about wind chimes. Kathy and I always loved them. In my dream, the wind died forever so they could never chime again, and they became tarnished and covered with cobwebs. It seemed so symbolic it wiped me out for weeks.

"Always when I thought of her, I thought of you and Raine, and all the years you could look back on together.

"In the meantime, the hunting was going sour too. Nothing was right any more. Then one day I found I out I loved her more than I ever knew I did, and, even more, I found I needed her . . . to make everything else right. So I came home.

"I had to get back," he declared. "I was so lost and so unsure for so long, in and out of myself like a light bulb loose in its socket. One day I'd be me, confident and brash, the next, totally limp and unreliable.

"It shook me . . . hard.

"It's unbelievable how you can suddenly become such a stranger to familiar places. Tanzania, the Selous, is spellbinding for me. It's always taken me beyond myself – where I wanted to go. But I was there just before I came home, and I felt like I no longer belonged. It was eerie. It hadn't changed; I had.

"On one of the days I was haywire, I botched an easy shot on a buffalo. Smacked him in the gut, of all things. I'd never done anything like that before. Ever. I was hunting with John Sutton. I've hunted with him a number of times over the years. John's good as gold, but crusty. He started cursing, balled hell out of me, wanted to know what the goddamn shit was wrong with me. He had every right.

"So there are John and I and two Swahili gun-boys, teetse-eaten and thorn-bitten, tracking a rank buffalo we shouldn't have had to worry with in the first damn place, and all of a sudden I come unhinged and cry for no reason at all . . . goddamned crying in the middle of a buffalo hunt!

"I don't think John ever knew the difference, thank God. It all looked like sweat. Five minutes later I was myself again and finished the job. But it threw me."

"Just what did happen, Keegan . . . with the hunting?" I said. It was a question I could no longer resist.

He was silent for a time. In the lower reaches of the riverbottom a big owl murmured a welcome to nightfall.

"I guess I just didn't believe in what I was doing anymore, Alva," he said finally. "It got to be too much about killing and too little about feeling. You started me different from that. I guess it finally caught up."

Like John Sutton that day in Tanzania, Keegan could not see, as we sat in the swelling darkness, that there were tears on my cheek. It had taken a long time, but I knew now that Kathy was right. Keegan was back. I was right to believe.

It was dark when we left the river. Overhead, the moon and stars commanded the heavens and the night was filled with stillness. Above the light disturbance of the leaves under our unhurried feet, another sound carried on the chill air, arresting us momentarily to listen. From wood's edge came the staccato bounce of a retreating deer. Then another.

"I love it, Alva, you know that," Keegan said wistfully. "I miss it. The wonder and the wander. I've got to get back."

"You'll find the way," I promised.

I could hear Seth Thomas striking nine as I turned the key in the side door lock, pushed the door open for Raine, and stepped behind her into the kitchen. She fumbled for the light switch. The brightness was disorienting for several moments, colliding with the remnants of our night vision. Glancing out the window, I could see the tail lamps on Keegan's truck climb onto the hardtop at the end of the drive and turn east into darkness. Raine took off her coat and immediately fell to unpacking the picnic basket and straightening around. I returned for the guns, pinning the soft case between arm and body, collecting a hard case with each hand and making my way like a cinch-bound mule from porch to study. I tripped the wall switch with an elbow, shifted my burden onto the couch, and exhaled.

It had been *some* day.

I moved the gift case to the coffee table, opened it and lifted free the Dakota rifle. I laid it in my lap and studied its eccentricity. What an exquisite tribute. A little optimistic, perhaps, at my age, but wonderful. Probably the thing that endeared it most was that it had been in the works for some time. Even with Keegan's Dakota connections, it must have been ordered months ago to get it here this quickly. Keegan had been trying, in his own way, to bridge the gap between us, even while I was trying in mine. And he might have misplaced for a time the ethics I had tried so hard to instill long ago, but he had not forgotten. They had returned to him, of his own impetus. I put it to rest that night, for good, all the years of absence and obsession, disappointment and pain. It was time. They would no longer stigmatize my existence, nor repress my affection for Keegan. His atonement was complete.

IV

Another November opened to a medley of old money color. Gone was the flamboyant heraldry of its precursor . . . the defiant effrontery of the maples, dogwoods, gums, and poplars . . . the opulent scarlets, pulsing vermilions, vibrating oranges, and energetic yellows . . . renounced for the stoic, quiescent hues of the elder guard. The oaks draped their great shoulders with cloaks of maroon and the hickories pulled on coats of aged tobacco gold. Summer's last line of defense surrendered to fall.

Nights were cold and midday was mellow. Morning found the green plumes of the pines hoary with frost and twilight huddled to earth under the make of the Hunter's Moon. Across the land, the verdant thatch of summer was withering and wasting, and the fields fell ever more gaunt. With growing fury, merciless north winds hurled punishing gusts to press a frigid warning, while all the world made ready. The initial shiver of winter had been felt and the year was admitting for the first time that it was growing old.

In paradox, November was old age at its best, bringing a penchant for tarrying at length with simple pleasures and the wisdom not to fight it. The result was Indian summer, a golden state of mind between yesterday and tomorrow. In it were invigorating, flawless mornings that rejuvenated the soul, aimless, nurturing noonings of lying on your back and staring into faultless blue skies and happy meanderings in afternoons sun-splattered with perfection. In it were a gun and a dog, the woods, waters, and wild things, the wistful fragrance of chimney smoke at dusk and the distant lights of home across the fields in the chill of evening. In it was Thanksgiving, the succulence of yesterday's turkey hunt, punkin' pie, people you love and the promise of the deer you would get on the morrow. At its close was the satisfaction that, whatever lay at hand, for once you had lived life to its fullest.

Each Christmas, I hoped for another year. Each autumn, I begged for the privilege of another November.

Keegan, Orrin and I lived it to the hilt, sometimes as a pair, sometimes a threesome. There was an undeniable urgency in it for me, born of premonition whether real or supposed. I spoke to no one of it, not even Raine. But I sought to enjoy its season as I had never before, to sense its every breath, to feel its every heartbeat, to give myself to it so completely that, should there never be another, there could be no room for regret.

It did not disappoint me. Within its spell, I found again with Keegan much of the fulfillment I had known so long ago, the totality you find only in the presence of the painfully few people in your life who are so singularly special. We wandered the fields and woods paths that had been freshly familiar to us those many years gone. Some had changed, of course, altered by time and dimension as also we had been. Nevertheless, in all some charm remained, waiting to be extracted by diligent reminiscence. Keegan and I reveled in doing so, sharing at length with Orrin the small, wonderful things that had composed the sum and substance of our lives then, when the only thought that had constrained the morrow was how best it might be spent. With each resurrected memory we became ever more easy.

Despite my best efforts at detaining it, the month refused to abide. It scurried past like stolen time, aging prematurely into its final days, leaving me with the same anticipatory morbidity I used to feel a millennium ago when I was a school kid in his last week of summer vacation. I strained to savor every fleeting minute, faced once more with the infinite monody that all good things must end and striving with all my being to defy the truth of it.

Thanksgiving dawned cold and still under a slick, gray sky. When I awoke, Raine's side of the bed was empty and she was already astir in the kitchen. The invitation was out for the traditional dinner, and fixings had recommenced well before first light. Shortly, Melissa and Kathy would be over to lend hands, Haley would be in from school to join the ranks and by early afternoon something wonderful would happen. Lying in bed, I could hear the radio downstairs softly droning an old-time hymn and, intermittently, the muffled clatter of cooking pans. The homey magnificence of steeping sweet potatoes had climbed the stairs and it was probably wishful, but I thought I also caught the beginnings of the turkey, corn pudding and oyster dressing. Excitement overcoming reluctance, I brushed the quilts aside and piled out onto the cold floor. Dressing quickly, I followed my nose to the kitchen. Raine was fashioning pie crusts and humming along with the radio. I put my hands on her hips, leaned over her shoulder and kissed her on the cheek.

She purred a tender "good morning" and whispered "Happy Thanksgiving." I kissed her again and returned the wish.

A tea kettle was whistling for relief on the stove top and the coffee was burping rhythmically into the glass bulb on the cap of the percolator. I inspected the latter, pulled a cup from the cupboard, and poured it half full.

"You're rushing it," Raine cautioned.

"Life's short," I said, tossing a grin at her and getting one back for the effort.

I sipped along slowly and then decided I was hungry. I got up and reached for a plate and two buttermilk biscuits from the warming bin. My old friend Garland Basford had sent some Georgia cane molasses up from Moultrie and a jar of mayhaw jelly. I loaded one biscuit with the one and the second with the other. Raine made a face and shook her head.

"Just go on about your rat killin', old woman," I said, "and don't mind me. I'll be out of your way presently. Got to go check on the dogs."

She blew through her mouth.

"When's Haley due?" I said.

"Mid-morning."

Good, I thought. *Couldn't have Thanksgiving without Haley.* I wished to hell Orrin would hurry up and marry that girl. If he didn't, maybe I would.

I finished my makeshift breakfast, grabbed my coat and hat off the peg, pulled them on and stepped outside. The air was damp and chilly, and a steady northerly breeze ruffled the hair at my temples. I turned my back to it and started toward the kennels. Halfway there I heard a car door slam and looked back to see Melissa and Dan making their way up the steps with arms full of bags and covered dishes. I waved a backhanded hello and marched on. I'd be up in a minute. Now I was anxious to see my dogs.

Wren, the springer pup, caught my approach and bounced out of her barrel in an exuberant clamor, racing around the run in streaks of liver and white as I neared. Roused by her alarm, the resident population spilled out in turn, mounting a general quarters uproar. It was a kind of music . . . unorchestrated, but appealing . . . the soprano clip of the fiests, the ripe tenor harmony of the Beagles, the baritone chorus of the pointing dogs and retrievers, the bawling bass of the hounds, the alto notes of the Boykin and springer. Dancing at the fence on hind feet and clamoring for position, each occupant bestowed a welcome fit for royalty and begged his or her opportunity at the day's hunt.

What a man my age was doing with 15 dogs was hard to say. Actually they weren't all mine. Three were Orrin's and two were Keegan's, and one other of the pointing dogs was Jim Lowdermilk's.

But that was little more than a technicality. They lived with me, and trusted in me, and the days of their lives ebbed and flowed with my passing. I loved each and all. I had seen most of them into the world, watched them pass the perils of puppyhood, trained them through headlong flights of addled essence, and basked in the brilliance of their prime. In the season of their perfection, we soared in a union of spirits through a mutual quest for completion and attained it together in a field of dreams. And when their season was past, I comforted them as best I could amid the despicable infirmities of old age and struggled to uphold my shattered soul as I was forced to bequeath their mortal remains to a lonely mound of earth. The ties that bound us could never be severed. They taught me the meaning of loyalty and honesty, and the value of constancy.

In the fire of their eyes, then and now, resided the affirmation that I had lived. I strove, each day, to persist in honor of their memory. They drove my existence and motivated my being, and in times of utmost need I drew on their heart and courage to persevere. They were the tap roots of my virility; the secret of my strength. I did not ever want to know life without dogs, and when my time came, it was to them I would look to endure death.

I worried about them now. What would happen to them when I was gone? Some would outlive me. It had come to that. Always before the injustice of normal expectancy had dictated otherwise. Now, one day too soon, they would be the ones left to grieve. Who would comfort them? Would they be loved and treated well, and most of all, be given the chance to do the one thing they lived for, to run and hunt the golden fields where the birds gathered or the moonless hollows where the night critters walked? I knew, of course, that Raine would care for them if she was here, but Raine was young no longer either and even should she survive me, there would quickly come a time when she could not manage.

I might expect that Dan and Melissa would take the Boykin or the springer and maybe one of the feists, but they already had seven other dogs of their own. What of my hounds and pointing dogs. Tell whined and bawled his impatience at me . . . the big, rangy rascal. Only a hunter could love a hound. I put my hand through the wire, let it rest atop his broad, black-and-tan head, and met his eyes. I knew how it must be. It was Orrin and Keegan that I counted on. I would ask them for their word. In this, they must not let me down.

When I returned to the house, Keegan's Suburban and Orrin's jeep were in the drive. Everyone was happily gathered in the kitchen, jesting and laughing. Dan was tucked into a corner out of the traffic, sitting backwards in a ladder-back chair, sucking an orange. Keegan was parked at the table with a mug of spiced cider, Orrin standing with his back against the counter munching a Winesap and dodging the women as they darted here and there in a cooking frenzy. The aroma of their collective efforts had grown to an intoxicating swelter.

"You boys waitin' for a hand-out or just generally gettin' in the way," I inquired, pulling loose the ties on Raine's apron as she hurried past.

"Generally getting in the way," the women sang in chorus.

"We're kind of supervisin'," offered Keegan. "We know that's usually your job, but since you'd gone to the dogs, we've made a meager attempt at filling in."

"The emphasis is on meager," Kathy opined.

"Didn't me and Dan manage the quality control on the sweet taters?" Keegan retorted.

"You ate one if that's what you mean," Kathy snorted.

"I can see I have gotten here in the nick of time," I said, tossing a look at Orrin. "Nothing you could do to take this atrocity in hand?"

"Not since you arrived," he teased. I cuffed him lightly on the ear.

Raine jumped in. "Don't the dogs have anything for you all to do this morning," she said.

"Matter of fact, they did have a suggestion or two," I reported.

"Well, you best be at it, so they can have you back here about one o'clock."

"Good advice," I admitted.

I walked to the study and came back with a shotgun and shell vest. I was already in my hunting boots, standard equipment for Thanksgiving Day.

"C'mon, young Orrin," I motioned, "those dogs of yours want to see if you've improved any since last time. Besides, you don't want Haley to know you've been mopin' around all morning waiting for her. You'll be housebound the rest of your natural life."

Raine squinted hard at me.

I gestured at Keegan and Dan. "You two can come along if you're whoa-broke."

Raine stepped over and gave me a peck on the cheek at the door, letting the batter in the bowl she was holding rest for a moment. "You're incorrigible," she vowed.

"If that means handsome and headstrong, I'll suffer it," I said.

She grinned.

We left the womenfolk be and spent the better part of the morning at quail on the Sommers Place. Orrin's two setter derbies, Pat and Mike, gave a much better account of the bird-finding than we did with the shooting. By 11:30 they had pointed four coveys, handling each with finished manners and grandstanding on three or four singles with nary a bobble. Exuberance only rarely over-ran obedience, a rather dazzling performance for a fiery set of youngsters. Orrin was proud. Me the more.

Switching about in pairs on the gunning privilege, we held to two guns on the rise, and downed 13 birds between us. Not an exemplary shooting display, but sufficient to keep the dogs happy and more than enough for our mood.

By design, we made the bottomland pastures of the Tillman farm just before noon. It had rained earnestly over the preceding few days, tapering, but not before the diminutive branch that resided in the low ground had been incited to rebellion, jumping its modest banks and flooding the adjacent sloughs. The combination of its recent recession and the prodigious rainfall had left sizable pools of surface water speckling the length of the drainage and had softened the fertile black earth to a gentle cohesion.

Across its entirety, the valley teemed with snipe. You could see the small bands rise and fall on fleet, rapier wings, skimming and banking the lowlands, flashing underbellies of silver with each flitting turn. Leashing the pointing dogs, we entrusted the balance of the hunt to Jodie, the Boykin. Save a couple of divided retrieves with the setters, she had been remanded to heel – until now. Sensing the offing, she danced and whirled beside me, piercing me with electric eyes, pleading release.

To maintain order, we elected the same gunning plan as before, posting only two guns to the fore, left and right, leaving the idle pair in reserve. Keegan and Orrin were awarded first honors. We made ready, the Boykin bunched and cocked her hindquarters, and I hit the whistle.

Galvanized with passion, the spaniel tore in a flattened, liver blur for the front.

"Close, Jodie!" I hollered.

She flinched slightly at my voice, breaking her forward drive and swinging far left, overwrought with exhilaration. I yelled again. She reversed, crossing ambitiously right, then cautioned herself and settled with the efficiency of a metronome into a companionable, quartering sweep. She had barely made the first flooded swale when the first flight of birds sprang to wing. A band of seven rolled starboard and jetted across Keegan's flank, voicing their irritation in short, raspy *scaips*. Two larger squads jumped a scant instant behind, wheeling and flaring in sequence over Orrin's head.

I hit the whistle sharply as the guns bounced up, Jodie slammed brakes and dropped to "Hup," and Keegan's Red Label 20 thumped the air. On the fringe of the bunched, fleeing squadron, a small, dusky clump of rapier geometry pitched and fell. Closely behind, another. Off Orrin's left shoulder, a lilting bird caromed obliquely off its bearing, avoiding the searing rush of 8s that passed dangerously past its tailfeathers. A companion only wingbeats behind was not so fortunate, running headlong into the second charge and blowing limply into the arms of gravity.

Jodie fidgeted, marking the falls.

"Hold, Jodie!"

As the shots rebounded against the marshy bottom, the dark earth ahead lurched again and belched five more bunches of careening birds. They shot by us on every side, in unnerving flits and bounces. Keegan missed, shoved in fresh shells as the ejectors jacked the cases past, and rallied in time to crumple a crossing left and an outbound right.

On Orrin's side, two birds fell in unison to a single charge, while a third shot by unscathed. Clawing the spent hulls from the chambers, Orrin jammed in one shell, dropped the other on the ground and fought his vest pocket for a replacement. Finding it, he slammed home the breech, banged the Fox to his shoulder and made good with both tries. Waves of trailing snipe blew past as Keegan loosed a final shot and then, suddenly, the air was empty.

The headlong silence of the filigreed tension was like a step off a blind cliff. Whining and wheezing, the setters slammed against their leashes, dancing and tangling.

For a moment my reflexes collapsed. Wresting them back, I glanced for the Boykin. Still in place, but barely. Mincing on hind legs, she begged the whistle. Two piercing notes sent her into a frenzy.

Scorching to the mark of the first fall, she gathered Keegan's bird to mouth, rushed it by my hand and sped to favor Orrin. Checking herself in mid-stride she circled, regained the disclosure of the breeze, closed in concentric semi-circles and stabbed the snipe with her nose. Soon all birds were in hand save the last.

Orrin's last had fallen to the water, a nondescript clump of wet feathers amid the grasses, and it took several minutes for the perplexed spaniel to unravel the mystery. Exhausting the alternatives and surmising the problem, she raced the edge of the pool with a high-headed inquest, extracting a faint clue. Reversing and correcting, she searched methodically for its source. A suspicious black knot was apprehended in an explosive spray of water and, shortly afterward, blissfully delivered to custody.

"Good girl, Jodie," Orrin praised.

She shook and wallowed, stationing beside me without command, smug and aloof. I reached to scratch an ear. She shunned it as a priggish young lady might fend an untoward advance, reminding me she was working.

Then Dan and I took a turn and we all tracked out of the Tillman bottom, thoroughly muddy and miserably happy with three limits of snipe. By the time we rounded up the Suburban, reached home and kenneled the dogs, it was 1:20. Hanging the birds to cool, we rushed for the house.

Raine took one look at us from the porch — fouled and splattered with a mix of black mud and Holstein offing — and refused admittance. Haley was behind her.

"Ooouh," she said, wincing at Orrin.

"Is that all I get," Orrin asked.

"Oooouh," she said.

"Don't fret Haley," I said, "he'll wash up nicely."

"Oooouh."

"You all go 'round and come in the back," Raine ordered. "And leave those boots on the porch. And get out of those pants."

"That'll be a sight," Haley snickered.

"Yeah, one you won't see," Orrin said.

"What're we supposed to wear," I said, begging the question.

"I'll throw out a clean pair of pants or two. Keegan ought to be able to get in one of yours," Raine declared. Keegan dropped his head and studied his feet.

Melissa and Kathy walked out. "There's an old pair in the back of the wagon for Dan," Melissa volunteered. "I'll get them."

"They've got holes in the seat," Dan objected.

"What am I supposed to do?" Orrin asked.

"I'll throw down some of Alva's pajama bottoms," Raine said sweetly. "I'm sure they'll be fine." Haley giggled.

"Be damned if I'm sittin' down to Thanksgiving dinner in a pair of pajamas," Orrin vowed, turning beet red.

"Go on around back . . ." Kathy pleaded, "we'll work out something."

When we got there, there were four clean sets of clothes on the washstand. Admit it or not, female intuition can be a wonderful thing.

We gathered at the table . . . steaming, colorful and fragrant with autumn harvest, so bountifully spread it could not have accepted another bowl, dish or platter . . . joined hands and returned thanks. Moments of silence closed our humble prayers. In them was the opportunity for private words of gratitude, for an unassuming petition from an overflowing heart. As sincerely as I knew how, I begged homage for our simple, country lifestyle, which at once seemed so grandly opulent, and for the gentle, enfolding reassurance of friends and family. For the most special day of November and for the privilege of living it. For upland fields and bottomland pastures. For little brown dogs on spaniel paws. There are times when the wealth of your blessings is inestimable.

For all its beauty, dinner was painfully fleet. By mid-afternoon Orrin and Haley were up and saying "good-bye," off to spend the balance of the holiday with Haley's folks in Edenton. Melissa was gathering and wrapping leftovers, and it would be only minutes, I knew, before she and Dan would excuse themselves and likewise depart for the Cameron household. It was all as should be, of course. We could be granted only a part of their lives now; the rest was given to others. Nonetheless, it was saddening that so wonderful an occasion must end so soon. The parting was harder for me now than it ever had been.

I shoved past a moment of helplessness and consoled myself with the hope that Keegan and Kathy would stay. Keegan's folks were with friends in New England and Kathy had lost both parents to the tragedy of a car accident years before. As for Raine and I, aside from Melissa and Dan, the few family ties that remained were tenuous and remote. The many beloved people around whom our earlier lives had been so deeply and richly woven had fallen away. All's left was each other.

We saw Orrin and Haley away, and then Melissa and Dan, watching them down the drive from the yard.

"That was us only a few years ago, Keegan," Kathy said, speaking of Orrin and Haley. "It's hard to believe; now we're the older generation. You may be a grandpaw some day before long."

"Let's don't hurry it, Granny," Keegan implored, wrapping his arm around her.

"Not much you can do about it," I said. "It hurries on its own."

"Just wait," Raine sighed. "Melissa will be 53 this year. Tell me that doesn't frost your punkin'."

"You've weathered well, Loraine," Keegan consoled.

"You held her in one hand, Alva, the day she was born . . . remember?" Raine said, staring vacantly down the drive.

"Two years later she was playing in the sandbox with Mattie, when Mattie was a puppy. A few more and she had up and married Dan. Where did it all go?"

There was a period of disengagement. It was a question without an answer, the ageless enigma of time and the river.

Raine caught herself. "I've been working on a new quilt," she said, brightening as she turned to Kathy.

"Let's see it," Kathy replied, starting with Raine for the steps.

I was relieved as they went inside, thankful that Kathy had accepted and that she and Keegan would be staying awhile.

Keegan and I ambled to the barn where the snipe and quail hung. Overhead, the sky remained gray and expressionless, without hint of the sun. Along the horizon, ashen clouds brooded in long twisted cords, stacked like wet sheets spin-cycled to the walls of a clothes washer.

"Almost favors snow," Keegan observed.

"Almost," I agreed. "Not quite cold enough maybe. Feels like low 40s."

"I wish it would . . . what a way to cap the day."

"Not much hope. Too far south. I can't remember it ever snowin' on Thanksgivin' Day . . . in 80 years . . . has on Christmas a few times. When I was a young'n in grade school, we always sang Over The River at Thanksgivin'."

Whimsically, I broke into the first two lines. Keegan picked up the second and here we were, two grown men with more snow in their hair than they could hope for on the ground, singin' Over The River in the barnyard:

> Over the river and through the woods, to Grandmother's house we go,
> The horse knows the way to carry the sleigh, through white and
> drifted snow-ow . . .

We held and emphasized the *snow-ow*. It was fun. It brought that capricious flight of emotion you get when you do something crazy in the midst of something serious.

"White and _drifted_ snow, dammit, and we can't get a flake," I cajoled.

"I always wanted to live where it snowed on Thanksgiving Day," I said. "Vermont or New Hampshire. Guess now I never will. Man can't have everything, I suppose. But you, dear Keegan, are a young feller. You still can."

"There's some gorgeous country in the Northwest," Keegan replied. "It would be easy."

"Well, why the hell aren't you there?" I wondered.

"Because you're _here_," he said, looking at me briefly. There was more than a trace of sincerity in his gaze and I was taken back for a moment.

"And Mama and Daddy are still here," he continued. "I think Kathy would do it. And Orrin is his own man now."

"Maybe I will someday," he said, after a stint of silence.

"It's good to have you back, Keegan," I said spontaneously. "There were a lot of empty years while you were away. You mean much to me."

I struggled hard with those last few words, as one man must when he reaches into his soul and extracts for another feelings of honest affection. But it was something I very much wanted to say to him, while there remained an opportunity.

My forthrightness disarmed him. He stopped and turned to me, struggling also with the clash between emotion and masculinity, wanting in the moment to be a boy again.

"It's good to be back," he said. He paused, fighting the well of sentiment in his eyes. "You made it all happen." He could go no further.

We sat on respective stall sills and cleaned the birds. The words between us were sparse and mindful while we immersed ourselves in drawing and plucking and searched for the footing back to levity. There seemed yet a ways to go. Keegan appeared ever more absorbed the nearer our task drew to completion.

"Let's take a ride, Alva," he said. "Let's go walk in the woods. There's somewhere I would like to go before the day closes. I want to put something right."

I wondered, but said nothing.

"Do I need a gun?" I asked.

"No," he said. "Not this time."

There was little more than an hour left in the day. I stopped at the house, stuck my head in the door and yelled to Raine and Kathy that we were leaving and to expect us about dark. They were absorbed with quiltery and were unusually complacent. I climbed in the Suburban. Keegan was waiting for me behind the wheel.

We rode only a short piece, to the McKinnley Place. Keegan steered the farm path past the house and tobacco barns and hog slats, wound through the fallow, silvered fields that stretched away behind the barn, and pulled to a stop under the great oak at the break of the low ground. I got out, shut the door gently and took a look back at the meager remnants of Mason McKinnley's existence. The house and outbuildings huddled in the distance at the hilltop, lifeless and gray against the cold. I remembered them in better times, when they were vibrant with children and dogs and joy and hope. Mason and Martha were good friends.

Keegan picked up an ambiguous woods trail that hid behind the oaks and fell off down the hill along a hardwood ridge. I knew where we were going now. I wasn't sure why.

The woodland was somber and retiring behind the burdened mask of the sky. Everywhere there was stillness. I followed as Keegan led. The trail seemed steeper than once it had, my legs less sure. How different it had been the last time we had passed this way when I, so confidently, had been the one to lead. Now I followed as we dropped lower and lower along the brow of the ridge until we reached the crown of the knoll that overlooked the small bottomland glade Keegan and I had hunted that prophetic afternoon so many years before, when the big owls had worked their clandestine magic. To the place where a moment of truth had spawned years of dissolution.

Keegan searched a minute, then stopped before the leaning maple in which he had sat that day. Above its lazy trunk, the stolid, black limbs wound skyward, branching and forking like the veins on the back of my hand. A pittance of pale red leaves clung forlornly to the terminal twigs of its drip-line, a few lonely soldiers left to guard a hopeless front. Below and west lay the little glade, still green with fern, and the intersecting creek that wandered intimately along its contour.

Keegan looked into the vacant limbs for several seconds, then directed his gaze to me.

"Alva, do you remember that afternoon years ago, when we hunted deer here and you heard those strange sounds?"

"Very well," I said.

"I lied to you that day, Alva. It's eaten at me every since."

Keegan paused . . . surprised, perhaps, that my face remained expressionless . . . then continued.

"That buck did come by me that day. Right up the rub-line, right by this tree, just like you thought. He was tremendous and I had the shot, point-blank."

"And you couldn't take it," I said quietly.

"I couldn't take it.

"He was the biggest thing I 'd ever seen. You know what it had been up until then . . . does and forkhorns. I wanted a big deer so bad. He was huge. I thought I was ready and I wasn't.

"I watched him all the way through this end of the bottom. I saw him stop and mill around, just as you did. Then he came right on out of the bottom and up the hill, straight to me.

"I had to watch him too long, Alva. He scared me. I couldn't believe what happened. I got hot and sick. I was sweating and I thought I was going to vomit, but I couldn't.

"I was shaking so hard I had to hold on to the tree. The sweat was pouring. By the time he got in front of me, I couldn't even breathe.

"Finally, I started gagging, gasping for air."

Keegan paused, then continued.

"That was what you heard. I thought I was going to pass out. On and on. I couldn't quit. My hands were like lead; the rifle weighed 50 pounds. I kept telling my arms to move and they wouldn't.

"The whole time, the buck never paid the least mind to it. He stopped once, listening. Then he just sauntered on like nothing was happening. I guess he thought it was owls.

"I did get the gun up, for what good it did. I don't think I even threw the safety. It was too late anyhow. He was gone then . . . had just melted away, into the thicket.

"By the time you got up here, I had recovered enough to put

up a front. But I was devastated inside . . . disheartened, angry and dazed. I had let everybody down. Myself. You. Most of all, me.

"So I lied to you . . . the only time ever."

He stopped, looking to me for a response.

"I guessed as much, Keegan, at the time."

"You never said anything."

"No."

"Why?"

"You were a boy then, still a boy. There was no dishonor in it. I had been there myself. I knew it wasn't easy. I thought it was better left alone.

"A man can't be at truth with somebody else until he's at truth with himself. Only when his confidence and humility overcome his pride. It takes a man a long time to come to that. Many never do.

"I worried about it later, when I realized how much it was affecting you. By then I had waited too long. If I had said something sooner, I might have saved you a lot of pain."

"No, Alva," he said, "you couldn't."

"You were right. It was something I had to do on my own. As for the pain, it took me to a lot of wonderful places I would never have known. Places that were worth the pain."

"What happened, Keegan?" I asked earnestly. "I understood the disappointment and the determination, but not the anger."

Keegan did not respond for several moments, gathering himself for the task. Resting a hand against the trunk of the tree, he lowered himself as if he was greatly burdened, to one of the large surface roots at its base. I did likewise.

"It's not easy to explain," he said. "Maybe it's one of those things you never really understand about yourself. It just happens and carries you along, like a feather in a stream, and all you know is that you have to go. Other people get caught up in it too, and there's always some regret. But it's not about somebody else. It's about you."

He looked at me. His gaze was resolute, almost accusing.

"I was trying so hard back then to be something I wanted to be, and was so frustrated that I couldn't.

"I tried harder than I ever had. And then when I thought it would happen, I had that day with the buck and it all fell apart. It took the heart out of me. Then I got mad.

"It kept working inside me, like a pile of maggots.

"Mostly I was angry with me, but partly I was mad at you."

The comment caught me off guard. Keegan recognized the surprise in my eyes, the question that was rising closely behind it.

"It wasn't easy living up to your standards, Alva, and I wanted too so badly. I could never do it. And when I failed you kept pushing me.

"You were never tolerant, you know. I loved and despised you for it, all the same time."

"The best never comes easy, Keegan. You have to give more if you want to go higher. I tried to show you that. I know now I pushed you more than I thought."

"I don't think you ever thought about it, Alva. It was just you.

"Oh, the lesson took. It was hard, but it took!" he said, eyes burning. "A few miles and years later. And I was thankful for it. When it did, I drove myself harder, harder than you ever did."

"I thought about it," I said, "mostly from my viewpoint I suppose. I thought about it a lot later, when you were off and gone all those years and I never saw you."

There was a period of detachment, then Keegan huffed, something between a laugh and a groan. "You know, the funny thing is I became just like you. The two most popular words for describing Keegan Jeffreys are insensitive and intolerant."

"Fine pair, ain't we?" I observed.

"Maybe. We've done things most people never will," he said seriously.

Keegan gazed at me with wonder in his eyes. "Everything seemed so easy for you back then . . . big deer, doubles on quail, callin' turkeys . . . showin' up boys."

His face lightened with the last few words.

"I had worked at it a long time, Keegan. That's the part you wouldn't see."

"You were a legend, Alva," he said.

I had been thinking of Keegan as the boy again until then. I had a bad habit of that. Suddenly I remembered who he was. This was a man, a man with world-class entries in every major trophy book in the sporting kingdom, a man who had encircled the world more times than I had been out of my home state, who had done things and seen things I would never, informing me that I was a legend!

"I was determined to do it, to be like you," Keegan continued, "just as I was bound to avenge myself for that day in this tree. So I just kept going and killing deer until I did. And after deer, it just naturally led to a lot of other places."

"You've done it," I said, "several times over."

"It kept burnin', drivin' at me. But I'm more comfortable now," he said.

"The urge is still strong. Not so much to prove myself any longer . . . not how big and how many any more . . . just to go, to be there. I love it, Alva, all of it. And I left things along the way, things I intend to find again.

"They may open the Sudan again soon; if so, it'll be grand for a time. If they do I'll go . . . and take Orrin, and Kathy too, if she'll come."

"You should," I said.

"Come along," he said honestly.

"I'm afraid my chance at Africa passed a while ago, Keegan. I let it slip by. I'll have to see it through you. You need to tell me more of it soon."

Dusk was settling into the glade below, chasing the retreating light to the ridgetop, much as it had all the years ago. After all the miles and years, life had come full circle. A boy had grown a man, and an old man had been pulled hard against a simple truth. You can only start a thing; you cannot know the path it will take nor where it will end.

"You've come far, Keegan," I said.

He stared away into the growing darkness of the bottom for several moments. The muscles in his jaw quivered slightly and then he turned to me, speaking in a quaking voice.

"I may have set the rudder, Alva, but you were the sail . . . you were always the sail."

Unsuccessfully, I fought the welling of the tears.

"You were the son I never had, Keegan. No man could have asked for better."

We sat for many minutes, maybe a little uncomfortable with the intimacy, letting the darkness engulf us. It was deathly quiet. On the distant hillsides, lights began to twinkle through the trees, and somewhere below, the creek could be overheard, sharing its notions with the night. Neither of us wanted to leave.

"We'd better go," I said finally. "Raine will be worrying."

Keegan gave me a hand up and we felt our way up the ridge. Three-quarters of the way to the top, I stopped for a breather. Far below, in the vague blackness of the bottom, a big owl called for the first time. Another answered at the fringe of hearing. Some small creature, probably a mouse, rustled a leaf. Then all was still.

We topped the hill and walked the last few yards to the truck. The hulking black trunk of the oak grew suddenly out of the darkness; overhead, its great fingers clutched queerly at the sky. Across the open fields the night spread away with a strange, tensioned uncertainty and the air was unduly damp and chill. The closeness of the truck cab was welcome. Keegan stirred the engine to life and we wallowed back up the rutted farm path. We rode in silence, alone with our thoughts. The lonely shape of an abandoned building shadowed past on either side, then the indistinct bulk of the house itself. I wondered if there were any trees left in the old orchard to the east. Winesaps. Mason loved Winesaps. The trees were his pride and joy.

I was lost in yesterdays again when Keegan slammed the brakes and the Suburban jolted to a stop.

"Alva, look!" he exclaimed, as I slapped a hand on the dash to catch myself.

He threw open his door, tumbled out, waved me to follow.

I opened the door and climbed into the night. At first there was nothing. And then I saw them, slipping silently past against the glow of the headlamps . . . tiny shards of snow.

V

Three weeks had passed since Thanksgiving and we were hard onto Christmas. I had not seen or heard from Keegan in the interim and I was mildly concerned. Where once his absence would have been a matter of course, it was now uncharacteristic, and I had grown accustomed again to his presence. It was Wednesday afternoon before the holiday, and Raine was hunkered over the kitchen table amidst joyous bolts of wrapping paper and a riot of ribbons, tying up the last of our presents. Orrin was off shopping, of all things, with Haley, and I was at loose ends, thinking I might as well grab up a shotgun and a dog and try the doves that had taken up in Clyde Overton's laid-out cornfield. I was halfway to the gun cabinet when someone tapped a car horn.

I glanced out the kitchen window on the way to the porch. The blue Suburban with the SCI, WTF and DU stickers on the rear window sat in the drive, so it had to be Kathy or Keegan. Either way, I was pleased.

It was Keegan. He opened the door and stepped out about the time I hit the porch, throwing up a hand. "Chris'mas, Alva," he called cheerfully.

"Chris'mas, Keegan," I said as I made the steps.

Behind the reflections on the glass of the truck there was an allusion of motion, something or someone else fidgeting on the front seat. Keegan leaned over to acknowledge it, saying something I could not hear. My first thought was a puppy, but it seemed larger. Making his way around the hood of the truck, Keegan crossed to the passenger door.

The heavy door swung partially open, on the losing end of a determined struggle, and a small pair of dirty tennis shoes popped out. Above them was a leached pair of bluejeans, one cuff up, the other down, with a raveled hole in one knee. Then came a Star Wars teeshirt with a small, blue jacket over it, a wriggle and finally an abundant thatch of blond hair under a camouflage cap. It was a boy.

In the process, a slingshot fell to the ground. He bent to retrieve it and his cap fell off, causing the long blond locks to spill into an unruly tumult over his forehead. With one hand, he brushed them back to submission, gathered up his cap and slapped it over his head a bit off-center. Stuffing the slingshot into a back pocket as he regained his feet, he moved to Keegan's side. He stood there studying me, with soft, appraising eyes, neither shy nor forward. Somewhere deep inside me the old kinship stirred.

"Alva, this is Brad," Keegan said. "He likes woods and wild things."

Keegan looked deeply into my eyes for several seconds and I into his. An ancient message carried between us, sifting down across the generations with a gentle affirmation.

"Brad, this is Mr. Treadlock," Keegan proceeded, turning to the boy. "He kinda likes wild things too."

The boy extended a small hand past an abbreviated coat sleeve. I took it in mine and a lot of years fell away. He withdrew it almost at once, ill at ease, studying me again with cautious green eyes. I smiled inside. He looked to be nine or ten. There was a fine innocence in his soft features and a malleable promise to his carriage. A careless tease of ginger freckles bridged his nose and a twinkling of down glistened on his cheeks like the tiny hairs on butterfly wings. But there was something more; I could see it in his eyes. There was a budding passion. I knew him well. He might have been me all the many years ago, or Keegan in his time, or Orrin in his. Through him the circle could be completed. Through him a man could grow to be a boy again. I wondered if fate had picked him for Keegan as it had Keegan for me.

The dogs were raising Cain at the kennel. Brad glanced furtively in their direction.

"You want to see the dogs, Brad?" I said.

"Yes-sir." I smiled inside again at the "Yes-sir."

I put an unpretentious hand on his shoulder and we started across the yard to the kennel. A shadow floated by our feet, traversed the corncrib and climbed the barn, stalling there and banking back upon itself. Its source soared lazily overhead, between sun and earth. Brad followed the buzzard intensely, enthralled with its size and proximity. It had been a while since I had known the utter fascination of a boy's eyes.

"I've been teaching Brad to shoot the last three weeks," Keegan said.

It was if Keegan's words unsnapped a lock. "We put a can on a log and I knocked it off," Brad boasted proudly. "We made this beanshooter too, see?" He pulled it from his pocket and thrust it at me. I took it and turned it slowly in my hands.

"It's a fine one too," I said. "You need to burn your initials on it somewhere. That way everybody will always know it's yours and that you made it."

He looked to Keegan for approval. Already, the adulation was there. I had forgotten how deeply it could run.

Keegan nodded.

Old Tell bawled an unearthly welcome and incited every other dog in the kennel to pandemonium. I hollered sharply and they quieted.

Brad walked to the trembling hound, hunkered down at the gate and offered a hand. Tell mouthed it piggishly, then ran his muzzle through the wire and ran a great, drooling tongue the length of Brad's face. The boy giggled and wiped the slobber away with a back of a sleeve.

I studied him appreciatively. He had the mettle.

"He's a big one!" Brad cried.

"He's a coon dog, Brad," Keegan explained. "You know those tracks we saw in the creek the other day. Well, that's what he's bred to hunt. He runs 'em up a tree and then barks for you to come."

Tell bawled a validation. Gypsy, his kennel mate, wailed a high-noted second. It prompted another robust chorus from the entire choir.

Brad made the rounds, stopping before each kennel run. Even Jake, captious rascal that he was, embraced the attention. The affinity between a boy and a dog is universal.

We strolled about the yard on our way back to the house, stopping to examine the steel traps hanging on the crib, an old pair of discarded hipboots by the shed, a lizard that had ventured beyond a crack in a barn timber to gather the warmth of the slanting sun, and a piece of crystal quartz that happened underfoot near the back steps. The afternoon was pleasantly warm and peaceful, perfect for idle venture.

"I've been promising Brad a squirrel hunt, Alva," Keegan ventured "This seems a fitting afternoon."

Brad's eyes grew big and round.

"I think it's a great afternoon!" he exclaimed. "It's a great afternoon, isn't it Mister Treadlock," he entreated, plying the leverage of my substantiation while begging Keegan with beseeching eyes.

"Want to come along," Keegan said, directing the question to me. "I thought we'd go walk a hickory ridge somewhere. Brad danced around us like a young colt put to pasture for the first time.

I wanted to go, but it really wasn't right. The day was Keegan's. Keegan's and Brad's.

"Maybe later," I replied. "Today should be yours."

"I'd really like for you to come, Alva."

I studied Keegan's face. There was more than an invitation there; there was a solicitation.

"Yes, I'd like that very much," I said. "Let me tell Raine."

"Oh . . . Alva," Keegan called as I headed inside, "think we might take the Remington?"

I turned to him and smiled.

Raine was waiting for me behind the kitchen door.

"I saw you three boys piddlin' out there," she said. "What's the small one's name?"

"Brad."

"Always loved little tow-headed boys," she said.

"Why didn't you ever give me one?" She put both hands against my chest.

I wrinkled my brow and blew through my throat and tried to step around her.

She wasn't to be put off.

"What time will you vagabonds be back?" she wanted to know.

"Pretty sly, aren't you old woman?" I said, sliding past and hurrying for the study. I pulled the little Sportsmaster from the cabinet, cased it, grabbed up a box of long rifles and rushed back past her for the door.

"Suppose you'll expect supper too," she said.

I brushed a curl aside and smacked her on the forehead. She caught my sleeve and pulled me back, making me kiss her quickly on the lips.

Guessed that meant we would get supper.

Keegan eased the Suburban down the drive and onto old NC 49, urging it to a leisurely pace past Watson's Store and Miller's Crossroads, and west at Hopewell Church toward the river. At Parker's Mill we bore south once more and climbed the long sloping toe of the Uwharries. From the vantage of the swelling incline, the earth spilled away below and west to veiled infinity, shrinking the subordinate headlands into prayerful congregations against the foot of the mountain. Beyond these lay the great river valley, wandering in serpentine loops among the ancient wrinkles and folds of the foothills. Westward still sprawled the distant highlands, their rolling shoulders cloaked in a mantle of cobalt and purple. Save the few wrinkled, brown clusters clinging to the oaks and the tawny, parchment-like raiment of the beeches, the leaves were gone. The hardwoods on the hillsides stood bashfully barren, leaving only the evergreens to color the steepening woodland. The sun floated three o'clock high, a golden medallion at the throat of an innocent blue sky, bathing the slopes with pastel washes of yellow. A fine December afternoon, it was, to be atop the world.

Brad was restless as a hoedown fiddle at a clogger's congress. He fidgeted tirelessly, spewed an endless interrogatory and trembled with excitement. For fear that he would short-circuit, we had to stop once to inspect a defunct but vibrantly fragrant skunk, and once again for him to pee behind a tree. Three miles farther Keegan hauled him to safety when he almost crawled out the window after a ditch-bank chipmunk. He was contagious. What could you be but happy?

The road began to crest and flatten as the contour of the mountain softened. A few miles ahead it would settle onto the congenial plateau known locally as Ridge's Mountain. On either side of its amiable backbone would arise a series of finger ridges, pointing away with a friendly inclination toward the respective horizons. It was a beautiful place to ramble, timbered with magnificent stands of oak, hickory, beech and poplar. The hills were full of bushytails. It was there we would hunt.

I was caught up in anticipation and lost in the sheer beauty of the surroundings, thinking just how lucky I was to be there when Keegan caught my eye in the mirror, reached across the back of the seat, and with nothing more than a smile handed me a long brown envelope.

I returned a quick, quizzical inquiry, but he did not reply.

I turned the envelope slowly in my hands, assaying its strangeness with wonder. Finally, I flipped it over and thumbed the flap. Inside was a thick white document, folded in thirds. Carefully I freed it from the envelope and spread it open. It was a legal instrument of sorts, formally composed, headed with a multiplicity of hereases and wherewiths, and sealed at the bottom of the first page with stamps of officialdom. I glanced at the mirror again, but Keegan was affixed to the road.

The language began to capture me, compelling me to study it with increasing intensity, as gradually it released to me its substance and meaning. Much of the legal jargon was confusing, but its crux I grasped clearly:

*By provision of GS128-17(b) and by decree of the instruments set forth and appended herewith, the tract of land lying within the Counties of Randolph and Montgomery, consisting of the 4217 acres encompassed by a boundary line arising on its western corner from an iron stake at the base of a large oak tree along the Uwharrie River and proceeding north by east 178 degrees for a distance of 4,843 feet to a square granite block at the eastern termination of a rock dam, and therefrom proceeding north by west 1,237 feet etc., etc., heretofore known as Burkhead Mountain, shall henceforth and forever more be known as **Treadlock Mountain** . . .*

. . . there is hereby created and enabled the Alva Aadley Treadlock Sporting Heritage Foundation, hereinafter known as the Treadlock Foundation, which shall hold in perpetual trust Treadlock Mountain, and all rights, privileges, and natural assets accordant thereto. The Treadlock Foundation shall be further benefited in

the attainment of its purpose by a capacitating endowment of three million, five-hundred thousand dollars, to include all future gains on principal from interest and investment accounts. To otherwise ensure, sustain, and augment its work, there are additionally created herein provisions which shall allow for expansion of the financial and physical assets of the Foundation through individual and corporate contribution and bequeath . . .

. . . there shall be created a Board of Directors . . . which shall be constituted of seven members to be appointed by the Trustees, each of whom shall be an active sportsperson chosen solely on the basis of his or her affection, interest, and concern for the stewardship, restoration, protection, and enjoyment of woodlands, waters, and wildlife, for the exemplary strength of his or her desire to share and perpetuate the State's outdoor sporting heritage through active community youth programs of enlightenment, information, and education regarding the privilege and rewards of ethical and scientifically-managed hunting and fishing, and for the sincerity of his or her belief that an honorable pursuit of such activities is uniquely constructive and nourishing to the well-being and character of the human spirit.

Finishing the third page, I fell back against the seat, stunned and befuddled. In course, my eyes fell on the mirror. Keegan was there. I wanted to speak, but could not. A half-minute passed before I could resume.

. . . It shall be the explicit purpose of the Treadlock Foundation to establish, enable, and sustain interactive programs of community involvement which shall make available to young people between the age of nine and fifteen years the opportunity to experience and enjoy the woods, waters, and wild things, to properly introduce to them the honorable pursuits of hunting and fishing, and all the trappings and traditions thereof, by association with knowledgeable, caring, and ethical sportspeople selected specifically for such aptitude and motivation, and to generally ensure to the full extent of its means, that every eligible boy and girl who desires such experience and instruction, shall not otherwise be contrived or deprived from the fundamental wholesomeness and character of the American sporting heritage . . .

I was stricken by the impact and could simply go no further. My stomach knotted and my breathing grew elevated and irregular. I felt a rush of heat. I wanted to speak, but my throat was constricted and the words just wouldn't come. I was outside myself, senseless.

Keegan pulled to the side of the road then, stopped the car and with an outstretched arm directed my attention far across the blue valley below, to the faint purple hill that most prominently towered the winding river.

"If you look between the notch of the two ridges, Alva, you can see your mountain."

It broke me down. Minutes passed before I could speak. Finally, the words formed.

"I *think* I understand this, Keegan . . . " I said limply.

"A Mentor Program, Alva, in your name, perpetually; Brad's the first beneficiary. To our knowledge it's the first privately endowed endeavor of its kind in the country. Before it's done we'll make it a national model."

I shook my head disbelievingly. "I don't deserve this, Keegan," I stammered.

"You just don't realize, Alva. All it takes is your name. The initial trust is being established by an endowment from Trident Securities, of course. Dad sponsored the motion himself. It passed the board of directors unanimously, on the first vote. Already we have monetary commitments from every major interest in the county, commercial and philantrophic. We can doubtlessly get some P-R support from the State as a part of the hunter education initiative if we want it.

"I've hardly begun on the national contacts. I've talked with Remington, Ruger, Winchester, Beretta, Dakota, Swarovski, Boyt, Matthews, Kimber, Orvis and Bean so far. Each and all welcome the chance to be a part of it . . . money, equipment, promotional support. Orrin ran it by Jordan Enterprises, Bass Pro and Mossy Oak; they've both pledged youth camo for every participant, indefinitely. And I haven't even started with the conservation organizations. I can assure you of SCI's endorsement and backing, the NSSF, of course and, believe me, there will be many others.

"We've had a small recruiting staff going since the first of November, just to seed the concept and secure the first few mentor matches. The response has been overwhelming. We've got people everywhere wanting to serve as mentors or nominate kids, the right kind of people and the right kind of kids. We're already screening the first dozen matches.

"It's only the beginning, Alva."

"But the mountain . . . " I groped, "how . . . ?"

"The mountain was mine. Dad deeded it to me years ago. This way, it'll always be there, as it is now . . . the way you and I would want it to be.

"The mountain will be the heartbeat of the Foundation . . . it'll give it life."

"It's all too much, Keegan."

"I've looked for a proper way to thank you for years, Alva, for bringing me along the way you did. I would have missed it all.

"Until now, I just didn't know how. Actually, it was Brad. He kind of happened along a while back and brought the idea with him. Besides, it's not altogether noble. I'm doing it partly for myself. It's a part of being complete again."

I was still numb. Numb and disoriented. "So great a thing to have started so simply," I marveled absently. "Wait 'til Raine hears . . ."

There were no words to express the gratitude I felt.

"Thank you, Keegan," I said, with all the feeling I could muster. It was not nearly enough.

Brad had been sitting quietly until now, a little wide-eyed and a bit in awe of the solemnity of our conversation. Impatience had finally sculpted the courage to override timidity.

"Aren't we going squirrel huntin'?" he moaned.

Keegan smiled at me, then the boy.

"Yes, boy," he said, "we're goin' squirrel huntin'."

We piled out of the truck in a trill of excitement. Brad hung to Keegan like a seedtick. I fell in behind.

Opening the back hatch and dropping the tailgate, Keegan reached for the gun case and slid the little Sportsmaster free. Brad's eyes brightened. I handed Keegan the box of cartridges from my pocket. He slid the box open, cradled the rifle, filled the magazine and pushed the rod home. Avoiding the bolt and flipping the safety, he left the chamber empty. Brad watched surgically the while, entranced by every move.

"Can I carry it?" he asked, when the process was complete.

"Soon enough," Keegan responded sternly. "Today you watch me. Watch how I carry it and think about what I've told you about safety. You can never be too careful in the woods, Brad. No matter how hard you try, someday something unexpected will happen.

"But if you're doin' what you ought to, every second of every minute, you'll probably get through it without killing yourself or somebody else. Don't ever forget that."

The boy was disappointed, but taken with the gravity of the lesson.

"Walk behind me or beside me, Brad," Keegan added. "We'll hunt this ridge and find us a squirrel."

He turned to me.

"Alva, since there're three of us, why don't Brad and I take one side of the ridge and you the other, and we'll walk it in shifts like you and I used to . . . just ease along in sight of one another and see if one of us can push a squirrel around to the other.

"If we find one, we'll see if young Brad here can scare him to death."

"Good," I nodded.

Brad was squirming with excitement.

"I've got to pee," he said, looking sheepishly up at Keegan.

"Well, go ahead," Keegan said. "But hurry up!" Brad stepped to the base of an oak and struggled with his zipper.

Keegan and I traded smiles. "Reckon it's the size of a red oak acorn yet," Keegan asked, grinning.

"I dunno," I laughed.

Keegan was happy. As happy as I had seen him since he had returned. The old voltage was in his eyes. Though he had hunted the far corners of the world, his zest for a backyard squirrel hunt remained as fresh as it had been the day he turned 13.

Brad tripped back, still fighting the zipper, this time in the opposite direction. All boy, he managed the three-quarter mark and called it done.

"Ready," Keegan asked.

"Ready," he declared, beaming.

We slipped off the crown of the mountain, onto the gentle slope of the ridge, with the sun streaming in, the rustle of leaves under our feet and Christmas only a few days away. Somewhere down the hill we would find a squirrel, and a boy would take a small step toward being a man, and Keegan and I would take another giant step back toward being a boy. The world would turn on, day by day, year by year, with the promise that it would happen again. It was not necessary now, I knew, that I be there. After Keegan, there would be Orrin, and after Orrin there would be Brad, and after . . . well, there'd be someone.

Life loomed pretty good for an old man. Orrin had finally come through. If I lived, I'd see he and Haley married in the spring, on the big rock in the middle of the river under the sycamores while the current sang and their dreams idled past. And the wind that brought the dreams would whisper through the trees and stir the wisps of hair on my Raine's forehead.

Keegan had said that I was a legend. Well . . . maybe. Maybe not. That really didn't matter much any longer. I had far more. I had a legacy.

And in it, there would always be a boy.

D usk was advancing rapidly now, expunging the purple smoke that billowed above the smoldering ruins of sunset. The evening chill was gathering amid the loneliness of the muted woodland. About us a capricious breeze swirled and expired, its icy breath turning and rattling the fallen leaves. An involuntary shudder called hunters to home.

"About the deer. You knew all along," Keegan said without breaking his gaze, " . . . all along."

"Yes."

"Just thinking about where it all started," he said, "and where it's all come."

"There was a lot of boy left in the man then," I said.

"There still is."

"Just enough," I replied.

I lingered behind for a moment, watching them up the ridge, the man and the boy, thinking about yesterday and tomorrow again. I smiled inside, at peace with myself. What was age, after all, but a wonderful contortion of memories.

I hurried along then, anxious for the soft light of a warm kitchen, anxious to tell my Raine.

Squaw

To every end, there is a beginning. For every beginning, a memory.

My most sacred recollections of Squaw do not find her among gum boots, guns and decoys, as it might, but in a sandbox with my two-year-old daughter, Melanie. I see her pug nose and the elfin highlights in her eyes as she sits splay-legged and pot-bellied, contemplating mischief, while her playmate works with great purpose to bury her front paws. Though it is about to suffer a juvenile setback, a tolerant patience is growing. It will become her staunchest trait.

For now, havoc prevails. Needle-sharp teeth give a coat-sleeve a roughhousing. The child squeals wildly and the black puppy backs and whirls like a wind-up toy. Until mid-afternoon finds two small souls adrift among the blankets, whimpering in unison, chasing dreams. A sibling bond is being forged. It will last both lifetimes.

Squaw was friend and guardian before she was field dog, especially to my daughter, and she took the one charge as seriously as the other. She shadowed Melanie religiously, harassing the caterpillars, fire trucks, ponies and other tag-alongs perpetually in tow, cavorting and growling with impish defiance at the cavorting and scolding she incited.

The high deck on the south side of the house was threatening to a child, and Squaw stayed in a nervous frenzy when we were there, placing herself between Melanie and the edge. Not unlike the day at the vet's, when at a gangly four months – gentle and submissive by nature – she waxed demonic when a mature Doberman was perceived a threat to Melanie and her mother. Hackles bristling, teeth barred, a growl in her throat, she placed herself between Melanie and Loretta, and the hulking Dobe.

"The Dobe backed off," Loretta likes to recall.

In later years she would instill the same respect in uninvited strangers who found their way to our door. Dogs are infallible judges of character. If Squaw didn't cotton to someone, we didn't either.

Amidst her domestic responsibilities, I worked in a little field training, suffering my daughter's wrath at the monopoly of her friend. The little Lab was a joy to train. There was progress every session. She learned "Sit" in a half-day, both voice and whistle command, and never forgot. At the end of a week, she would "Stay" while I circled the house. "Here" was natural. Basic hand signals took about two months. She had a strong water entry for a young lady, marked well land or water, and lived to retrieve. Soon she was handling multiple fetches on bumpers with ease, then was rapidly on to feathers. She coveted tethered pigeons and shackled mallards, her returns soft and direct. When she heard the gun for the first time, she was a polished dog on yard drills. By the end of her first shooting season, she was green-steady to wing and shot. She was like malleable iron, strong to the core, but bent and shaped as willed.

Like most shackled souls who escape domesticity for random flights of adventure, Squaw managed a Jekyll-Hyde existence during the accrual of her field credentials. Emerging from training and hunting sojourns scratched and bleeding from greenbriers, slimy with garlands of algae and reeking of marsh mud, she would work that miraculous canine transformation that left her fresh and shining by evening, when she and Melanie trooped off to bed. Our lights-out check would find them in the blissful slumber of youth, loose blond curls on a pillow of obsidian.

"Lass and lassie," Loretta would declare, snuggling the covers up tight and kissing them both goodnight.

Soon it was Melanie's turn at schooling and Squaw's place to mourn. She would retreat to Melanie's room, pining away the hours, auditing the comings-and-goings of the household as we might watch a clock, until 2:30 of each afternoon when she would run to the screen door for the happy reunion. Hard to tell who was most joyful. Weekends, free of good-byes, were Valhalla.

After a time, our daughter would invite schoolmates over, and it was a whimsically wonderful thing watching four chattering little girls, a colorful assortment of dolls and teddy bears, sharing a tea setting and the latest "gossip" with a black lady Lab decked out in Sunday hat, scarf, sweater and heels.

I would borrow the Lab now and then for hunting escapades. Melanie was forever miffed, because it was the only time Squaw would readily forsake her. Dancing and whining at the sight of the gun, Squaw would bound for the door, moaning and fretting for freedom, while Melanie stood by with a pout on her face.

Coming five, Squaw was into her prime, proficient and easy. Waterfowl hunts would excite her and she was an honest water dog – doing journeyman duty as well as a flushing dog on woodcock and snipe – but the love of her life was doves. In her era, legal shooting began high noon. It took a dog with grit to suffer the sweltering, southern September afternoons in the direct sun. She never faltered, retaining her zest in the most smoldering, soppy heat and humidity, sitting alertly by my side marking the falls. She would often gather multiple limits, retrieving for my friends after I'd shot out – and never tiring of it. Remarkable really, since we were shooting three and four days a week then, during the early season, and the legal bag was 18 birds.

I never saw her happier than when Melanie came along. She immediately established station alongside her closest friend, and no matter who shot them, would deliver downed birds to Melanie rather than to me or our friends. I never scolded or corrected her for it. I couldn't. We'd simply divide the bag at the end of the day. When Melanie couldn't go, I would gain again her good graces and she would work for one and all. But she would not be enticed into play, or be petted, by anyone.

"The gun," she said, "was business."

Squaw was my first real retriever. I'd had a "drop" – Papa was a pointer and Mama was a setter – a few years prior by the name of Chance. He was a cracking good pointing dog and a fare-you-well at fetch. Chance was a big, on-his-toes Rip-Rap dog, white-and-black, saddled and heavily ticked. Many times, when we were through with quail we'd abandon the uplands and slip off to some swamp bottom to shoot a roosting flight of wood ducks. Chance relished the water and served honorably in the marsh, even on the big-time throw of the Pamlico and the breakwaters of the Outer Banks. When we weren't waterfowling, he'd post duty at doves. But it was an untoward coalition. Until Squaw came along, and I learned for the first time how really valuable a non-slip retriever could be. I can remember times she had to search long and hard for a bird, after I'd given up, but I cannot readily recall a time after Squaw was two years old that she failed. And that claim covers a lot of territory.

Gunning over her, watching her work, was a soulful pleasure. Confidence in her gave me shots I would have passed otherwise, either to range or troubled cover. Friends begged to go because she afforded them similar option. I would take the Elsie Smith trap gun, 30-inch, full-and-full, restrict myself to the highest incoming or widest crossing birds. The challenge was formidable. Not only the shooting, but as delightfully, the handling. Steering Squaw by mouth, hand and whistle, into the long blind retrieves. Birds shot at 40 and 50 yards would sometimes drift a hundred before plummeting. It would take us a while sometimes, but eventually she'd work it out. She'd hunt and hunt and hunt far across a field for fallen doves, lost-and-gained to sight amid the heat vapors, stopping to whistle for revised orders, then searching on. At last, her nose would capture a wisp of scent and jerk her head around. Her tail would quicken and she would correct her line, tracing the breeze to the find.

"Heigh-ho." The joy hers, though as equally mine.

She'd clip back, head and tail set like quotation marks about the stiff, straight line of her back and the dignity of her stride.

"Hey. Look. Look at me."

One splendid September we hunted doves every day the first segment of the season, just the two of us. A series of unseasonable cold fronts marched down from the north, sweeping away the stagnant haze of summer with the replenishing breath of fall, bringing color to pallid skies. Heaven touching Earth, as only it does in autumn, and we made the best of it. Hunting Sampson County in North Carolina that year, we located a large flock of birds in picked corn the very first day. When I glassed the lay of it from the truck, the rise and fall of the feeding birds looked like gray swells over a fitful sea. For six weeks over ten square miles we followed that bunch of birds, from cucumbers to croton, melons to squash, cotton to corn.

Grand, the time. Squaw would sit in front of me, covering the rear. I could tell by the flash of her eyes, the crouch of her shoulders, when birds were approaching from behind.

"Steady, Girl."

We'd hunker. Then I'd take them as they passed, going away. Concentrating on doubles and triples, and wind-driven speedsters at peculiar angles. It was top-drawer. I missed and I hit, but we were in no hurry to fill the bag. Simple put, we were happy —"free as a feelin' in the wind," to borrow a favorite line. I think of that time each year as September rolls around. If I were to be granted a few days of my life to relive, one would find me there.

Of my shooting friends, Jim Dean was Squaw's favorite. He was easy on the nose, his manner was mellow and he was good for a retrieve now and then. The three of us shared some good times. There was an afternoon of wood ducks on an East Coast millpond, when early season limits were yet more than liberal. I can sense it still, the tag end of a glorious day in October. The sun was dying, draining the blood-red glow from the sweetgums on the Alder Tag Point, with it the last legal shooting hour was closing. The sky was waning to indigo, the treeline and shoreline melting to obscurity as the shadows deepened.

I was worried. Squaw as well. Her eyes kept searching skyward, and she fidgeted and fretted. I cautioned her and she looked at me, annoyed. Time was running close. Only a few minutes left.

Then it came. Muffled in the far lower reaches of the lake, the floating, plaintive note of a lone wood duck. In the solitude of near dusk, it was haunting. Thrilling.

I caught six silhouettes, four forward, two trailing, over Jim's makeshift blind in the distant buckbrush. The advance guard for a virtual siege of homing woodies. The lead bird spun, afflicted into a cartwheeling descent to the water, and then the thud of Jim's gun thumped the stillness. Another fell from a second wave.

Squaw was up, whining and trembling, glued to the direction of the shot. Now we had our own business to attend. Two drakes and a hen rode set wings low and front. I took one incoming and turned to catch another near the peak of its looping vertical ascent. As quickly as I could reload, two crossing birds climbed away, unscathed as I emptied the gun. A distant bird loomed in periphery over the treeline, and at the buck of the Smith folded into the top of a great sycamore.

"Squaw!"

She had marked the fall, was straining to go. At my hail she was off, in a crash and shatter of water. I missed again, connected again, as the shooting day expired.

Four times the Lab was back. Three times a drake, once a hen. Nary a bobble. Harlequin colors in raven-black jaws, the composition stunning.

"Not bad, M'Lady." I grabbed her collar and she arched her neck, pulling herself up and over the gunwale. Shook heartily. Ignored me. Business, you know.

The shooting had expired, but not the occasion. I eased back along to Jim, paddling idly. Squaw picked up a couple of errant birds for him and then we loafed in a meandering journey back to the truck. Darkness had fallen. Stars blinked against the night. Among them wings cut the air, sizzle and rush, and group after group of birds dropped into pockets and corners in a melee of splashes. Jim lit his pipe and settled back against a boat paddle, his free hand buried behind Squaw's ear.

"What say, Old Dog." She wagged her tail, stretched across the seat and laid her muzzle on his knee.

I turned one last time, toward the lapsing glow of day, with an unspoken word of thanks. We were hunters born again.

Squaw had long since become essential to a successful trip. It was far more than utility. Snuggled under a cedar blowdown in the quiet of a January snow, I relished the kinship in her eyes as we exchanged anxious glances over the ringnecks avoiding the decoys, and a special peace as the snowflakes sifted – one by one – through the green branches and onto her black muzzle. In the cold rain or driving sleet of a broad, windswept and desolate marsh, waiting the long hours through for a wedge of geese, the comfort of her presence brought an inner satisfaction I had never known. Numb to the bone I sat, many times, watching her shiver in icy water, icicles tacked to her chin, the eaves of her belly, her tail so heavy with rime she could not lift it, teeth chattering in rhythm with my own. We endured it all, because we loved it all – together. It was a matter of wildness and pride, and neither of us ever let the other down.

She and I, against the worst, and there's nothing like miserable and happy at the same time. Especially with a friend. After Squaw, I could never again be content without a dog at my side.

A ll too swiftly the years passed, bringing the change they always do. Squaw's life turned the corner from autumn to winter and Melanie wondered into adolescence. Loretta and I looked twice and discovered we were 30-something. For us, every moment with Squaw was mellow and Melanie was a happy reflection in the mirror of our passage. Yet, there was about it all an inescapable sense of apprehension – a time not distant, when we would lose them both. The sandbox seemed long ago, far away. Though again . . . wasn't it just yesterday?

Dolls, tea sets and other little-girl things committed to attic and shelf, Melanie spent more and more of her life in "addled essence," engaging the person she was coming to be. She would ride her bike relentlessly up and down our country path, or sit for hours on her favorite outcropping of rock along the pond dam, staring over the water. She noticed Squaw less now, but the Lab was undeterred. Despite her advanced age Squaw ran dutifully alongside the bicycle mile after mile, tongue in the dust, and sat as steadfastly by the rock at the pond as if she were a part of it. A kind word now and then was enough.

As Melanie abandoned her childhood, much that would regain its worth in later life was laid aside, sacrificed to the values of the present. Squaw would suffer with the departure, as would Loretta and I. But Melanie would come back to us one day. Ever how hard she might wish, she could not, to Squaw. We tried to tell her that. But, then, she would not understand.

There came a time when her blossoming femininity demanded a nicety that relegated dog hair and fragrance less than Dior to separate quarters. Come bedtime in the evenings, painfully we would hear her from our room above: "No Squaw. No."

And then her door would slam. The door to her bedroom, that might as surely have been the door to her heart.

Squaw had slept with Melanie every night for 12 years. Enduring a succession of room guests, including hamsters, lizards, rabbits, birds, turtles and a kid goat, but as surely as they came and went, she alone was allowed to stay. Now she could not understand or accept her exile. For weeks, she stayed at Melanie's door the long nights through, whining softly and pawing now and then, gently at the sill. Only to be scolded by the one person she had trusted most in the world. She would never come upstairs to sleep with us. She adopted a corner in the kitchen near Melanie's room, pining there each evening for the rest of her days. The rites of passage inflict greatest pain on those who do not make the journey.

I began walking to the pond afternoons after supper, in the gloaming of dusk, encouraging Squaw to follow. I threw a few birds for her and it helped, temporarily. Gradually she came around. Much of her domestic stewardship was transferred to Loretta, demanding her presence about daily chores as though she were appointed and accountable. Her gentle countenance, so void of intrusion it was almost a suggestion, became as comforting and essential to my wife on the farm as it was to me on hunting outings.

Life for Squaw, in her 12th year, was tranquil. After breakfast, there were stables to clean and if the smith had been there, a few old pieces of hoof trimmings to gnaw on. At the kennels there were balls and sticks to worry, and the setters to put in place and milk bone treats after cleaning duties had been attended. Gardening rounds brought invigorating wallows in the cool, moist earth under the tomato plants or siestas in the wood mulch under the roses. Noontime was a pleasant stroll down the path and through the pasture for the mail. Housework was a good excuse for a nap. Melanie was home at three. Supper waited at six. Then there was the evening security watch, a matter of maintaining a sort of on-call, supine alert the night through.

"Goodnight, girl," Loretta would call to her every evening after she had taken her corner near Melanie's door. "We know you're here. Nothing to fear." You could hear her tail thump the floor.

In Squaw's final September, Jim Dean's son Scott and I hunted with her on a coastal plains hog farm. It was the last episode in her lifelong love affair with doves. By calendar it was autumn, but summer clung by a death grip. Heat devils danced over the stumps of the amputated corn, and the air lay thick and offensive upon the land as heavy blankets on a warm night's bed. Dust puffed from the powdered soil with every step, hanging over the field in loitering clouds. It was dead calm, not the intimation of a breeze.

By the end of the day we were soaked with sweat, sunburned, as dirty as West Virginia coal miners. And about as giddy as a goose in a grain bin. If I could script my perfect dove hunt, it would play out like that afternoon with Scott and Squaw amidst the heat and the dust and the hogs.

The birds came steadily – doubles, triples, fives and tens – and at the height of the flight circled in great gangs, rallying again and again for the next assault. We took up stands among the cedars along a fenceline between the field and the hog pasture pond. Pigs were squealing and lids on feed bins were banging, and on the other side of the pond tractors were groaning, picking corn and amid the noise and the dirt and the sun and the sweat, doves were whistling. It was one more fine hell of a shoot.

You could make it as easy or hard on yourself as you wanted. You needed only to pick any of a dozen different shots, and if you missed, there were as many chances more. They never quit. The field lay east-west and they came north-south, in steel-gray battalions, until sunset. We shot the barrels hot. Intermittently you had to stop and pant, just absorb it all, appreciate the privilege. We had it alone, just the three of us. Camelot on the wings of September.

I enjoyed that afternoon, not so much for myself, as for a hard-bitten old Lab due one last day of glory and for a boy seeing and feeling it for the first time. It was a Godsend. Squaw retrieved doves in the stifling heat and dust as only a veteran could – a bit slower maybe, but no less sure. Retrieved until her tongue was swollen and her body wobbled on its underpinnings, but the fire in her eyes and the determination in her heart never waned. When the shooting was done and the sun was low, I leaned back against a fencepost for a time, letting my senses drink in the story. Squaw by my side as all the times before, watching the birds trade by, glancing at me impatiently, waiting for the gun. Her muzzle was grizzled and gray now. How I wished it was no more than the January snow, sifting through cedar in the days of her prime. How fortunate I had been.

We got up and ambled down the fenceline to Scott. He was halfway on the 12-bird limit and down to five shells. His spirits drooped, dismayed with his shooting. Squaw and I accepted his cause.

I threw him a fresh box of high-brass 7 1/2s and laid out another for confidence. Squaw set up station by his knee. Scott had never taken a limit of doves. There would never be a better time.

The boy set his jaw, then missed seven birds straight. He looked at me helplessly. I waved it off. Squaw shifted nervously.

"Just relax, Scott," I said, "pick a bird, follow it through, push past, _pull._" Another miss. He looked at me, eyes filled with doubt. With two fingers I motioned him on.

The day was closing and the flight had slowed. A worrying man would have had reason. Then a swift, high incomer caught the brunt of Scott's frustration in a shower of feathers and the timing chain clicked. Just behind, a fast-crossing bird flared, fought for altitude, crumpled into the top of a red oak.

"_Squaw!_" She was off. An unseen pair from behind, loafing in on the breeze, catching us flat-footed – hit the afterburners – twisting in an accelerating spiral, pulling out left and right, speeding away. Scott waited out their worst, swung past and under the left – _Whoom_ – connected hard, spun, swinging right – _Whoom_ – missed – pulled again, _Whoom._ A puff of white, a trailing feather and the bird wilted in mid-air, collapsing into a feathered knot and both doves were on the ground.

Yes. YES! Three hulls later and Squaw had made the trip six times. The day was won, duty done. Scott bent to accept the last bird from her, applauding the honor, then turning to me with a smile on his face the measure of a crescent moon.

A tired old Lab fetched her last limit of doves, and a boy gained his first. A small happening in an infinitely small corner of the globe. But in the multiplicity of such happenings across the planet rests the renewal of human spirit and hope for the world.

Squaw left us suddenly on a scorching summer day in her 13th year. She died without imposition, as she had lived. When Loretta found her body late that afternoon, there was no sign of struggle and there had been no sound. It was as if she did not want to trouble us, even with death. We placed her passing around midday.

Shortly after noon that same day, Melanie received a telephone call from the Barbizon Agency. Though she would know in a few hours the deepest sadness of her young life, she had her first grown-up job. For every ending, there is a beginning.

Chapter 16

"*I'll Never Marry...*"

I 'll never marry a man who hunts and fishes!" my 13-year-old daughter spouted, peering disdainfully over her mother's shoulder. A pretty little pout came with the proclamation.

"Hello to you too," I ventured. Too late. Nose in the wind, she was already en route to the immaculate asylum of her bedroom. Deep in the bowels of the house, I heard the door slam.

It wasn't really that bad. Trent, the Lab, and I were recently extricated from a set-to with backwater greenheads. Held our own too. But, we'd gotten turned around after dark and wandered onto a mud flat. Slogging and wallowing out of that, we'd stumbled into the creek channel, and I went in over my waders and lost my gun. I'd spent 20 minutes in icy water, gulping duckweed and groping blindly in the muck before it surrendered itself to be found. Then after we made shore we got into the switchcane and greenbriers, and once we fought free of those, the stickbriers and grapevines took over. When it all finally broke into Claude Bullock's cow pasture, the footing got a little squishy and despite my distinct caution to the contrary, Trent might have rolled a time or two, or worse. And, well, you've got the picture. The usual turn in the marsh.

Now, on the threshold begging entrance, what with the mud, slime, scratches and incense, maybe we were for the moment a bit sulfurous. Thirty minutes before the hearth, however, and Trent would work that miraculous dry-cleaning trick dogs manage and be glistening obsidian again. With a little soap and fresh water, I'd be newly respectable too.

The welcome I got from my wife, who had suffered my misdirected comings and goings for 19 years, was warm.

"Your supper was on the table an hour ago," she said, running the sentences together for effect, "and I've apologized to Sammy and Nida and told them you were still off somewhere on some damn duck hunt and since it was supposed to be for you, I guessed they'd just have to hold their party for somebody else some other time.

"Come, Trent," she said, letting the Lab in.

Warm is a matter of perspective, you see. It was her tone, only a six on a ten-point scale, that told me she was merely vexed. Believe me, I know a ten when I see it. A ten means forget the venison steaks on Monday, and Wednesday won't be spaghetti night anymore for a couple of weeks. But this was a six. It was only as she turned for the kitchen and I saw the icy glint of her eye that I knew what side of the bed I would sleep on. Well . . . maybe a seven.

"Yes ma'am," I said humbly. With a limit of plump mallards hanging under the barn, I could afford a little benevolence. After supper I'd change the bed linens. I'd learned long before that a wash of humility, like tepid rain on snow and soft flannel sheets, hasten a thaw.

Meanwhile, though, it was a trifle airy on the back porch. For all the heat, it can be downright cold in the chill of a woman's scorn.

Three years later, Melanie had grown "inkles," breasts if you will, a term she coined herself and for which I may claim no credit, much less explanation. It's noteworthy, however, because as beautifully as a butterfly chrysalis, my daughter had morphed into an alluring young woman and we were fraught with boys. First, there was the football jock with the William Perry neck and the hot hands. Then the wimpy kid with the Adams apple that shook hands like a broken pump-handle and talked like a mouse in a mitten. Then a whole string of in-betweeners that wore the driveway thin. In time somehow, in Melanie's eyes, they all got weeded down to one . . . the one she swore she would never go out with again after their first date. Later I came to believe it had something to do with the erstwhile disclosure that he owned a coon dog.

When I conducted his interview, I chanced upon the revelation that the lad also did a dab of squirrel and rabbit hunting.

"You mentioned this to my daughter?" I asked apprehensively.

"No, sir."

"Well, boy, a little advice," I whispered. "She's kinda curious about fur and feathers just now. Wouldn't hurt to wait a bit, you know, just until you see how things go."

"Yes, sir."

I cringed the first time the beagles went A.W.O.L. and he showed up late. Almost chanced a word on his behalf, but resisted for fear of tainting the brew. Between the rut and the strut, you learn that passion works its own kind of prejudice. I'd save the argument, offer to round up the beagles behind the scenes, and count on the hormones. Sure enough, after the usual stint of acclimation, turmoil and trepidation, we were planning a wedding. I held my breath through the "I dos," silently spurred the preacher for the declaration and celebrated a proper son-in-law.

From squirrels and rabbits, it hasn't been all that much of a stretch to ducks and quail and woodcock and grouse. The boy learns fast. I've been accused of corruption, but not indicted, and ten years down the tracks there hasn't been a divorce on either end.

If you're facing this kind of thing with your own son or daughter in the near future, take a cue. Muster your cunning. Remember, preserving our sporting heritage is more than paying your Ducks Unlimited dues.

The rewards keep coming. Last spring Teddy was piddling around in the yard on a bright May morning, when suddenly a turkey gobbled point-blank. He flew into the house, jerked on some camo, grabbed up his call, mustered Melanie into a set of oversized coveralls – a floppy pair of brogans and a bee-keepers mask – and pulled her hobbling down the back path to a calling station beside a sawdust pile. The gobbler was in the mood and Melanie sat with her heart thumping pirouettes as he strutted his stuff, and two trailing jakes walked by, close enough to count pin-feathers.

I basked in the glow for the next three months as she related it to anyone who would listen, and puffed with pride as this creature of the malls, normally on the hunt for Liz Claiborne and Pierre Cardin, begged my counsel on Russell and Realtree. My baby girl grown had rediscovered for her own the incomparable lure of the wild, at the hands of the man she would never marry.

Lately, however, I must report a slight setback. I don't rightly recall which of my recent transgressions sent Loretta off again. But abruptly, it was *deja vu*.

"I'm going to tell my granddaughter never to marry a man that hunts and fishes!" she stormed.

I tried to hide it. But she had to notice the smug look on my face.

199

The Jubilation Buck

Deer. The rhythm of their travel was telling, similar to that of a human, but a bit lighter, a bit more careful and calculated. There were two, one leading, one trailing. Walking at ease and closing.

The thing I didn't know was where they were. The hearing in my right ear is dull, argument for protection against years of magnum shotshells and heavy rifles. It's difficult to make out distance or direction of a sound. I have to remain immobile until I have a deer in sight. An abomination of first order for a bowhunter.

So I was sitting when I wanted to be standing, with my bow across my lap. By the time I was able to tell they were behind and left, I had the lead animal, a doe, in the corner of my eye. She was walking quietly, alert, with no sign of alarm. It must stay that way. She was the front guard, no doubt good at it. The deer behind had stopped, waiting for an okay. This was the one that drew my interest. The doe passed at 15 yards, unaware. So far, the advantage was mine. Somehow I had to get up.

No hope now. The trailing deer was moving again, slow and deliberate, on the path of its companion. Now, against the knot in my throat, thudded the beat of my heart.

The big sign had erupted ten days before. A six-inch cedar, rubbed, gouged and mutilated, several wrung-off saplings, punctuating an early scrapeline that traversed the neck of pine woods between a large cut-over and a creek-bottom thicket. The signature of a good buck and I had recognized it at once. I had hunted this same buck for the past two seasons. He had proven a formidable adversary. I admired him greatly.

Restless days and sleepless nights had gone into my setup. Three days more for the scent to cool after the stand was hung. Seven more still to gain the blessing of the wind. To spite the wait, I was late getting away. Shadows were long, the afternoon almost done. But now a deer was moving toward me – not 15 minutes after I had arrived – and the paths of our lives would soon cross. *Would it be him?* Seconds more, an eternity, and I would know.

He emerged in the periphery of my vision like a specter resurrected from a hundred armchair dreams. Gray and vaunted, he came, under high, heavy beams and long, polished tines. He traveled with an air of superiority, even arrogance, and the sovereignty of it left me fighting for control.

Alongside now, he stopped and lifted his head. Though I was pasted to the tree, he sensed my presence. I breathed deep and slow, avoiding eye contact, concentrating on absolute deception. I must beat him if there would be the chance. He was frozen, taut, reading every minute rise and fall of my chest. Growing jittery, threatening to bolt. I held my breath. He shook his head defiantly, took a few bounding hops on stiff legs, then stopped again to look at me. I had not moved. At last, he seemed satisfied, dropped his head, continued along the track of the doe.

A few steps more and he would pass behind a small cedar and a sparse line of maple saplings. It would be my only chance. The move must be quick and smooth. When the leaf screen was between us, I eased up and drew my bow in one motion. Thirty yards out, he had stopped with his nose to the ground. The distance was greater than I would have liked, but the shot was there. The sight pin settled behind his shoulder and I talked myself through the release and follow-through.

The *wh-um-ph* of the bow thumped the silence, the shaft was away. The buck vaulted wildly sideways, tore with the doe for the creek bottom.

In the instant, a wave of heat and nausea flashed head-to-toe and I grew dangerously light-headed. I was shaking and sweating, my hearing deadened by the pounding of my heart. The ground beneath the tree spun like the deck of a carousel. I managed the seat of the stand, hung onto the tree, panted like a dog fraught with heat exhaustion. I had only looked at the antlers once, no more, but the deer was big.

I waited 20 minutes, couldn't stand it any longer, then climbed down. I thought the shot was good, that the buck would not travel far.

At the spot he had stood, I searched for my arrow. Nothing. Twenty, thirty yards along the path of his flight, nothing still. By the time I had worked out 50 yards, with no trace of a hit, I was getting worried. The cooling red-purple cap of the sun was slipping toward the horizon, through the lace of the trees. Light was dropping fast. Anxiously, I took up a wide, quartering pattern that would intersect his line of retreat. Forty yards on I found what I was looking for – splotches of dark red blood leading toward the creek-bottom thicket. The trail was heavy, on the ground and on the undergrowth where he had passed. Anticipation soared. I thought to find him in the next 50 yards.

But the blood trail grew thin, dwindling to a drop here and there. Finally, I was on hands-and-knees, inching along to pick the small flecks of blood from the measled pigment of the freshly fallen gum leaves. Confidence shaken, I was worried anew. The sign read uncertainly for a vital hit, and I had no arrow to substantiate the difference.

My troubles were compounded by the fading light. Dusk was deepening and I had lost the trail altogether. Forty yards on, proceeding on instinct, I found one faint red smear on a pine needle. A moment later I heard the buck get up, only a few feet ahead. Instantly I stopped, straining to hear. The night was eerie still and the tortured limbs of the second-growth thicket reached like gnarled, grasping fingers toward the blackened sky. He was moving slowly away. For spellbinding moments I could sense him picking his way through the thicket. Until there remained nothing but silence.

Somewhere down the creek bottom, a big owl hooted . . . once . . . twice. I felt the boy rise in the man.

In the slight depression where the buck had bedded, there was only a slight smear of blood. It was obvious now he was not hit as well as I had hoped. My suspicion was a shoulder wound; there had been no paunch sign. I had not taken a wild, unreasonable shot. What had gone wrong, I could not say. The burn of nausea was rising in the hollow of my stomach again. Sickening, it was, that the kill had not been clean. He did not deserve the lingering pain.

Should I follow or back away? He would likely lie down again. I should let him. If I kept pushing, on a wound that was less than debilitating, he might find the reserve to leave the area completely. To never be found. I should leave. Leave and be back at first light.

I draped the only thing I had, an old green poncho, over a limb to mark my place and backtracked out of the thicket.

Reaching home, I called Teddy, the man my little girl married. There was yet the chasm of a generation between us, the distance aside from blood between the father and the son. The uneasiness still, that harbored on shaky pilings between matrimony and patrimony. But more and more we were finding time together. What was absent in blood, and confounded by law, was finding validation in common passion. The boy loved to hunt and fish. He reminded me a lot of . . . well, he reminded me a lot of *me*. I needed help, and there would be no better time or place, to ask.

When he recognized my voice, urgent and alto, he knew it had to do with deer.

"Where is he?" he said.

"Ughhm," I sighed.

"I don't like the sound of *that*," he said.

"How big?"

"A big eight, maybe a ten," I guessed.

I told him the story.

"Lord!" he said.

"Can you go with me," I asked. "Be there first light?"

"I'm supposed to work. I'll try. If I can make it, I'll be over an hour 'fore day."

"Hope so," I said. "I need young nerves."

All was done that could be done. Now came the long wait for morning. At ten p.m. I turned in, hoping to rest. I should have known better. The demons in my head tortured my mind to an overload, ruling out any possibility of sleep. Somewhere in the dark and deep of the woods, hurt and vulnerable, was a bowhunting trophy I had pursued for years. A dozen things could happen before dawn. While I was lying on my back, doing nothing.

I tumbled out of bed, reached for the phone. The "Hello" was Teddy's.

"If that was your deer out there in the woods, what would you do?" I said.

"I'd be looking."

"Let's go," I said.

I heard a door slam at the other end of the phone.

There was a new voice at the receiver. Melanie's. "He's on his way," she said. "He was already dressed when you called . . . was just before calling you."

I smiled. She may have married the right man.

We made the thicket just after midnight. Three times I sent Teddy into the tangle, trying in vain to direct him to the poncho. Then I went in three times more, with the same empty result.

"Damn," I swore. We'd wasted an hour and my head was muddled.

"All I know is to go back and pick up where you found first blood," Teddy said. "Trace it back."

Ten minutes of casting around and I had the initial trail. It was less distinct now, mostly dry. On every drop was a frenzy of ants. The smaller drops were being obliterated rapidly. We were right to come on. It took 45 minutes of crawling, the two of us, to trace its path back into the thicket to the poncho. We found the bed, where the buck had lain, and ten feet on one small drop of blood. Then we hit a dead end. There was a wash ahead, shoulder deep, grown up in saplings. It led downhill to the creek. The bank on the far side would have been a good, uphill jump for the buck, and we doubted he had made it. Maybe. I took the wash and Teddy worked the far bank deeper into the thicket. Both of us were crawling at a snail's pace, the night pitch black beyond the tiny circles of our lights.

The wash seemed the logical egress. It would have provided cover and declining elevation. But it proved barren to its end. The small red ticking on the fallen gum leaves was like an endless vein of fool's gold. I gave up and joined Teddy, now 50 yards farther into the thicket. We looked meticulously for another 30 minutes, quartering on all fours. Nothing.

Teddy lay on his back in the leaves. The night was deep, full of stars. I checked my watch: 2:25. We were tired, lay there dozing in-and-out, contemplating our dilemma. We had arrived with optimism, determined to find this deer. Determined we remained, but for the moment our hopes were taking a beating. We could not know that this was only the start. That the ordeal would eventuate the emotional equivalent of a rollercoaster.

"I don't understand it," Teddy said. "By all rights he should have taken that ditch to the creek. They usually go downhill. It's hard to believe he would have jumped it, and anyhow, we've looked this side out good."

We lay in introspection another five minutes. Then it hit us both at the same time!

"He never crossed the ditch," we said in unison.

I was glad Teddy was here. He had good instincts, and my head was swimming in an amalgam of disappointment, bafflement and regret.

We fell over each other batting through the thicket to reach the ditch again and the last drop of blood we had left well over an hour ago. Less than a minute later we found another. Then a few feet farther along the lip of the ditch, another. It gleamed ruby-red in the brilliant beam of Teddy's coon light. Whooping with delight, we were back in business.

The trail was meager, but steady. At the lower end of the wash, it led east, deeper into the thicket, running parallel to the creek some 60 yards below. A tiny drop here, another there, located only with painstaking care. Everywhere we found a drop of blood, I placed a bit of tissue paper. By the trail of tissue, you could fix the general direction of travel. A quarter-mile from where I had shot him, the buck had horseshoed, backtracking.

Then once again, everything dried up. We searched and searched, me on the thicket hillside, Teddy along the creek where we felt he had gone. We closed ranks 30 minutes later, downtrodden, sinking to our knees in exhaustion.

"Lord," Teddy exclaimed. He had taken to praying again. "I got to tell you," he said, "I came thinking we could do it . . . find this deer. A time or two tonight I thought we would. But now I don't know. There's just no blood."

I didn't respond. I just felt sick inside. We lay down again, and this time must have slept for a half-hour. As I woke, Teddy was climbing to his feet.

"I'm going back along the creek and look some more. He had to cross somewhere," he declared. There was no quit in the boy. I liked that. Picking up on the hillside again, I searched farther east. Maybe he looped again. But the premise took me nowhere. I was suffering another twinge of despair when Teddy yelled.

"I've got blood!"

I fought my way toward his voice, mindless of the stinging

branches and clawing catbrier. He was standing alongside the creek at a deer crossing 80 yards from our departure point. With his hand, he pulled aside the overhanging cover along the creek bank and directed his light to one small green leaf at the edge of the water. On it was a pinhead speck of blood.

"Boy . . . you're good," I said. He grinned.

"Lucky's more like it. I just kept working the creek bank back and forth, and finally, there it was."

Grit, I was thinking. _Sheer grit._

We crossed the creek, began looking anew, hopes resurrected. There were several beaver ponds in the area, together with long bottom wetlands stretching east and west; a lesser swale bordering a tributary branch and leading south. I worked west, Teddy east. We met a long while later. Not a thing, either way. Combining forces, we searched a good way up the swale. Not a sign. Despondent, we made our way back to the creek crossing. This time, all truly seemed lost. It was the lowest point of the night.

"Just not meant to be," I supposed.

"There was a time, earlier, I really felt we could hang in and find this buck," Teddy said again, "but I don't feel good about it any longer. There's just that one tick of blood – maybe a couple of tracks – the last two hours."

In the pit of my stomach the nausea was churning again, like the toss of the sea. First light was still an hour away. We settled into the leaves to wait. Come day, we'd make one last attempt. There was silence between us. The last hour of darkness was endless. Finally, about the ghostly depths of the creek-bottom, the black of night traded into the faint gray of day. Thin tendrils of vapor rose gently from the beaver ponds and massed slowly into morning mist, veiling the old-growth stand of oaks, gums and poplars that guarded the lowlands. We were fain to stir, lulled by its tranquility, reluctant to disturb its peace. Reluctant, as well, to press our fate.

A t last, when it was light enough to see without the lights, we pulled ourselves stiffly up from the leaves and stretched loose the kinks. "I'm going back up the creek and look one last time," Teddy said. "Maybe I'll get lucky again." I didn't think he really believed it.

Neither of us could muster any real enthusiasm. Even less after another empty hour. I had been 200 yards down the creek, combing either side, and was returning to search again the crossing for the umpteenth time. When Teddy's exuberant whoop boomed through the stillness.

"Blood!" he shouted. "A good bit of it."

"Where?" I yelled.

"Up the branch swale."

I took off running. When I got there my lungs were pumping, but it wasn't from the sprint. Teddy pointed to a big red splotch along the west side of the branch, to another no more than a foot ahead of the first.

"I came within a few feet of this last night," Teddy said breathlessly. "If I had come a few feet farther . . . we'd have found it then."

"Well, you've found it now. That's what's important."

Abruptly, the blood trail had resumed, was growing stronger with every step. It was as readily visible as a stop sign and Teddy was ahead, pointing it out as we went. Our hearts were soaring. Leap-frogging splotch-to-splotch we pressed on, excitement growing in bounds, like the foothills ascending a mountain range. Crowding toward a peak.

Then my back grew stiff and I straightened to stretch. When I did I saw him.

It took a moment for my mind to accept the truth of my eyes, and even then it asked for a confirmation. In the instant I was sure, I hollered.

"There he is, Teddy! THERE HE IS!"

"You're kiddin'," he exclaimed, in utter disbelief.

"No. There he is!"

He was lying 20 yards ahead on the far side of an ancient, fallen log, gray as the morning mist. He had fallen facing his backtrail. This was his place, and he had returned to it in the end.

We held back, emotions swelling, admiration, euphoria and remorse. Until the relief of our search could no longer be contained and erupted into cloudbursts of joy. We grabbed each other in a bear hug, dancing through the briers and the honeysuckle like lunatics, crying and laughing and whooping in unfettered jubilation.

The buck was grand. Kneeling beside him, I traced with fingertips the height of the tall, burnished beams, the graceful curve of his muzzle.

"Ten," Teddy marveled, finishing a tally of the tines.

I collapsed against a stump, drinking it all in. I wanted to remember this precisely as it was, as ever it would be. Before the bark of the crows broke the cathedral stillness of the bottom. Before the first rays of the morning sun chased the shadows from the glade and lit the fires in the maples on the hillside, freshly scarlet with the rush of autumn.

I glanced at my watch. Eight o'clock of another day. Fourteen hours since it had begun, 14 long, stricken and happy hours we would not forget so long as we lived. Greater than the memory of the deer . . . grand as he was . . . the way it all felt – the fine, simple sense of mutual pride in being honest to the hunt, in staying with something until it was carried to its end, when all hob said it was hopeless.

I had gained a great buck with the bow. And I had gained a son-in-law. Folks said it happened at the wedding. It didn't. It happened that night in the deer woods . . .

Over the Jubilation Buck.

Chapter 18

In A May Way

Ever notice the world's in a rush beyond a reason?

Makes me wanna go fishin'. Not off to the Varzuga, Islamorada or Papagayo Bay – not just now – but somewhere it ain't much trouble to get there, and when you do, it ain't that far to come back. Somewhere it don't take a truckload of gear and the worry it got there, somewhere there ain't an airport, a customs cop or a taxi-driver named Sergei trying his best to explain to me something I'm troubled to understand.

Just now I want to be somewhere laid back and by – someplace shy to the eye – someplace you'd have to look hard to find me even should you try. Some modest little black-green puddle of water I've known as long and intimately as my lover's freckles, someplace as quiet as it's quaint . . . somewhere safe and sheltered where the wind don't blow.

Don't want to be in any hurry; don't want to have to wait on nobody to go; don't need to wonder why it's so danged simply hard just to say "no." I just want to be with me. Pull the pickles and get down to the potato salad, and there's a lot to be said for solitude, sloth and simplicity.

I've not got the toothache; I ain't peevish with the pox; I ain't hammered my thumb. It's not that I'm mad, so much as I'm glad, just that there's also this gnawing trace of sad.

No need to worry; no need to ask am I "okay?"

I'm in a May way.

Blame it on the moon.

If my granpa was here, he'd say I's "out of sorts." Which means my compass is spinning somewhere between Paradise and Purgatory. Disoriented momentarily by mystic notion as confounding as the Bermuda Triangle. But he ain't, and I don't know how else to explain except to say that he had more than a little to do with the condition. Certain May days on the same moon he was that way too, hung mid-step where the paths split, and now he's long gone and he ain't wrote back to say where. All of which is maybe to say, when a man trades rainbows in Idaho for backyard sunfish, he needs a reason better than his cow came home.

But here it is, the moon's been coming full for nigh a week – first time for the month – and I can smell them as sweetly as Nancy Richardson's perfume the first time I was downwind of her at our high school homecoming parade. The bluegills are bedding. It's about the same effect, begging me to crash upon the rocks of renaissance, neglecting all else in return.

So I'll piddle til late-afternoon, fetch up his little four-weight, study but forget the wind-knots in the leader as mostly last year I did. I'll cram a few black ants and a popping bug in my pocket, whistle up my dog, drive the four miles to the old house-place – what once was a home. I'll stop by the smokehouse, retrieve the old gray hat where he hung it on a peg, mosey 200 yards on down the path past the garden to the pond. If there was still a chicken lot along the way, I'd bring a pole and a Maxwell can, stop off like once we did and dig a few worms. Not the measly red ones you can buy today, oozy and yellow when they shrink from the barb, but the old-timey, gray juicy ones with the fat pink waistband you found under the leaf mold and manure – big enough to cover the hook and take it like a man.

Then . . . well . . . I'm in a fly-rod mood anyway, Granny's been gone long as Granpa, and most of the chickens went and flew off with her. There's still her lilac bush by the way . . . we'll tarry to watch the swallowtails, as inebriated by the blossoms as I am by the bluegills . . . and a little farther on, there'll be his bees, droning joyfully about the white hives by the greening meadow, in the hazy rays of the drooping sun.

The little pond will be waiting as I remember, a peaceful tapestry of sunlight and shadow, as we steal silently into the boat. Disturbed only by the *chewuungh* of a largemouth, as somewhere from the darkness under the willows comes a swipe at a dragonfly. Gently I'll push off, the dog to the bow and me for the stern. I'll lay by Granpa's rod, fire up his burnt-out pipe under the battered old fedora, unlimber the paddle he carved out of a hick'ry slab – same day he made me a pop-gun for a cedar ball – one gusty, long-away day 'twas March.

The 12-foot, plank-bottomed dory that he built as well, suffers now a mite to leak, but the dog won't complain. My pants are turned up to my knees, the water and slime of the algae feels warm and squishy on my bare feet, and it's a short, easy scull to the head where the beds will lay. Back-paddling, standing as we near, I can see them now, round as silver-dollars, shiny to the sand.

Upon each hovers the restive silhouette of a fish, 'bout as thick in the back as a swollen thumb and as broad to the beam as a butter saucer. Whirling, charging, retreating, fins flaring translucent and yellow-bright, each fights furiously in figure-8s to save from its neighbors the ripening legacy of its diminutive kingdom. The shallow flat is seething with the battles, a swirl here, a rip and chase there.

From a distance the little rod can load and limber at ease, I'll beg the boat to rest, strip off a shake of line. The water churns with a hundred small hopes. I've caught salmon on streamers and steelheads on flies; still my hands tremble to tie on a #16 ant and it's hard to know why. A couple of light hauls, the little rod answers in geometric poetry to my will, the line lifts, rolls and unfolds . . . and the tiny fly lights as gently as thistledown. As if it is afraid to touch the water. For instantly, a half-dozen, frenzied swirls erupt, a sharp little thump carries tip to thumbnail, and the tiny cane bows and dances more merrily than an Irish jig.

There'll be a half-dozen ol' blue-black, copper-headed males, wide as the palm and fingers of your spread-wide hand, that pee in your lap when you take hold of 'em to ask the hook out. But mostly I'll wonder . . . that a man who's had the privilege of hundred-pound sails, the might of a marlin, the blister of a blue, can still find such a simple fine time with a few ounces of bream . . .

On it will be, at the lazy lift and lay of the line, for as long as I shall wish – until twilight steals the day from the sun, until at last I decide I'm done. Until in the gloaming I'll hoist two-fingers of Macallan about as old as I am – to bitter-sweet, carefree days that can never be again the way they were, but have come now and ever to be, the way they are.

Tomorrow I'll do it again. Tomorrow and tomorrow.

Later that evening, when I reach home, there'll be a message wending. From Pat Pendergast at The Fly Shop in California.

"The Copper River, in June, do you suppose?"

"Yes . . ." I'll suppose.

I'll have recovered by then. The first moon of May will have waned.

Chapter 19

Belle's Era

The journey to the mailbox should have been exciting. There was a flawless, expectant stillness to the air, as if the world held its breath in waiting. Dense, leaden clouds layered the bottom of an ashen sky, leaving the fields gaunt and drawn in the penetrating chill, the woods and thickets huddled and lonely. Sparrows and juncos anxiously worked the fencerows, bunching and foraging with frenzied urgency. Absent the usual malediction, a line of crows lugged slowly by. It was compelling, unmistakable . . . the promise of snowfall.

But the memory was too fresh. He would have loved this day, for there were only a few such in any year, even more rarely at the tag end of February. The birds would move. Always before snow or ice, the birds would move.

The mail was uninspiring. She turned and started for the house, undeterred from the mood of the moment. Murray Britt had been intrinsic in her life. He and Mary had no natural children of their own, but the fascinations of their antiquated, country lifestyle were irresistible to two generations of nieces and nephews. Never beleaguered by social convention, the veneer of their existence betrayed the culture and fervor of their lives. The barn and outbuildings, ancient and drab, stood around doubtfully on splayed legs. The same turn-of-the-century farmhouse was their home for 48 years. From the outside, it would have appeared plebeian, even unkept. For at least half that time it had worn the tattered remnants of its maiden coat of paint. But inside was a wealth of period music, antiques, books and oils that would have been the obelisk of any elitist townhouse. And out back was a neatly kept kennel run with tap water and a sewage lagoon. It was a reflection of their simple creed . . . passion without pretense. The old house weathered the storms on its own terms, gracefully, as they did.

He had made special of her from the beginning. From the time he turned her and her third birthday frock into a barn stall full of marauding, seven-week July pups, he had won her heart. It was her first lesson, of many, from him on what was most important in life. Forever an outdoorsman and dog man, he kept ranks of pointing dogs and legions of hounds. For all the years of her childhood and even after she was grown with family, he would show up on an anonymous impulse with a box-full of dogs and an invitation to go a-huntin', totally oblivious to the possibility that anything in life could be more important to the moment. More often than not it wasn't. She could mark the memorable events of their relationship by epochs of dogs . . . by Jake, Sadie, Belle, Pat or Gabe. As he habitually remarked, "If it hadn' got a dog in it, I never cared much for it." Most of all he cared for pointing dogs and quail hunts.

She snugged her coat to her neck, taken with a sudden awareness that the chill was growing. It was then, also, that she became conscious of the crunch of gravel under tire rubber at the end of the drive. The car was unfamiliar, an older, generic sedan that had once been a more virtuous blue. It was proceeding up the drive and she stopped to wait, slightly ill at ease. As it neared, it appeared that the driver was the only passenger, an older man with white hair. She began to relax.

"Pardon me, miss, would you by chance be Nida Giddens?" he inquired, as he pulled alongside. His face was gentle, his countenance comforting.

"Yes . . ." she responded, cautiously intrigued at her spoken name. "Can I help you?"

"Please forgive the imposition, but I wonder if we might talk for a few minutes."

He climbed out of the car and steadied himself with the assistance of a cane. "Arthritis, the doctors say," he said, answering the unspoken question "an abomination of age, I'm afraid."

He wore khaki trousers, a frayed-at-the-fringes, cinnamon sport coat of corduroy that contrasted pleasingly with the sterling tones of his hair and mustache, and lacerated hunting boots with leached toes. She liked him immediately.

"I'm Frank Gupton." He extended a hand and an affable smile. She accepted both.

"I'm sure you don't know me, but I hope you will come to forgive my intrusion. We can sit in the car if you like," he gestured, "but it's all the same to you, I'd as soon sit by the fence and enjoy the day."

"Yes, thanks," she replied. "I would prefer that." She led the way to a nearby fence corner with a comfortable bench of earth, her curiosity rising. "What would you like to talk with me about?" The stillness punctuated the question.

"Bird-hunting, actually," he smiled.

"Bird-hunting!??"

"Yes, I have gathered that subject is not unfamiliar to you. Do you mind if I call you Nida?"

"No . . . I mean yes, please." Bird hunting!? she was repeating to herself silently, incredulously.

"Do you know the significance of this day," he asked.

"No." More than you know . . . she had started to say.

"It's the last day of the quail season. And could you ever find a better one?"

"No, it's perfect," she agreed.

"As perfect as it is, there is another, even more special to me. Fifteen years ago. I was a bit younger and sprier then, still kicking up a little dust. Red was still here . . . a lifelong friend. We both kept dogs and bird-hunted. We loved it more than anything.

"Fifteen years ago almost to the day, the bird season had wound down to the last Saturday. We had about worn our local territory out by then, and were up for a change of scenery. Somebody had told Red about a laid-back crossroads two counties south that was thick with quail, so we loaded up the guns and the dogs and were on the way about 4:30 in the morning, excited as schoolboys with a substitute teacher.

"It was a beautiful day for February, which usually goes limp and balmy on its gasping breath. Different from today, but nice nonetheless. The morning dawned bright and yellow over a heavy frost, and when the first rays of the sun hit the tops of the pines, the highlights in the ice looked like Christmas candles. The weatherman was promising light winds and afternoon temperatures that would never get out of the 40s. It was all ahead of us . . . bittersweet though, being the last day and all . . . and we were feeling mellow.

"Just as the sun climbed high enough to put a halo around the field edges, with the land still mostly in shadows and all those fires in the frost, my old hunting buddy Red looked out the car window and said, 'Don't want anything more than this . . . never wanted anything more.'

"I'll never forget that. We never said a lot to each other. Wasn't necessary."

His tale was warming nicely. Yet she fought the urge to ask him why on earth he had arrived out of nowhere to tell it. Why to _her?_ But the lull and tenor of the old man's voice was captivating and an interruption would have been unsouthern.

"The country turned out to be everything we had hoped for," he continued. . . . "very few houses. Laid-out beanfields everywhere, patches of scrub lespedeza . . . briery heads in old grownup weedfields, broomsedge here and there. Now and then there was an old garden plot gone to seed, an abandoned hog lot or a cast-off tobacco bed. You could read quail into every nook and cranny of it."

"It was like that everywhere when I was growing up," Nida said.

The old man paused and pulled two sticks of horehound candy from his coat pocket. She smiled. It had been a long time since she had seen horehound candy.

"Care for a piece," he offered.

"Yes, thanks."

They pulled silently on the candy for a minute or so. The chill was growing ever more convincing under the somber sky, the air dampening as the afternoon waned. It would start soon.

"Did it turn out as well as you hoped," she asked.

"Yes," he said gently.

"We rode around awhile admiring the territory until we found an inviting field with no poster signs. We weren't in the habit of hunting without permission, but there wasn't a house anywhere close, and we were so excited over the prospects we decided to go ahead. It didn't sit well though and before we got halfway across the field we decided to gather up the dogs and find somebody to ask. It wasn't easy; the dogs were full of vinegar and in no mood to get back in the box.

"But we finally rounded 'em up and leas'ed 'em. We had almost made it back to our car when an old, beat-up, green pickup came by, slowed down like it was going to stop and then went on. In a couple of minutes it came back.

"Red," I said, "we're in for a chewing," as the old truck pulled up and stopped. It had gouges in every fender, the paint was flaking in spots, hanging like loose bark on a sycamore tree, and it kept running for 15 seconds after the switch was killed. Red looked at me wall-eyed.

"The driver got out and looked at us. He was middle-aged and in farming garb, two days worth of stubble on his chin, obviously a local. "Where you boys from?' he asked. No show of emotion either way.

Red took all kinds of pains telling him and begging the situation. I thought he was doing pretty good, so I just kept my mouth shut and tried to look genuinely pitiful and repentant. About midway through Red's apologetic diatribe, the man's face began to lighten a bit around the corners and Red, sensing progress, turned it on all the more.

"Finally, the fellow interrupted. "Listen," he said, smiling for the first time, "why don't you boys just load your dogs in the back and go hunting with me."

"I looked at Red in complete disbelief. He had a strange grin on his face like he had one foot in heaven and a promise for the other."

"I guess so," Nida said, laughing, fully invested now in the story. "You went, I guess?"

"Wasn't a minute's debate. We generally hung pretty tight to ourselves, but this man had a way, and no doubt knew the country and everybody in it. He introduced himself, we shook hands all around and started loading guns and dogs into that old truck. We had three pointers, Pete, Bell and Duke – pretty good dogs. But Bell hated to back and would steal a point when you weren't watching. We didn't know what to expect dog-wise from our host, but wanted to be on our best behavior, so we left Bell in the box. We climbed into what was left of the front seat, me in the middle with the floor shift and an old Fox Model B between my legs, and rode a mile or two down the road. Red was beside himself, talking more than he had for the past three years.

"When we got to the first field we were going to hunt and turned out, eight bird dogs got out of the box! Or seven anyway. One was a question mark. He had four of the biggest, raw-boned, double-nosed pointer dogs we had ever seen, a strapping lemon-and-white pup on a check cord, and one small bitch that could almost have passed for a rabbit or a deerhound. That little dog could cover more ground than any dog I have ever seen, before or since. In polite company, she would have been liver-and-white, but the liver was more of a washed-out brown and the white was a sort of tobacco-stain yellow. She blended with the cover so well you could barely see her, so he ran her with a bell around her neck.

"Oh, what a morning. Clear and still, with a bite in the air . . . patches of frost still splattered around. We hadn't been down 20 minutes when the little bitch pointed. She was flying down a long edge when she smelled those birds and swapped ends like her nose was nailed to a wall. She took two mincing steps and snapped into a point . . . and left skid marks in the dirt where her toenails dug in. *God, it was nice.* The covey had fed about 40 yards into beanfield stubble and she was reading them the bill of rights.

"I had followed bird dogs for 38 years, but the next few moments were easily the most moving of my hunting life. The sun was hard in our back, 9:30 high, in that forever blue, crystal sky, and the light reached over our shoulders and cut that little bitch out of her ground shadow like a carving relieved from a block of yellow fieldstone. Seven other dogs arrived on the scene from five different directions, all in turn, and caved at the withers like they had been cleaved, honoring the find. The pup was last up and a peaceable "whoa" was all it took. They ended up in a semi-circle – *eight* dogs! The intensity was electrifying. It was eloquent. Breathtakingly eloquent."

"I would loved to have seen it," Nida said, tears welling. "Once, when I hunted with my uncle, we had five dogs standing. It's mesmerizing. You want to lock the moment away and relish it forever. It's like a Christmas present in special paper with something wonderful inside, but too pretty to unwrap."

"We savored it for quite awhile before we kicked the birds up. When they went out, Red killed two, I got one and the fellow we were hunting with knocked down three! It went that way, more or less, most of the way. We called it quits about mid-afternoon with 16 birds in the bag. We thanked our benefactor profusely, this man who had been a virtual stranger only a few hours before. Whatever we said was inadequate.

The conversation at home that night was the best Red and I ever had. For the first time we tried to tell each other how much the years between us had meant, tried to relive a lot of the wonderful times we had enjoyed outdoors."

For the second and last time, Frank Gupton paused in his account and looked away for long moments across the shadowy landscape. Waiting mutely, Nida Giddens respected his silence. His story was beautiful, but there remained the question in her mind. At last, he turned and looked at her with softened eyes.

"Nida, we hunted that day near the little community of Turkey in Sampson County. The man we hunted with, who so generously gave us that exquisite, final day of the bird season 15 years ago, was your uncle, Murray Britt. He was the finest hunter and quail shot I have ever had the privilege of associating with. Red felt the same way. To this day, when someone mentions sportsmanship, I tell them about that day and Murray Britt.

"I read his obituary in the paper in December. He died just three months after Red. The family note mentioned a niece, Nida Giddens, of Creedmoor. I live in Oxford, near the Brasstown Road. When I saw it I knew I had to come and see you. I don't know how much longer I'll be here; it was a way of thanking him again, one last time.

"I asked around and found out where you lived. I purposely waited until today to come so it would be an anniversary of sorts. I thought you would want to hear it. I hope I haven't upset you too badly. I wish I could say I ordered the day; it seems made for the purpose. Makes you wonder."

Nida Giddens was struggling to compose herself, trying to speak through the constriction in her throat and the tears in her eyes, and the mixture of pain and gratitude in her heart. He took her hand. "Call me sometime," he said softly, as he rose to leave.

She tightened her grip on his hand, speaking a profound "thank you" with her eyes. The gravel whispered under the tires again and he was gone.

For a long time she sat and stared into the eternal gray of the sky, trying to comprehend the magnitude of the day. How could it have possibly happened as it had? It defied reason. But the years had imparted the wisdom to leave it be, to accept it for the simple blessing it was. Perhaps there truly are angels among us.

The little bitch would have been Belle. She became as much of a legend in her time as her uncle in his. She, herself, would have been 30-something then, endeavoring to weave a teaching career between the assiduous threads of family responsibilities in a different corner of the world. Her uncle would have already been well into his 50s. She thought about the time that had transpired since, and his passing, reminded acutely of the irrevocable velocity of the years.

The puppy on the check cord would have been Luke or maybe Joe, she thought, as she gathered herself and started for the house once more. It was his trademark, a puppy on a check cord. So it must always be with men who set their worth by the measure of their dogs, find a passageway to tomorrow in faithful, hazel eyes, and wrap their memories in eras that hasten by on canine feet.

Almost as an illusion, the first notion of snow was on the air . . . tiny, vagabond flakes faintly stealing by, caught against the cathedral green of the pines . . . their faint ticking against the tinder leaves a welcome intimation.

Dusk was near. She could hear the clamor of the dogs at the kennel. Jarrod must be feeding. He was 15 now. Almost off the check cord.

Mantengu

We walk abreast to the fallen animal – an Irishman, an Englishman and a Zulu – the affinity between us heightened by the complicity of the moment, and given the tempestuous historical tapestry of Africa, the paradox is inescapable.

In another time we were bitterest of enemies. In another time there was ever between us clashes of freedom or conquest. Most poignantly with the Zulu, in this his homeland. For not distant from this peaceful plain below the Drakensbergs, at Dundee and afterward

Rorke's Drift, his people defeated my people and my people defeated his people. Though the hatred has mostly bred away, and the anger behind has been whisk aside, grain over grain, like dry windblown sand. While the legacy of it all is the pride.

Now it is only I who shoulders a weapon, for wholly genial reasons, and bad gone worse, I who would readily trust my life to Garry Kelly, the Irishman, and Enoch Mantengu, the black man by my side. Already I have learned to depend upon him implicitly, the Zulu, to follow precisely his spoor even as he lifts his foot from a warm track. It is the path that has carried us stealthily and successfully through a half-dozen stalks, avoiding the stab and the slap of the bush, and twice dispatched the puff-adders that have sulked in my stead. For he knows the KwaZulu as the veins that mole the back of his hands, this adept and stolid man of the highveldt, thrice by blood, once by essence removed from a warring chieftain of *Mfecane*. I respect him for that, and already he has taught me things, the ritual of the first animal to fall:

"Lokho okufanele kuthathwa ngegazi kukhokhwe ngokomoya."

"What has been taken in blood must be given back in spirit."

There is a trinity between the land, the sky and its creatures, I have learned from him, that must never be forgotten. Lest there be ghosts behind to trod a man's soul.

Maybe more than all, he has explained, not in his words, which I do not always understand, but in custom, that Africa is a bountiful land, the most benevolent on earth. That it is tempting to forget midst the excess and thrill of her that there are, nonetheless, talismen to be paid. That, if you ask her for the latch-key to her best, you will come to know that she is not always easy. You are there on her terms, and because she herself is the dream is not the guarantee that she will grant you yours. Not immediately. Not the first time – perhaps not the last. It is careless to assume of Africa. Perhaps, as Enoch, it is better to think of it as genderless.

He does not pretend it, but Enoch Mantengu is a man of some wealth. He has his cattle, his three wives and five children. He comes from an affluent family that owns sugar cane fields near the Town of Mtubatuba. Because of his good fortune there is jealousy among his neighbors, but you would not know that either. He's a jovial fellow, who flies above it. *Mantengu,* reconstructed to English, becomes "bird," and about him there has circled a flight of wit and a steadfast pleasantness. Until now.

Now in his fixed brown eyes there is a hardness growing, dark and pestilent, that I have not seen before.

We have reached the gemsbok, and there is something, from the 200-yard vantage of the shot, we have not known. Something ugly and sinister. Around the base of its stiletto horns is a snarl of steel wire, and about its upper neck the lethal loop of the throttle itself. Already it has sliced its way through the hide, deeply into the striated muscle beneath and into the windpipe. Gore and pus ooze in purulent trickles from the circumference of the incision and the flies blow round.

In a day or two more the work of the snare would have been done. Unknowing, I have killed mercifully.

"Bloody awful poachers," Garry mutters. Were it only for food, there could be some indulgence, but this is for the market.

Mantengu speaks cruelly, still, with his eyes. Normally he would have laughed and teased at my success. I do not know him any longer.

The sun is dying over the mountains. Around us the veldt is melting under the long slanting rays, the molecular golden color of the plain climbing and suffusing into the air itself. On the backside of the hills the shadows are painting their mysteries against the morrow. But the evil of the scene defies the beauty. The rising darkness is not altogether the night.

I can no longer see the black man's eyes, only read the insult in his stance.

"Mantengu has worked extensively against poaching on private ranches," the Irishman will explain to me afterwards. "He has been very successful. This was due to his rather brutal way of handling the people he caught.

"The poachers were terrified of him and because of this did not try their luck.

"It is against his belief, the poaching."

So it would be, I thought, remembering all he has taught me. His Gods would be spurned.

I am disgusted as equally. It is temporarily overpowering, killing an animal in Africa. A mix of space, sky, sun, earth, place and spirit sewn together by several moments of remorse. Locked in unison with the forever mystery of the hunt, how within a microsecond of time, destiny can close an immeasurable distance between two lives and one ceases while the other continues. Yet – symbolically – both continue at once. But now the passage has been marred. Mantengu would understand.

The Irishman and the Zulu speak. In native tongue. I wonder what they are saying. There is the momentary glint of anger in Kelly's eyes as well as he turns to me, like the flicker of impatient light off a cold steel dagger.

"We'll spend a bit of time searching in the morning," he vows. "You'll understand, of course."

It is Mantengu, at dawn, who directs the hunt. For men this time and it is eerie. I study the razor sharp edge of the panga he carries, wonder what would happen should we capture someone. How far does the justice go?

"Enoch thinks as Shaka Zulu," the Irishman has said. "If you do wrong you are punished – the worse the crime the more vicious the punishment. He says the Zulus know only one way and that is a strong law. Anything else is weak and will be overrun.

"He does not believe in Western leniency."

Sometimes . . . as now, I decide, neither do I.

The black man finds more snares. Obviously something more, a telling clue. There is much camp talk, native rhythm, the next several days. Words I am not meant to hear. I suppose what may have happened.

He has not returned as yet, Mantengu, the companion I have known.

He will not return until the warthog I shoot two days hence. After we have spoken, dutifully, to the Gods once more. The animal is good, and once over he teases my success, straddling the pig and flashing a toothy grin.

"Inyama imnandi," he spurts, laughing broadly.

"Delicious meat."

He is the bird again and I am glad he is my friend.

Because I have learned a thing more.

We never defeated him at all, and in the ways that count, he was never my enemy.

Chapter 21
Letter to Louis

December 21, 2003

Mr. Louis Venter, PH
Imba Safaris
Limpopo Province, Steenbok, S Africa

Dear Louis,

The part of me that came back has made home. The rest waits with you, begging my return. You'll likely not notice it, for it's mostly molecular, tied up in first light and a yearning for the francolin to call . . . for their melodious soliloquy to dawn and dusk, which your Dad always said "announces so perfectly" hunting time.

If an extra and depleted cup of tea is left to recur mysteriously each morning upon the sideboard, a few extra bars of Dutch granola are absent from the jar, I'll beg your pardon. Tis merely the repast that has bided my time until you arrived, and which completed my reverie

226

as we examined together the day before us, long before the rest of the camp was astir. Possibly you shall harbor no recollection of it, yet sense strangely that something has happened. If so, do not worry; all is well. And should you and your client-of-present feel upon the quiet morning air the strange rush of a breeze as you depart from the lodge to the hunting car, only you will know it as the clamber of my anticipation, the flight of my spirit. And I will intrude no further that day . . . the wonder of a hunt we must share alone, as hopefully again we shall. Some day ahead, once the miles close amore.

Meanwhile, I shall be waiting as eagerly on the dawn of each morrow, to wish us off once more, to bid you, always, good fortune. You will not see me, but trust that I am there.

The portion of me that has left keeps the echoes. Of the kudu and waterbok – every minute, moment and morsel of them. Of all the things we shared. Smallest to greatest. "Fascination" must originally have been an African word, for nowhere else on earth is it so richly and plentifully apparent. You were remarkably patient in embellishing for me the wonder of else and all.

So much knowledge, so much passion, so much feeling – so much of life, unjaded by convention – you have gathered for such a young man. How wonderfully refreshing and heartening in this oftentimes stale old world. The next time you sit upon the high brink of the Valley in the last of winter, wonder at it all across the vast bowl of the plain, the ceaseless wander of the River, the distant escarpment and riverine treeline that guards the welcome of Botswana – the only thing promising and green upon the entire earthscape – as we did under the blood-orange death of the sun that September afternoon, whisper with the twilight a wish for me. In Africaans. For ever, I relish the lift and tumble of the words.

You know, of course, that the hunt and death of the kudu bull that seventh morning was one of the most profoundly affecting incidents of my life. The thing you do not know is that, in the considerable realm of my sporting endeavors, it is the foremost episode of my life. Kudu have held something deeply spiritual for me, that nothing other has, and certainly I am not the first to be so afflicted. It's hard to kill something you cannot separate from yourself.

A young lady in the Natal last year, after I had unsuccessfully sought a fine bull, said to me: "Perhaps he is your spirit animal and you are not meant to kill him." She may have been right, for as we watched him totter and then finally fall – the pride and the majesty crumple – under the irony of a Weeping Wattle tree, no less, it felt for a time I had killed a piece of myself.

I wept, of course, for I am made that way. Could not avoid it, then nor again. Have thought much of it since . . . would I – could I – even do it again? If so, only the way we did it then.

But without apology, as we examined afterward in the ancient company of the baobab tree, I am a hunter. I love the hunt, always have, always will. And as sure as my pulse beats I will hunt again, and soon, for a man seeks the nearest well when he is thirsty. Even so, I will remember faithfully every inch and innuendo of our hunt for this one splendid animal. He is a matter of greatest pride to me, and the overwhelming few minutes that brought time, space and destiny to close between the three of us, so that we took him, are marked indelibly upon the calendar of my life: the seventh day of Remember, in the month of Forever.

I shall not forget as well, your words upon his demise. It's difficult to embellish silence in such an extreme moment. Only rarely it happens. But when at last you said to me, as we lingered to certain his passing, "You may touch your animal now, Sir," the effect was flawless. Like closing with your trembling fingers upon the soft, warm nape of your ladylove the golden clasp on the finest string of pearls. I've never had any other PH, guide or outfitter say just that to me, anywhere else in the world. It simply says again what could be said before. You are a young man of exemplary sensibility and character, and God knows, the planet needs a lot more like you.

But to adorn it all with the gift of the great waterbok on my 61st birthday. When you would relinquish no moment nor matter in the quest . . . beseeched the Gods of the Hunt to let it happen. Be-Josephat if it didn't – and I guess we both know now that, somehow, it was meant too. Nevertheless, always I am beholding to you.

So now you have known the best and worst of me, the strongest and weakest, in a way no other man has, and it is between us, and us alone, as long as we either shall live, and the best I can hope for is that the difference was small.

It's hard to say in sum what our time together meant to me. Maybe by giving you something I might not otherwise. For there is a slightest inference of impropriety in it, and in any event, not a ready thing to pass between a PH and a client.

But it occurred to me at several intervals during our hunt that by age, you could be my son, and how utterly proud I could be were it so. Tell your Dad he did an awfully lot right. And congratulate yourself for the rest.

Never compromise your sensibilities of fair play, for regardless of how many times life will challenge them, there is nonetheless and always the right or wrong of a thing.

My very best wishes for you and Hilary of a long, fruitful and blissful life together, upon the ceremony of your betrothal. May the *Tokoloshe* flounder forever in the dust of your happiness.

Until . . . and again,

Mike

Chapter 22

Wisdom Birds

There are words of old Maine rarely spoken
. . . *Pumpkin Sweet . . . Nonsuch . . . Maiden's
Blush*. Words that formed the names . . .
Greening, Duchess, Pippin. Words imbedded in
the aspirations of the Mid-Coast pioneers who
turned their backs to the sea, forged inland and
hacked farms out of the great forests between
the Kennebec and Penobscot.

Words that whisper of the families that once cleared the fields,
that gathered up the stones and placed the winding fences and laid
the old orchards by. Of centuries that turned more placidly on the
axle of time. Of a place and being, both hard and gentle, contingent
upon the Earth and the moon, the sun and the sky.

Gone now the pioneers, given back to the land; mostly gone the
farms, abandoned to forest. Only the old apples remain, descendants
of descendants of descendants. They flourish in the woodland
coverts, alongside the ancient rock walls, perpetuated by the trace and

travel of wild things. Only occasionally now, someone will pause by one of the many old trees, heavy with fruit, remember the words and call their names . . . *Wolf River, Ribston Pippin, Greening Sweet.*

Only the forest listens. For around and about the apple trees, in succession after succession, thickets of alder and aspen grow. Bush and brier. Beech and oak. On them the fruit is borne: elderberry, blackberry, raspberry, cranberry, hazelnut, beechnut and acorn.

To the coverts of apple, brier and beech come the birds. And to the birds come the men and women who hunt them.

It is raining softly. It patters gently upon the grass. Quietly, I slip among the ancient apple trees, circling a small, thicketed draw jeweled with highbush cranberries. Gun ready, I'm stealing along to close our stratagem. In the country road on the far side Teddy is stationed. I can make him out faintly against the ribbon of dirt. Upon the green hillside between us waits a woman in a glistening orange slicker and beside her, a black-and-white dog.

In place now, I tip a hand to the lady-in-waiting. A touch, and to the task dashes the spaniel. Quartering the slope, using the dampened breeze, it patters a practiced pattern toward the larder of cranberries. Its stub tail is popping furiously. The tingle of expectancy swells with each quartering cast. I raise the shotgun to port, cautioning myself to relax.

"Bird, Blue . . . find 'eh bird," the woman encourages in scarcely a whisper, loosely directing the search from the hillside with soft whistles and body language.

Abruptly the Springer goes happy, whipping tightening S'es against the wind. She gathers the scent, stabs the cover. There's a *whumph* of pinions on the heavy air, a female voice screeches *"B-I-RRR-D!"* with the soprano urgency of a fire whistle and a grouse blows out.

Immediately, I tense . . . then loosen. It will go Teddy's way. Leveling and beating low for the woods, it will cross the road, directly by him I'm hoping. Again I hear the piercing scream of the woman, then the muffled swish of another flush even as Teddy's twenty claps twice. Too late, I catch the dusky silhouette skimming the lacy ceiling of the thicket. I snap away a shot, but the bird is safely by me.

Yet another grouse is up, climbing and rolling to port into a murky head of timber.

As suddenly, it's over. From a distance I perceive the clamor of congratulations. The woman, the dog and the son my daughter married are standing together, admiring something. I know what it is. I rush to share his face and his words. Great cause for celebration, a first grouse.

As I arrive, the bird is still breast-up in a palm. I ask for the privilege. Proudly, Teddy hands the grouse to me.

I touch the feathers, fluff and smooth the ruff with the back of a finger.

"Nothing on your end?" the lady asks. She knows the answer.

"Just my usual opportunity to miss," I concede, returning the bird to Teddy. I smile obligingly, knowing I'll bowl the next tail-over-tea-kettle. She smiles back.

Over the ensuing three days our hunt will go as delightfully, and I will come to greatly admire this small, resilient, middle-aged woman who loves equally springer spaniels, the woods of Maine and ruffed grouse. There is something very special about Jo-Ann Moody. Not the least of which is her uncanny ability to predict the unpredictable.

She's the perpetrator of Maine Game Bird Guides, a small, dedicated hunting service out of Belfast. No deer. No ducks. Just grouse and woodcock.

"I only do birds," she says, eyes bright and moist with passion.

Ebullient, effervescent, resolute, Moody is herself a bird hunter to the fingertips. Her few days off are spent with her dogs and a gun. She's a jovial person, given to seek and appreciate humor from everyday living, particularly as it concerns grouse hunting. She's seen a lot of it and hunting with her is ever shy a dry moment.

Off-season, she's 294 days abuzz, training her dogs. It shows.

"Course, the other girls aren't anything like I am."

Jo-Ann Moody was brought up in a hunting family, three boys and three girls. "Course, the girls aren't anything like I am," she declares. "I just happened to love the outdoors." Usually brothers won't let a kid sister tag along, "but mine did," she recalls with a laugh.

She started out hunting deer and rabbit. But one day somebody gave her a dog, part beagle, part Brittany. Cindy would be the beginning of her life-long affair with grouse and dogs. Because Cindy wasn't interested in rabbits. She only did birds.

"I was 16 or 17. This dog on her own wanted to hunt grouse! She taught me a lot. Smartened me up. I remember her fondly, though she made me mad – don't they all at some point? – she was always out too far. I'd yell and scream at her to get in here, and flush more birds than she ever did. So I learned to shut up. Then she'd check in more.

"She had an awful good nose, and she'd bark before the birds got up, so you could get ready."

"He said, 'You go hunting, don't you? Well, take somebody.'"

Some years later, the hunting service came quite naturally. A brother started guiding a year before her with a local outfitter. The outfitter needed another guide. Her brother said, "Why don't you do it."

"I can't be a guide," she stammered. "I don't know how to guide."

"You go hunting, don't you," he retorted.

"Yes."

"Well, take somebody."

She did, and has ever since. Eleven years into her own business now, she has clients worldwide. Her demeanor and zeal encourage serious bird-hunters. Most book year-to-year.

Along with her extrasensory ability to predict exactly where the birds will exit a given piece of cover, "blocking" as a style of hunting distinguishes both Moody's hunting operation and her considerable success.

Most of her working covers are small, less than five acres . . . thick strips, fingers and heads stippled with apples and berries . . . bordered by fields, roads or woods paths. Essentially, one gun goes into the cover with the guide to take flushes over the dog and the other drifts post-to-post along the perimeter, covering exit routes for birds that escape the man inside. In particularly onerous coverts, both guns are stationed outside, and only guide and dog go in.

It's a force play – the birds have to go – and it works!

A dog's death is the price you pay for a priceless possession."

"I remember that from somewhere," Moody says. It hallmarks her feelings for her springer spaniels. She got her first, Bonnie, by accident. She's 30 years along with them now, into the fifth generation. Breeding, whelping, training and hunting her own.

At present, there are Blue, Bess and Dee. She prefers females.

"They give you more," she vows.

Her training regimen, split between field, home and hearth, is heavy on bonding, sparse of discipline. In a lot of years around sporting dogs, I've seen no greater exhibition of rapport between dog and handler than Jo-Ann Moody and her springers.

"I don't know what it is," she admits. "People think I'm so good at this. I would be nothing without my dogs – absolutely nothing. Every summer I lose my confidence. Then I start taking the dogs out, watch them work. It all comes back. I know I can do it again."

Pre-dawn. Against the illumination of the head-lamps, the wipers are slapping at the raindrops splattering the windshield. Above them you can hear the sizzle of the tires on the wet pavement. We have seen the sun only the first afternoon, when we arrived and idled before the hunt at the Belfast Harbor Inn, hypnotized by the slipstream of sailboats in the reflection of autumn color from the hills overlooking Penobscot Bay. Now, on our last morning, it is again dark and dripping. Gloomy as a grave-digger's funeral.

All about us the hills are kindled with the incendiary hues of a New England October and not a ray to torch them.

Nevertheless, we are expectant. Our outing with Moody's cohort Jim Cunningham the afternoon before proved surprisingly fortuitous. No doubt the birds would have foraged more fervently granted fair footing, and a hell of a lot more comfortably, but we still flighted nine grouse and a dozen woodcock.

We bend our way northward along a portion of the 30-mile-long bay, the largest inlet in Maine, toward our jumping off point at Searsport. Were the night clear and moonlit, the lights and even the hulk of the old forts, George and Point, garrisoned in the early wars of territory and independence, would be visible across the shimmering water.

Along the winding road the old seafarer's mansions loom, emerging impressionistically out of the night behind rain-streaked window glasses. Wraithfully white. Hauntingly nostalgic. At the height of each, a widow's walk glows softly against the gloam. Does someone still wait there?

Moody bears inland. Soon we are on country roads. Climbing rolling hills. Dawn is breaking. Here and there are rambling farmhouses, brooding domicile, barn and outbuildings under one roof to thwart the bitterness of winter chores.

Along the graveled road, fields of blueberry tumble down undulating hillsides, crimson with fall frost, stitched with the serpentine travel of the gray stone walls. Rushing at their lower fringes into the painted hardwoods, the fields collide with the forest, and the colors splash like shattered water.

We spend a soaking morning working the wild apples, then wooded fingers thick with berries that dissect lush, green pastures. By noon, wet but happy, we have extracted seven birds. Teddy adeptly acquires another brace. I, meanwhile, continue to wander the Valley of the Shadow, rutted in the wickedest shooting slump since Snider McCombs (you had to know him) back-bored my BB gun.

Lunch is brighter. We stumble across the quaint crossroads of Brooks on the apron of the Kennebec and Moose River valleys. Remember when you were a kid and your folks drove you past the local bread factory – that heavenly, get-in-your-pores aroma of baking loaves? Well, there's a blithe little oven at 3 West Main, with a small restaurant tacked on, called *As You Wish Bakery*. Just follow your nose.

Tell 'em what you want, what you really, really want, and if they don't have it, they'll do it . . . from scratch. Great sandwiches too. I had a homey roast beef, though in my condition I would probably have been better served with the "Cluck & Moo," or better yet, their "Bull's Eye."

We take in another schedule of covers, flushing three or four birds, waylaying only the one that miscalculates and slices by Teddy.

L ate afternoon finds us on public land. The Maine DNR and the Ruffed Grouse Society have collaborated, cultivating hoards of crabapples in strips and heads bordering meadows and timber. While the majority of Moody's covers are private, the public project's a hot bet if the hunting pressure is light. We were wagering that the steady bath had most hunters sequestered. And there was a particular old Wisdom Bird there we wanted to test one last time. Evading Moody and company all season, he had hoodooed us the first day, ghosting out ahead of Teddy's best efforts at a super-sneak.

Had he known, of course, he could have drifted by me quite safely.

We are right about the absence of competition. The only person we encounter is Jo-Ann's son Steve and his dog Teddy. Yep, another one. Steve's in an outdoor trade.

"Too wet to work," he grins.

We team for a while, moving more birds, but lucklessly. Meanwhile, the rain intensifies into a pesky downpour off my hat brim. My shoulders are cold and clammy. After three days, the deluge has penetrated my best defenses, even wicking down my socks into Gore-Tex boots.

Breaking off, we bid Steve farewell and make for the cover that hosts the Wisdom Bird. En route we take a quick horseshoe detour and collect a nice cockbird that banks inexplicably off home-free to chase down my errant charge of $7 \, ^1/2$s. Redeeming, but a good shot short of salvation.

Stealthily, we broach the chosen cover. Three-year-old Bess tips along at a mannerly heel by Moody's leg.

Beforehand, we have tossed the dice. Teddy will swing high and wide, use the rain, circle in from the far end and try to intercept the old boy going out. I'll melt myself into the dark edge along the lower, off-side, stay abreast of Bess; maybe the cagey rascal will alter tricks and roll out my way. Jo-Ann motions an inaudible release. Bess is out and busy in the strip. Here and there I glimpse a patch of liver-and-white on a crazed stump of tail. Three-quarters of the way, she's hotly birdy. Nerves tighten. I strain at the moment, eyes intently skyward, tensing for the thud of Teddy's gun.

Nothing. The suspense drains sadly away. Now we must live for the next time.

Teddy is waiting at the end of the strip. "I heard him," he laments softly, "I *think.*"

I chuckle at the familiarity.

We stand around at loose ends with droopy shoulders, draining like an over-worked downspout. None of us really wants to quit. But it is pouring.

"Well," Moody suggests, "we could leave here and there's this little head of cranberries . . . "

I'm smiling openly again. She stops mid-sentence and looks at me cleverly. I look back.

Before me is this stoic, take-no-prisoners little woman, hair plastered in curly, wet ringlets to her scalp (never wears headgear —

"can't hear," she fusses), drenched top-knot to toe-nail. It's 4:30 in the afternoon; we're seven hours and close to 20 covers on the far side of where we started, and she's tromped straight through the meanest, thickest muddle each could offer. It's raining Dalmatians and now she's got this one more.

Now I know how it was Joshua Chamberlain held Little Round Top.

Chapter 23

Warm Yellow Kitchen

I t is dark below. Raindrops clamor helplessly at the small window by his shoulder, driven in itinerant streaks across the glass by the travel of the airstream. The emptiness of the night absorbs his thoughts like blotted ink.

Somewhere close beneath, at last, is Memphis. Memphis, 218 Waterford Road, and home. Listing for a time, the plane rolls left upon its wing and swings, then slowly levels. The engines surge, loaf, then surge again, gentling the Boeing into a landing descent. Alternately, the jet glides and stoops for the runway. Captive to its motion, he feels himself following in weightless stairsteps.

Through bleary eyes, he glances at his watch. Two-twelve in the morning, Central.

Suddenly the low, murky clouds lift and the earth rushes up. In the near distance, a small city of lights queerly looms and ahead the runway markers stretch away as regimentally as a march of militia. The wheels grab the asphalt and the fuselage shudders. Thunderously, the engines reverse and roar, the brakes catch and the forward force of the plane dies as if arrested by the retarding grasp of some great giant. Docilely now, the aircraft taxis to the terminal and brakes to a halt.

Outside, the rain beats a steady tattoo into the puddles on the tarmac. Baggage attendants and maintenance crew rush about the shadows in glistening slickers.

He sits absently, spending the last moments of the trip in introspect, acceding the trace of relief. He's thankfully there and back again.

This time it was Cameroon and bongo. The time before, Alaska and king salmon. Before that, Scotland and grouse.

For a spell, once more, the wildness has been satiated, the restlessness quieted. His longing now is for home.

Home and Stephy.

The cabin speaker blared in a pinched monotone: "On behalf of Delta Airlines, we'd like to welcome you to Memphis International. Federal regulations require that you remain seated until the captain has turned off the safety belt signs and your flight is ready for deboarding. Thank you for choosing . . ."

For all the many years she has understood. From their first dates as high school sweethearts, long ago and far away, when the fish bit late or the puppy ignored sunset. And even later, as she learned that the terms of their endearment would forever hover around dusk, when the deer walked or the turkeys needed roosting, and dawn, when the ducks flew. When, time and again, his implacable wanderlust compressed their precious few hours between the whims of some wild thing and her father's 11 o'clock curfew.

There was an immense part of him that would never be contained or civilized, and would ever leave her waiting, and even knowing that, a few years afterward she had promised her life and love to him.

In the decades since, he had sometimes wondered why.

For he was ever prone to go, as surely as water is given to flow, and there were times he had not been there for her.

Searching his reflection in the window glass earnestly for a moment, his features sobered.

He could not remember a time that she had not been there for him.

The deboarding signal thumped with a blunt chime.

He waited past the initial press of passengers and slipped into line, onto the aisle way and into the terminal. Pensively, he threaded his way through the staggered concourse toward the baggage claim.

In the early years she had followed. That portion of their life together had passed more swiftly than he would have wished. Inevitably, perhaps, for it had much to do with the gentleness he so adored in her. Though she understood the intensity of his quest, she would never match it. She loved the adventure, but more, she cherished the constancy and grace of home, and the easel of her small studio.

"Go," she said. "I'll keep the dogs fed and the covers warm."

She had made it all possible. She was the melody of his song. And ever she watched and waited for him, in a warm, yellow kitchen.

He'd been comin' home from somewhere or the other for 40 years, and the most comforting sight of all as he finally made the back porch was Stephy stirring around in the soft light of a warm, yellow kitchen. When she was younger, the back-lighting always put an alluring glimmer in her long brown hair. He would stand quietly in the shadows of the porch for several minutes sometimes, simply reveling in it. Listening to her humming in his mind, as she always did when she was happy. Supper had waited on a low burner many a night when he was a younger man. There was a son and daughter to prove it. And a grandson, who had killed his first deer the fall before, and who would soon go in search of wildness with him too, as Andy had. And the little girl with hair the color and texture of sun-kissed cornsilk, who beleaguered her "Grandunny" to keep every pup in the latest setter litter.

Stephy's hair was silvered now with the striving and, yes, perhaps the waiting. As was his. It no longer fell in the long fine tresses about her shoulders. Her face was tautened by caring and wrinkled with giving . . . and she was more lovely than ever she had been. And still she was his and still she waited for him.

"Thank God," he whispered softly.

So it must always be. He wished to live one day longer than Stephy, and one day only.

He retrieved the considerable duffel, the rifle cases, slid them to a corner, found a cart and ferried it all to the loading station. A ticket attendant there consented to guard it. A chilly bluster of wind nudged him defiantly as he pushed past the door to the parking pavilion. Rain pelted his face. It was black and dark. The struggling security lights wore faint silver halos in the fog.

Reaching the Discovery, he punched in the entry code, flung aside the door, clambered onto the seat. Slamming the door behind him, he recovered for a moment, safe and dry. Minutes later he was loaded and southbound on the freeway.

He wanted to hold her now. Feel her against him. Hear the ageless promise again.

The wipers slapped softly across the windshield. The road was empty and dreary.

She'd be in her blue velvet robe – have the coffee hot.

His ear bent to the tune on the radio. Unbelievably – Gary Morris' _Wind Beneath My Wings_. He'd never comprehend it – how Fate sometimes embellished the proper moment. If Fate it truly was.

Only a few more miles now, of the thousands. He pressured the accelerator pedal, watched the speedometer needle climb another five miles-per-hour.

He considered the things it had taken to make his existence complete. Forever he was incontent to compromise. Major interests in three profitable corporations. Enough rifles to fill Stoeger's fall inventory, fly gear to mount any excursion between Bristol Bay and the Cays, a shotgun for every occasion. Three of London's best.

Wealth and freedom. Everything for every season.

Well and good, he thought, as he swung the wheel into the last turn. But the fortune of his life waited just ahead, as unpretentiously as it always had, in a warm yellow kitchen.

Chapter 24
Daughter of My Daughter

There's a new granddaughter in my life. The daughter of my daughter. Two little girls now. Always there would have been the one.

Sixteen years coming, she is the gift seemed not to be. Even after the disbelief was shaken and she had made herself obvious, she was a tease. Female all the way. Defying the prophesy of the ultra-sound, confounding her doctors with a tomboyish heartbeat. Keeping us guessing. Trying us by surprise, insisting her way into the world 20 days north of due.

But the night before she was born I caught the shadow of a heron against the make of the moon. The chimney smoke had laid flat and pale, and the Guernsey cow in Sutton Miller's pasture lowed three times before a rooster crowed false-dawn. One day I'd explain to her the country augury of all that, as wondrously as her great-grandmother had to me, so that one day again she could explain it to another, the little girl of her own.

I'll admit she scares me a bit now. Such a wisp of a thing, to stake such a profound claim on my heart. I hadn't really expected that, until she was a mite older. I've worked up the courage to hold her once, rocked her till she fell asleep. Studying her in the cradle, she looked like she belonged midst a litter of setter pups.

I'm a trifle impatient, I guess. I'm restless for the day she can take my hand, follow the Lab for a walk. Discover a terrapin in the path, look up at grandpaw and ask "Why?" I'll stoop and pick it up – she'll giggle when my old knees crack – and it'll be about the size of a 50-cent piece, and I'll stuff it in the little watch pocket of her overalls and show her how to look at its belly and tell the time. The way someone did the once for me. Think that'd be rushing things? Maybe when she's four we'll find in October a thick, brown woolly caterpillar and I can tell her why the winter's gonna be hard. Or what good's a doodlebug on a ball of manure?

I've so much to explain.

We'll play in the mud, I imagine, cause even little girls know the best things in life are dirty, and we'll clean her up before she goes home and not tell her mother. We'll catch lightning bugs and keep them in a jar, and collect pollywogs and sneak them past Granny into a bathtub of water. And do you reckon when she hunkers down and stares the first toad in the face, works up the nerve to gather him up, I should really tell her that's how you get warts. Would she believe me still, when later she finds it's not so?

I can't wait to see her eyes grow big and bright when we find the wren's nest in an egg basket in the corner of the barn. When three gaping yellow mouths pop up on diminutive stems begging breakfast.

"Grandpaw," she'll gush, *"can we take them home?"* And I'll take pains to tell her they're already home. And could she listen quietly, she'd hear their Mama fussing, asking us to be about things of our own.

One day in snow under cedar we'll spy a rabbit in its bed and follow the spoor of a fox, see a turkey even, or maybe a deer. Another little avenue of wonder will throw open its door. So that again I can rejoice with her glee. And with a trace of sadness, wish again for the little boy that was me.

I'll work hard to awaken for her a yearning for woods, waters and wild things like you awaken in a good pointer a slavering for birds, because I know when she's grown and older she'll come back to it each day, that despite the immensity of pretense in the world, it will ever anchor her life in what's real and right, and always be the chapel that harbors her soul.

I'll bring her to believe that all things are kin, great and small, that a titmouse or an oak sprout is as important as she and her grandpaw to the better nature of the world. That arrogance is a spurious thing. That if you belittle the life of any other creature, you belittle your own.

There's so much to tell her . . . such a task ahead. We'll build a bow-and-arrow, fashion a whirly-gig, put together from a gum sprout a popgun that shoots cedar balls. Not long after, would you think, I could drop by the farm store, buy her a BB gun and knock together the makings of a rabbit gum?

I expect eventually she'll shoot something with the BB gun and it'll die. A field mouse maybe, or a wood thrush. And she'll cry. And right then and there I'll have her to know there's nothing in God's world wrong with that. The crying or the shooting. That it's one more part of coming grown. Not songbirds or field mice anymore, but later, that maybe she'll choose to shoot something else. Like a kudu or a Dall ram. Just so long as she should remember one thing. The only way you can reasonably take a life is by respecting it as you do your own.

There'll come the day not long after I'll teach her what I know about a rod and a gun. Groom her from the little wayfaring wood's lass I've started to an alluring young sportswoman come into her own.

I'll try hard to remember two things.

I'll teach her to hunt before I teach her to shoot. For there is a valuable and civil difference between quest and conquest. And I'll teach her to read the water before I teach her to fish. I want her to think always of the way, ahead of the means.

When I'm done, I want her roll-cast to unlimber to the water as the kiss of thistledown, her bird gun to scratch down quail as nicely as wishes tumble from Christmas trees. I want her to be the living counterpart of the *Sporting Classics* calendar girl, with all the laddy-bucks brought up hunting and fishing panting after her magnetism, loveliness and skill. I want her to be just proper enough to put them off and just enough of a flirt to lure them on. And one day when the stars come right, I want her to put a ring on one, 'cause I don't think she could marry better than a sporting man.

Besides, I reckon the one that walks the tall cotton past both me and her Daddy might figure out somewhere near her worth.

I want her to believe in the power of her imagination, the compulsion of a dream. To never rest short of the mountain, for the triumph of a hill.

From there, she'll find wings of her own.

So that one day I'll hope to go to Africa with her the first time, to wilderness Alaska, and maybe Siam . . .

"Course, 'fore that happens," the old friend I'm promising all this to reminded me gently, "you'll be about ten years gone."

And I looked at him through the tear he planted in my eye, and wished . . .

"Maybe not to her."

Chapter 25

Old Horses

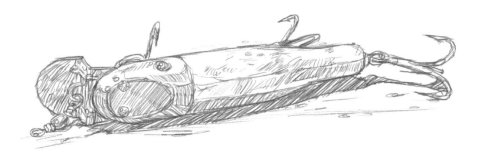

I f ever imagination towered to its apogee, consider the flight of Horace Ball.

Time had just cracked the door to the 20th century, Orville and Wilbur Wright were a whistle-and-a-whack away from the airplane, the first pitch was being launched for the inaugural World Series and Henry Ford was about to crank up the Model T. Astounding aspirations all, historic in their sphere. But scarcely more fanciful than the night dreams of Ball, janitor of the county courthouse in Paw Paw, Michigan.

Of the members of the Moonlight Fishing Club, a bunch of black bass insomniacs hard-put to fish open daylight, none was more original than Horace Ball. In the courthouse basement – about the time James Heddon was whittling his first "plug" frog along the Dowagiac River a few miles across the pike – Ball was carving wooden lures of his own. The difference was as spooky as the shadows under a fishing moon. While Heddon mused of frogs and minnows, Ball's creations seem almost surreal, conceived wondrously in the netherworld between flesh and phantasm.

Witness his first, the No. 1 Floating Bait, "for night or moonlight fishing," granddaddy of the many "peckerhead" lures of the era. Cause in shape and collar it looked wildly like a . . . well, polite folk called it a "woodpecker" bait. In succession would come the Dreadnought – a delightfully monstrous, gang-trebled contraption that resembled an old timey, double spool-bobbin – the wall-nosed Zig-Zag, the capricious Ladybug Wiggler and "1916's Newest," The Bug, a psychedelic rhinoceros beetle. Point was, they all caught fish – and fisherman.

So began the Moonlight Bait Company, most imaginative of the earliest wooden bait manufacturers, with some of the most captivating geometry in the history of fishing. Down by the Dowagiac River again, native Pottawattamie for *"many fishes,"* Jim Heddon would counter with his first catalogue, which in 1902 offered a single surface bait, the old "Slope Nose" Expert, in a single pattern: sky-blue head and cream-white body. Rapidly in its wake would come a parade of three- and five-trebled, underwater "Dowagiac Minnows," Nos. 100, 150, 1900 Near Surface and 450 "Killer." Among a growing choice of patterns was the bedazzling flash of "gold flitter."

In Kalamazoo, catching the swell of a growing tide, William Shakespeare, Jr., who cut his teeth on early multiplying reels and invented the "level wind," was adding his own line of manufactured lures: foremost the axle-and-spindle "Revolution," a gurgle bait with "Mickey Mouse" props. In 1909 his company slogan was "Built Like A Watch."

A short cast across the Indiana border in South Bend, F.G. Worden, who had been making "bucktail baits" since 1894, caught the word and chips piled for his first run of baits, featuring hand-welded hooks from England. Each lure called for a minimum of 50 hands-taking operations. Over in Garrett, piscatorial genius Henry Dills was hard at work on the first of the "Creek Chub" Minnows, the No. 100 Wiggler. As old Earnest Pfleuger, an Ohio neighbor who had emigrated from Germany, best known for hooks, rods and metal lures, quickly introduced the Luminous Crystal Minnow, the Monarch and the Neverfail, deadly famous in their day. In Chicago, "Smilin' Bill" Jamison cranked off a gaggle of distinguished lures, a special box for every one, including the Struggling Mouse, Nemo and Humdinger. Even Winchester, the venerable arms-maker, levered some action for a time with a Winchester Bait Minnow. As a host of smaller makers like Art Winnie, Jacob Hansen and J.T. McCormick climbed aboard, with artful creations of gum, cedar and pine dubbed the Stump Dodger, Spoon Jack Minnow and McCormick Mermaid.

From simple cottage industry erupted a creative revolution that, in all variations and another 50 years, would render as masterfully as any could one of the most beloved folk craft forms ever invented: the glass-eyed, wooden bass plug.

For the first decade of the new century, Michigan to Ohio, courthouses, kitchens, barnyards and benches were smoking with fresh woodshavings as the budding companies of Moonlight, Heddon, Pfleuger, Shakespeare and South Bend battled for lion's share of a blazing new fishing market. Heddon asked best in one of its first catalogues, "Are You A Bait Caster?" playing to the rocketing popularity of baitcasting countrywide, burgeoning since the perfection of the Kentucky watchmaker reels by Snyder, Meek, Milam and Talbot 50-odd years before. Jeweled, German silver reels, black bass and artificial casting lures were the trendiest draw since "doodle-socking." And the hottest ticket of all was the wooden minnow.

So demonstrably a story goes, that in a frenzy to dry the paint on an early "Rush Order," Mrs. Heddon over-baked a batch in the kitchen stove, creating what became a wildly fashionable pattern: green fancy (crackled) back minnow. It would be one of "blue-dozens" of finishes livening Heddon's classic lures, which in their prime were being created at the rate of 12,000 to 15,000 a day. Sienna crackle back, yellow perch, pike, rainbow and shiner were other vintage favorites.

Creek Chub, meanwhile, innovated a special, mesh-painting process for producing a lifelike scale effect (later selling half the patent to Heddon), using it for the duration of its years to virtualize a 145 different baits in 75 patterns. Moonlight, before folding to Paw Paw in 1928, pitched its whimsical little Ladybugs, in sparkling blends of "air-brushed" colors. And Pfleuger, for its Pal-O-Mine Series, conjured some of the zaniest manifestations in the fishing kingdom, including Cracked Green "Argyle," a dizzying impression of polki-dots, and "Scramble," a marbleized, multi-color suggestive of several hues of enamel, stirred but refusing to mix.

As sharply vibrant were the advertising hooks. "It's new. It's sensational. It's revolutionary," Creek Chub vowed in 1933 when it introduced its pioneering Series 4100 Jigger, an early "sonic' bait." "The River Runt Does the Stunt," Heddon said as emphatically of one of the most famous lures in its history. The Biff Bass Spiral, College Edition, would "Fool the College Bred Fish." And Shakespeare, red-lighting one of its hottest numbers, captured in allegory the beguiling appeal of all vintage lures, suggesting seductively: "Like a Thing Bewitched, It Seems to Weave, a Weird Enchanting Spell."

My, what a spell indeed.

Since the advent of the National Fishing Lure Collectors Club in 1976, old bass plugs, the boxes they came in and the pitches that made them famous, are among the hottest of America's collectibles. Serious collectors tally into the thousands, rare lures, such as Heddon's No. 1300 Black Sucker, easily command five figures, and bullish buying is nudging the market ever skyward.

For many of us though, who loved them first and most, I suspect it started differently. Not as a collection, but as a condition. I imagine the most fortunate of us took a liking to old bass plugs about the time we took a liking to old men.

Old men who smelled sorta sweet and sour, who reeked of black coffee and smoking tobacco, the dank, dark dirt from the tin can they kept the nightcrawlers in, and something more on their breath we couldn't be sure about. Old men who wore battered felt hats, shabby gray suit-coats and a watch on a string. Old gadabouts that habited tea-colored millponds, the days their bones ached, the mood of the moon. Old men who came along when bass fishing still had most of its mystery and all of its magic. When the nearest thing to a bass tournament was the annual contest at the general store, and baitcasting was as perfectly art as artifice.

Old codgers, you'll remember, who'd favor a boy with the bow seat of a little, home-made scow. Cluck him along in front of a one-lunger Martin to where the channel hugged the bank, and a pot-bellied chub would hold. Who'd spread open a dinged and hip-roofed metal box, where inside glass-eyed, wooden minnows schooled like workings in a kaleidoscope. Wise old men who could choose from among them some entrancing figment of fish foolery, prop their glasses on their noses, tie it on a braided line tethered to a Bristol rod and a Coxe reel. Hand it to the boy, scull the boat lazily along from the stern, and leave him first cast. Patient old rounders who'd pick out backlashes, show a youngster hope and how.

Sprouting in the years just after the Big War, I was apprentice to several such gents. Old Horses who took me to tow fore they petered out and taught me the measure of the big-mouthed, line-sided fishes that cruised in packs along the banks of the creeks, beneath the lucent green water of the pools. Those shadowy-and-silver invitations of fin and fancy that taunted me mercilessly. That would have nothing to do with the worms I readily caught the sunfish on, and seemed so arrogantly above the plebian possibilities of a corkstopper and a cut pole. A professor at a state university would tell me one day later they were members of the same family, the homely robin red-breasts and punkinseeds that fought for my hook, and those loftier piscatorial riddles the old men called bass. Never believed it then. Won't now.

One day, when I was nine, I learned wholly by accident you could fool 'em with a grasshopper. The hapless critter sputtered by, lost his rudder and plopped *spla-dunk* into the May-Dab Hole. Two breaststrokes and it sounded like somebody lost a lip-lock on a siphon hose. All was left was a suck-hole. Never figured though, until the old men came along, you could hope the same with a chunk of wood.

"He didn't either," they said of ol' Jim Heddon, a beekeeper and newspublisher man, "til he whittled that first plug frog. Looked like a elephant bullet what smacked a brick wall.

"Chunked it there in the water, and low-un-behold a bass struck it," they told me. "Tacked some hooks on another and plugged up some more. Then started carvin' 'em for friends. Fore he knowed it, near ever'body wanted 'em.

"Not jus' frogs but minners too, with collars 'er spinners on 'em so they'd kick up a fuss through the water. An' pretty soon after that," they vowed, "ever'body's brother wanted 'em 'cause bait-casters was growin' like tater sprouts, an' all these other folks got in the business."

They told me first and best, those old men, the lore of it all. It was more fascinating than any ghost story I'd ever heard. I'd ask them to tell me again and again. Cause they'd been there, lived it. Cause I was head-over-tailcap in love with bass by then. With old men, and rods and plugs and reels, with black stumps guarding quiet little pockets in lilypads, and red-wing blackbirds and anything else that had to do with them.

Then they'd show me from the box one of the first baits, carved about the time Congress minted the Gold Standard – an old red-and-white Bolton Bass Hog – clinch it on and catch a fish. And next a South Bend Panetella, the color of a rainbow and shaped sorta like the cheroot, popular 'bout the time Walt Disney came up with Mickey Mouse. After that a Creek Chub Wiggle-Fish, perch scale with a tin tail, just like the one George Perry had caught the biggest bass ever on, they said. Out of the Ocmulgee River, down in Georgia one June morning of '32, just ten years before I was born.

It was like mending the breach of the years . . . closing the two ends together with a jeweled clasp. I'd ask them to go through the box, every bait, tell me lure and lore. Frogs and beetles, crayfish and crabs, minnows and mice. More colors than a Crayola box. Spinners and sputters, poppers and chuggers. Things that spat and things that skittered, things that could be jiggled, bobbled or jiggered. Things that zigged and things that zagged, others that wiggled and some that wagged. This one had a spoon and that one a spout; these came with lips and those came without. Some were forthrightly familiar; others quare as doubt.

They gave me a few to start my own box. A Heddon Lucky 13, a South Bend Bass-Oreno, a Creek Chub Injured Minnow. A few others I begged on my own. Fore long I had a dozen. I loved the way they stared up at me, through goblet eyes, from the trays.

With them I struck out to earn my spurs. To catch big bass. To gain a place among the old men. On a South Bend Plunk-Oreno and a Dalton Special, one day later when I was 16, I chugged up a couple of bedding bass better than ten pounds out of Back Creek Lake. They had fished there often, the old men. I hoped those left were proud.

All these years now, I remember them best by their signatures. Mr. C.H. Wood was a top-water man. The world could have stopped with a Creek Chub Darter and a perch Heddon Basser, cause he'd still been happy, as that was all he threw. By dawn's silver light, with mists climbing the chill air, along the deep banks by the Green Branch run. M.A. Conner would have cottoned to old

Horace Ball, for Alvin was a night fisherman. He taught me to scull
the little boat along silently as a whisper, to fish dark nights, to wear
clothes that matched it and watch out for wasp nests. He swore by a
Creek Chub Ding-Bat, the surface model with the plunker head. He'd
blurp it along, raise the biggest ol' chub in the lake right at the boat,
roach every hair on my head. Old Tom Thaxton loved to troll the
lunker-lairs, mutter along over the wander of the river, knocking on
every sunken stump and oxbow. He ran old glass-eyed River Runts,
the early ones, on home-done trailer rigs, had a box-full . . . deep-
diving Creek Chub Wag-Tails, Heddon Crab Wigglers . . . long after
they were extinct in hardware stores. Eck Bullins flung a red-headed
Zaragossa, scarred and hook-scored from "walking the dog" with the
behemouths of Badin Lake. Sometimes I see him still, when I walk
one of my own.

After the old men, old bass plugs were like chiggers, an itch
you had to scratch. I begged ever one I could, in smallest part for
the fancy of it, more because they caught big fish. Guess I would
have amassed a collection five years sooner, except a Yank named
Nick Crème came along with a plastic worm. And somebody from
Sweden flew over a flashy red, free-spool baitcasting reel that had
"Am*bass*adeur" as its middle name, which you could throw them on.
For a time I wandered from old lures.

Maybe I was luckier than most. Providentially, just before I
escaped college, another old man happened along. J.C. Banks. Plugged
up the whoppin'est string of bigmouths ever from a nearby city lake,
on a Heddon Jointed Vamp. Did it once-over a week later on a jointed
Creek Chub Pikie. One of the 50 million or so Creek Chub sold in its
time. Like most old hands, his benevolence outweighed his pride, and
he confided in us boys.

It was love all over again. The marriage of an Ambassadeur
5000 reel and a vintage 5/8s-of-an-ounce, glass-eyed plug was the
sweetest union I ever attended. I started collecting newly, with a
passion. Old Heddon Flap-Tails in Grey Mouse, with ears and
whiskers, that tolled big ol' bass plumb out on the banks on an
inky black night. They'd blast it right at your feet, like somebody
chunked in a cinder block. Tad Pollys that scooted backwards, like
a skedaddling crawfish. S.O.S.s that purred the top like contented
kittens. Creek Chub Dingers with horsehair legs, that bounced
through the stumps like the marble on a pin-ball machine.

Pfleuger Pal-O-Mines and South Bend Babe-Orenos, bloop-along Jitterbugs, handy little wooden Midget-Digits and graceful old Moonlight Pikaroons.

For the next ten years I caught a lot of lugger bass on old plugs. Forty years later I still do.

Friends tell me now my old baits are worth a tidy sum of money. I wouldn't know . . .

I value them most by the old men who left them to me.

Chapter 26

The Stormwalker Buck

T he hallway was acrid with the stench of sterility. Wooden-faced attendants in white, blue and green scurried to and fro in urgent sprints, gravely studying pages on clipboards, rushing multi-storied trays of glassware, syringes and instruments past, dodging and weaving their way toward an endless ultimatum. From an obscure nursing station, a paging speaker blurted a perfunctory summons. On either side of the extensive corridor, numbered doors in boringly uniform ranks guarded the portals of blandly appointed rooms. A few were open. Through the breach of privacy, gaunt and hollow faces returned vacant stares above bed-ridden torsos. Mercifully, most were closed, leaving only to contemplation the nature of their wards, shielding from view the humiliation, pain and inevitability of infirmity. It was his first intensive care visit, and little more than he had imagined it to be.

Feeling dreadfully vulnerable, he followed the directional signs past yet another intersecting passage, past soul-bound convalescents confirmed to walkers and wheelchairs, past more chambers and faces. He wished he were somewhere else . . . anywhere else. Finally, a door plaque read 6731, the brass shield below – "Donated by Sam P. Cranford, Jr., in memory of . . . " Somebody important, he supposed. The door was slightly ajar. He took a breath and nudged it open.

Inside, there was silence. His eyes searched the room, uncertain of what to expect, coming to rest on the end of a bed and the small covered mound erected by feet under bed sheets. The occupant was hidden by a partially drawn curtain. Detained by apprehension, he could hear the burdened labor of irregular breathing. He winced, then gently pulled the curtain aside. Instantly, his gaze locked into the eyes of his grandfather, into a face withered and pale.

In it he could sense the hurt, but more, the bewilderment and resolution. He had seen it many times before in the eyes of other wild creatures . . . once the defiance had waned . . . an acknowledgment of certainty, a derision of wits and privilege. His spirit revolted. It was a travesty . . . for this man who had never known incapacitation, who for his 94 years had lived beyond walls. For this man who had known high, quiet places and crisp, clean air, who had watched eagles scream their supremacy to canyons far below, who had heard the elk regurgitate the voice of the wilderness in an icy dawn.

"Hey, boy," the old man murmured softly, his eyes flaming, then ebbing.

"Hey, grandpaw."

His hand caught the bony fingers that feebly beckoned, holding them for several moments. They were cold and sallow. Loosely, he dropped into a chair.

Loops of clear plastic tubing flowed from his grandfather's nose and mouth, and climbed circuitously from the i.v. tap in his forearm, encircling his face and upper body in a semi-ordered tangle.

"You look like a backlash," he stammered unconsciously.

The old man started a laugh that faltered into a grimace. "Don't do that, boy," he said weakly, but with an edge of humor, a hint of a smile.

He fumbled for words. None seemed to fit.

"It's all right, Devin," his grandfather whispered.

They sat quietly for many minutes, letting the silence resurrect all that lay between them. The emotion rose and fell, permitting finally a moment of composure.

"I saw him again, Grandpaw."

The harrowed face lifted from the pillow, turning, registering acknowledgment.

"Tell me . . . everything."

"A December snow, Grandpaw. I saw him in a December snow."

The old man's face softened. December snows were rare in the South. He had not known. For a week, day had followed night in an insensible swirl, a chasm of disorientation. Where before he would have witnessed the first tiny flake, marveled at the exquisite blessing of it, he had not known.

"Tell me," he urged again, settling limply back into the pillow.

"He was with a doe. He stepped into . . ."

"No, boy," the old man interrupted, "tell me *everything.*"

He realized, then, the supplication in his grandfather's voice, understood its significance. He stalled, choosing the words.

"It was rare, Grandpaw, beautifully so. You knew it from the start. The dawn was chill and damp, just the hint of a breeze, the clouds stacked in cords. It'd brighten a little, then fester again; the sun was strugglin', but never got through. Just before noon, it gave up. The air felt close and clean, and the temperature was droppin' . . . the woods so still you could hear your breathing. You could feel it comin'.

"Yes," his grandfather said quietly.

"It started just before four. You could barely see it at first. Just little bits of ice ticking the leaves. Then the first small flakes started sifting down, then more and more, bigger and bigger.

"I was walking that logging path above the McDowell Place, Grandpaw. You can see forever from up there. I stopped and looked across the hollows, toward the mountains. They looked cold. Cold and blue and distant. The snow was coming hard then, thicker and thicker. Until you could no longer see the mountains, barely make out the next hollow."

Pausing, Devin studied his grandfather. The old man lay upon his back, breathing evenly, eyes taut with expectancy.

"A wind had sprung up. The snow would swirl, then idle. It was white and layered on my mustache, wet and cold against my tongue. There was just me and the woods, and the wind and the snow. I felt wild and free, Grandpaw . . . wild and free."

"Yes, boy . . . *yes*," the quaking voice said.

"I heard her coming then, running. The leaves were still dry. She came out of the hollow, jumped the path and disappeared into all the haze. Not 30 yards ahead. I threw the safety and listened. Time wore on, the snow kept coming and I kept straining to hear. There was nothing. But I knew the buck was there. I could feel it. Like you told me I would.

"All at once, there was this strange feeling on my neck and I whirled around. And it was *him*. Standing there, in the middle of the road, against the white of the snow. Fading in and out of it like a mirage. He was huge. He's got drop-tines this year, Grandpaw. Drop-tines. He's got to be in his prime."

Devin was flushed. His blood was pumping, his breath growing faster with the exertion of the tale. There was flame again in his grandfather's eyes.

"We stood there lookin' at each other, Grandpaw . . . I couldn't move. My arms felt like lead. They wouldn't listen to my brain. I felt numb all over. Ever'thing moved in slow motion. Finally, he just melted off, in the fallin' snow. I never even got the rifle up."

There was a moment of silence.

"Were you sorry?" the quaking voice asked.

". . . No," Devin said after a time.

His response resonated against his conscience. "I want him, Grandpaw. But every time it's like this."

"It's been willed, Devin."

Devin looked into the old man's pale gray eyes. "Does that mean I'll never get him?" he asked.

"I don't know. But if it comes to it and you don't, remember what happened along the way."

The reply was frail. The old man was tiring now. Attempting a terse smile, he sank back to the pillow again, closing his eyes, surrendering to the imploring darkness. Once more his face was fleshless and pallid, his body drawn with pain and fatigue, his breath hampered and wheezy. In moments he was far away.

For a time his breathing seemed to falter, and Devin shuddered inside, hurled hard against a mistaken finality – then the scarce rise and fall of his chest resumed. Devin remained apprehensive, leaden with fear. He thought of his grandmother, 11 years gone. He thought of a wood stove in a warm kitchen, of warming bins full of cornbread, her cheerful fare-thee-well, and the happiness he felt the many times, gun in arm, he had followed his grandfather, out the back door and into pre-dawn. He thought of the hours remaining in his childhood. They would expire for good, he thought, when his grandfather was gone. Quietly he stood and stole outside.

The trip to the elevator was much as before . . . fraught with depletion, painful with living cadavers, each a poor, pitiful soul awaiting restitution. His mind fought for a kindlier perspective, but try as he might, it was elusive. Gratefully, he welcomed the blunt ding of the elevator bell.

It was different here, 30 feet below. Normal, everyday people gathered along the walls, happy people of all ages, laughing and talking, buoyant with renewal. Smiling candy-stripers flitted by. The paint was bright. His step lightened and his spirits lifted, lofted by anticipation. He made his way by the viewing ward, its glass tiers teeming with Disney characters, its ceiling spangled with twirling mobiles. The glass held at bay a half-dozen knots of closely pressed, ogling and cooing onlookers. Cameras flashed.

His pulse-beat quickened as he reached the door of his daughter's room. It was partly open. He started in, only to be detained by the shift nurse.

"Afternoon, Mr. Lockhart, back so soon?" she teased.

"Couldn't stay away from you," Devin replied.

"Careful, your wife's inside," she laughed. "We're helping Abby spruce up a bit right now. It'll only be a few minutes. You can wait around the corner if you like. I'll holler at you when we're done."

Devin walked to the designated alcove, catching the water fountain on the way. He sank into one end of a comfortably cushioned couch, oblivious to the three onlookers who eyed his arrival with idle curiosity.

Unimaginable, he mused, the whirlwind of events tied up in the last two days. It had him reeling, still suspended somewhere between astonishment and reality. In the middle of the forenight, first Cliff had called to anxiously advise that Abby's time was at hand and they were rushing to Moses Cone . . . to please meet them there as soon as possible . . . and only seconds behind, came the emergency alert from 911 that his grandfather was dangerously ill and being transported to emergency care at the same facility. Seven hours later his only daughter had given birth to a baby boy, and in the space of a new heartbeat, he was a grandfather himself. He had missed the actual event, unable to join the rest of the family in the birthing room, biding in the emergency wing while the man who had anchored his life since his own birth hovered between the Here and the Hereafter. The clash of happy and sad, life between a smile and a tear, forever the saga of humankind.

He had seen his grandson only briefly through the glass, but in the measure he'd felt a completion he had never before. Since that moment, his grandfather had stabilized, though his condition was yet grave. He yearned now to see his new grandson once more, perhaps, even, to hold him in his arms.

And beneath it all, 48 hours before, was the stormwalker buck – looming out of a cold December snow, esoterically but undeniably interwoven through it all as surely as life has beginning, being, and end . . . as surely as there were winters, woods and Lockharts.

T hree years had passed since he had first encountered the great whitetail, and the image was as indelible as eternity. He had found the massive signpost rub late in the previous year, after the winds and rains and cold had laid bare the final secrets of the slough. He had searched for other sign until he had narrowed the buck to his core and within the succeeding summer, he had laid his plan. In September, which seemed as if it might never arrive, he had donned knee-boots and stolen softly down the tiny watercourse that meandered the swamp, as deftly as he could.

The marsh had been lush with spotted touch-me-nots, billowing through the lowland and spilling gaily over the banks of the branch, pendant with the diminutive orange flowers that glistened like drops of honey against the mid-afternoon sun. Bees and monarch butterflies busied the blossoms; the air fairly sang with their energy. And high overhead, a redtail hawk was riding lazy circles in a sapphire sky. With painstaking caution he had tipped toward his destination, each step an excruciating shuffle calculated for stealth. All seemed serene.

But then came the distant roll and rumble of thunder, a hot sweep of wind and in scant minutes the sun was lost to a great thunderhead. Under it the black clouds seethed and gathered and the day brooded into a premature dusk. He never reached the stand in the lower limbs of the sycamore that guarded the branch where it funneled into the mouth of the buckbrush. Swiftly, awesomely, the storm advanced. The wind grew until tree trunks groaned and overhead the lowland canopy roared and bucked with violent gusts, until the ashen air was littered with flying leaves and torn branches. Before him, the sky was an angry black fury. Madness strolled the tortured clouds on jagged stilts of lightning and the thunder crashed maniacally in its wake. At the pinnacle of its wrath, the fury had descended.

Rain fell first in ponderous, wind-driven drops, then stinging, cascading sheets and finally, in an implacable deluge. One upon another, great splintering shafts of electricity seared the air and drove their deadly bolts into the earth, and the blistering rent of their passing and the overwhelming force of the thunder were as one. Burning for the hunt, he had waited too long, hoping the storm would skirt the low-lying bottom, and now he was caught without shelter in a cauldron of mayhem.

Scrambling up the bank of the branch against the pelting rain, he had felt the fear at his chest as the lightning spent itself relentlessly, so close that it sucked the breath from him and the air was sulfurous with its residue. He had hurried but a few retreating steps more when the great buck had arisen from his bed, not 20 yards abreast. Suddenly, amid the furor of the storm, he was aware of hide and horns and bounding motion. In the faint light the deer had appeared unbelievably massive, his body huge and knotted with muscle, his great rack squared and heavy.

The buck had bounced away for ten yards and hesitated, halting in the driving rain, the flash of the lightning, the thud of the thunder, to look back at him. He could feel the animal's staggering power, the tremble it left in his flesh. His fingers had fiddled clumsily with an arrow in the bow quiver, extracting it only to find it rattling against the riser in his excitement. He got it nocked amid an onslaught of adrenaline and found somehow that he could not raise the bow. It was then that the buck had turned slowly, flicked his tail once with practiced confidence and dissolved into the tempest.

He had been many days recovering, and then only superficially. It affected him so abstrusely that he had told no one, not even his grandfather, with whom he normally shared all. Why, he had not wholly understood.

He did not see the proud buck during the hunting season the following year, though he had worked and hungered relentlessly to do so. It was afterward, on a peculiarly balmy day in mid-winter, when the blush of spring was barely perceptible upon the February woodline, when he and Maggie had picnicked by the Almstead Pool and walked the river glen. The air lapsed thick and tepid, and through the afternoon a queer yellow light grew in the overcast sky and the breezes became restive. There was an aura of impending doom, an insidious presence you could sense but not completely grasp nor understand. They had grown uneasy, their concern heightening as they retraced the ancient wagon path to the truck in the impending dusk.

One moment the way was empty and the next he was standing there, the same buck. Devin had frozen mid-step and cautioned

Maggie likewise, and they had stared reciprocally for a long minute. The buck had not yet shed and the high, spreading beams were even more massive, the length of the tines breathtaking, the confidence in his carriage magnificent. He had taken several steps toward them, even, and in those moments the first raindrops fell and a warm breeze brushed by. It had affected him deeply. Then the buck had tossed his head, whirled and sauntered on. They could hear his soft, unhurried footprints upon the leaves for a distance.

That evening, in the small hours of early morning, an unseasonable burst of tornadoes had torn through the night, devising devastation and death. It left him to wonder for a long time.

It triggered a memory from a day long before, when he was first blooded on whitetail, and a small doe lay before him, and his spirits had danced at a fever pitch. Until he had known for the first time the biting sting of remorse, and the first tear had fallen. Looking to his grandfather, he had tried to wring meaning from it all.

"Life follows death, Devin," his grandfather had said, "and there will be other deer to replace the one you have killed. But there is for each of us who chooses to hunt, a deeper thing. One day you will know, but the years must pass. It is something I can tell you of myself, but cannot pass to you, something you must come to on your own."

He had looked at his elder with great perplexity, and his grandfather had chosen his final words with care.

"One day there'll be a boy fawn born, Devin, and one day when he is grown, he will come to you. When he does you will know it."

Years had passed, 44 of them.

He had finally related to his grandfather the essence of both encounters, and further, as always the old man wished, every minute detail. The old man had pulled upon his pipe and listened intently. Then his grandfather had looked at him at length, almost unconsciously, as if he was no longer there, but had traveled alone to some shrouded distance.

"Mine came when I was 46," the old man had said then. "I'm still not sure what it meant. Not totally. It was as inescapable as premonition and just as hard to define.

"And I've never gotten over it. Never will.

"But I've lived long enough to know this, Devin. Certain things, the things that are most deeply seeded in each of us, grow until they steer our souls, and sometime in our lives they will emerge in some strange and special way, a way that will defy coincidence.

"You can't time it, and a man's a fool to try. It comes in its season and graces your life . . . and never comes again. And for the rest of your days, you can never dismiss it.

"With us, Devin, you and me – it's deer."

The old man had paused then, for quite a time, and Devin had sat anxiously, wanting him to continue.

"I had seen big deer before, killed big deer before," his grandfather had finally said, "but none like this one." The old man's chin had rested in the fork of his hand and his head had rocked slowly with disbelief. "Our lives crossed four times," he said, "every time within a week of my birthday.

"I knew he was special the first time I saw him. Not because he was big. Because he reached something inside me that had never been touched. And every day I've been in the woods since, it's been different.

"As long as I've lived, it's been a mystery to me, Devin," he had said, "how two lives come to twine together in some wild place in a few seconds of destiny. I know, we go out and try our best to make it happen, and sometimes we think we do, and maybe that's so. But then something like your buck comes along as one has never before, does something to you that's never happened before.

"And either one of you could have been a hundred other places either occasion. So you're left to think . . . of all the seconds and minutes and hours and years it took for the mere possibility, *how*, in those particular few seconds on those few square yards, did it come to happen as it did?

"The answer brings you to your knees."

Devin had not asked more then, because all the while his grandfather was speaking he was searching within himself, as his grandfather had said he must. But there was the one thing he had to ask.

"You never killed him, Grandpaw?"

His grandfather had looked at him, and then away, into the distance. "I had him, boy. I had it all. Much as I ever could."

Ever, the old man had been gifted at tying moment with matter.

"Mr. Lockhart? . . . Mr. Lockhart?" Someone laid a small, gentle hand on his shoulder. It was the shift nurse.

"You didn't answer for a moment," she smiled. "I thought you were dozing. You can see your grandson now."

He climbed out of the couch and followed her to Abby's room. His pulse thumped in his throat as he opened the door.

Abby beamed from the bed. The baby was at her breast. The pediatricians encouraged breast-feeding now-a-days. It was important, just as it was important for newborn puppies to get the first milk of their dam.

He overcame a momentary wave of embarrassment, moved to her side and kissed her on the cheek. Maggie smiled from the side chair, enjoying his obvious discomfort.

"You okay, shug?" he asked.

"Marvelous, Daddy. Isn't he beautiful?"

He looked at his grandson, wrinkled and red. He had finished feeding. "Truly," he lied.

"How's Grandpa Travis?" she said.

"Stable for now. I'm not sure how long."

"He's failing, Ab," he added after a pause.

She could discern the dread in his eyes and the tears welled in her own. "I so hope he can at least see Bran, Daddy," she implored. "It'll only be tomorrow."

"Me too, Ab . . . me too."

He could not take his eyes off his grandson, so new, so small, so innocent of yesterdays and full of tomorrows. *Please God*, he whispered to himself, *grant me the chance . . . .. to tell him of the past and share some tomorrows, as grandpaw has with me.*

With perfect timing, Abby snugged the blanket to the tiny body, gathered it in her arms and raised it to him.

"Hold your grandson, Daddy," she said. In her arms was the gift that only she could give, the age-old promise of blood and renewal.

It was three weeks later before his life reached a semblance of order and advance. In the interim, there had been both intense joy and incomprehensible sadness. His grandson had made it home; his grandfather had not. One new life, one old, a beginning, an end. Travis Lockhart never saw his great grandson. It was the cerebral occlusion that had brought on the coma and sealed his doom, the doctors declared, and all of medicine had failed to stem the inevitable. Of the explanations that might be offered, it was the least plausible.

The burial brought the closure the old man had willed, and now the tombstone above his grandmother's grave was complete.

It was almost two years afterward, on a placid November Tuesday, when Devin Lockhart walked with his bow into the wildwood glade that nestled a tiny depression between Back Creek and Carraway Mountain. About him, the giant trunks of poplar, maple and gum stretched upward in towering obelisks toward a chaste blue sky. Two hours from the horizon a tiring sun lazed through their ramparts in slender golden shafts, stair-stepping the shadows and disclosing the reclusive ferns with anomalous splashes of light. Ahead, he could hear the gabble of the creek as it stumbled over the stones in its harried rush to the Uwharrie, and from his heart lifted a song of tranquility.

He had not known that he would hunt this afternoon. His two o'clock appointment had canceled and he had quickly reshuffled the priorities and engineered a departure. Just as all seemed clear, Maggie had called on the cell phone, stranded on NC 49 with a punctured tire and simultaneously, his fretting secretary had intervened with a frantic request that he proof the Blanchard contract before four. Nettled by irritation, it had seemed hopeless for a time. Ten minutes later, Maggie again – Jim Renfrow, a neighbor, had happened along and would take care of the flat – go ahead. With that he'd taken the chance on his secretary: a glance and Blanchard was back in her hands.

He needed the escape. Most of all, he needed the woods. Strangely today, his mind had dwelled in yesterday and burned for the freedom of solitude.

Neither had the glade been his first thought of destination. The promise was better in several closer and more convenient places. But again, his mind was of confounded purpose today and in its quest for contentment the glade had beckoned.

There were two options for the hunt: a stand by the elbow of the creek, where an old but reliable staging trail stole out of the deep hillside timber, or along the oak ridge just outside the thick second-growth where the heavy mast crop would concentrate the does. The latter was the more likely, as the rut was imminent. He would never really know why he chose the creek.

For a quarter-hour a sunspot had favored the maple stand, 30 feet above the curl of the creek, and he drifted semi-consciously under its mesmerizing caress. The hushed air waxed warm and mellow. The flanks of the mountain burned in umber, maroon and gold. Diamonds of light skipped over the shimmering surface of the water where the sun tripped through the trees and distantly, a wood hen tattooed a half-hearted sonata into a beetle-killed pine. Mood-stained with impressions of autumn, the land was lazy.

The small bank of wispy, gray clouds that arose over the western treeline garnered scant notice. Just another small brushstroke on an kaleidoscopic canvas. The feeble breath of its birth scarcely stirred the leaves and on the hillside, the squirrels still bounced in staccato flurries among the oaks. Inconspicuously, it gathered and proliferated until it amassed into sooty tiers that spread outwardly from the horizon and crept silently toward the sun. It was the eclipsing light that first brought it to his attention, that and the sullen silence, and by then it was a fully grown squall-line that had swallowed the sun and blackened the sky. And in utter surprise, it threw itself upon him

Within an eerie collusion of night and day, he could hear the roar of the advancing wind long before it arrived. He could see the tortured limbs and whirling leaves as it bore toward him, sense the presaging closure of the clouds overhead, feel the unsettling rise of anxiety at the pit of his diaphragm. Bracing himself against the tree, he groped for a handhold. Then it was at him, hurling into his face with alarming force and a sinister spattering of raindrops, and the battered and groaning maple listed dangerously ground-ward.

It was as he fought to regain his wits, as the mighty gust subsided, lowering his head against the whipping rain and assailing after-bluster, that he saw them. Two does, barely distinguishable in the darkness, and closely behind them, the Stormwalker Buck!

In the murky light he was devastatingly grand, an aura of great, white beams and fencepost tines, palmated drop-points and overpowering supremacy. Devin could feel it running through him, subordinating the rant of the wind, obliterating the sting of the rain, enslaving everything of life into the moment and the meeting. Struggling against it, steadying himself uncertainly against the plunging trunk, he sought to draw the bow – and could not. The blow was too great and he was brought stiffly back to its reality. Around him swirled a furious and disconcerting cacophony of swaying trees and flying debris. Beneath its roar, the small glade shrank and shivered.

Desperate seconds ticked away, as anxiously he waited for an instant of opportunity. Within a derelict lull, he tried once more. Amid a sea of vertigo, he could sense the bow breaking over, the string yielding, the fletching at his mouth. His fingers felt foreign against his jaw, the tug of the draw weight crazily detached. He fought for a familiar anchor point, as the undisciplined sight pin danced recklessly across the buck's chest. In that instant he comprehended the senselessness of his efforts. He knew his shot could never be true. He eased down the bow and panted, heart pounding, head spinning.

Ruthlessly, the moment and the predicament ate at him. There would never be another chance. It must be now, if ever, between him and the great deer below. Their encounters had already defied all reason. Fighting the brake of his conscience, he started to pull the bow once more, uncertain that he could allow himself to complete the task.

It would play its hand now . . . the same fate that had confounded their destiny from the beginning. Another roaring gust pummeled the maple, the limbs in its crown groaned hideously and its trunk shuddered to its roots. Thrown askew with a half-drawn bow, grappling for stability, he clasped both arms to the tree. And the unthinkable occurred. In a galvanized instant, he felt the bow slip from his hand. He watched as it fell, slowly away it seemed, as it might in a dream, bouncing in retarded motion limb-to-limb as the arrow was wrenched from the string and the ground rose up to claim it. Had it not been for the din of the melee, he would have heard the sickening thud of its impact.

He stared helplessly down at it, numbed to the bone with disbelief, as gall phlegmed his throat. _How? Why?_

There was only the emptiness now. The opportunity lost. The growing nausea.

The deer were still there, surmising the bow to be another falling limb.

The does were nervous and milling, the buck, as always, unperturbed and aloof. But about him somehow, there was a difference. Now that the quest had been wrested away, Devin noticed it for the first time. And the brunt of the revelation struck him irreparably.

It was the difference he had seen in his grandfather in those last few months . . . the drag of time and the river, the toll of strife and struggle, the hopelessness of being sovereign again.

Motionless, the great buck stood, the gray wisdom in his face ghostly white in the gloaming, the weight of the years pulling at his paunch, the dimple in his loins portending the lapse of his supremacy.

In that instant, he knew they would never meet again.

He clung to the few seconds remaining as he would some day the last few seconds of his life, wandering within the wonder of their passing. Stealthily, the does trailed away into the darkness of the forest. Turning to follow, the buck hesitated momentarily, then was swallowed behind them.

Minutes later the woods quieted. The trailing edge of the cloudbank lifted from the sun and its rays chased away the darkness. Soon, the world was serene again. The meteorologists would say afterward that an extemporaneous low-pressure pocket had arisen from the southwest, spawning a rapidly moving and particularly intense front of local turbulence. How it arose so forcefully within a prevailing high would require a greater explanation.

Until the sun was buried into the loam of the horizon, Devin sat in the maple tree, searching for the order in it all.

He would never have the great buck now. He knew that. Yet he was at peace. The revelation was complete. To him had come this one matchless thing that he had never been meant to possess, nor could ever fully understand, no matter how intensely he would yearn. Withheld from him until he had gained the wisdom to appreciate its singularity, it had come in a way that it never could again, and now it was beyond his reach, forever.

It was better this way, he thought. There must always be magic in a mundane world, else life is less the living. This the hunter knows more than any other.

His grandfather was at his ear. "You had him, boy. As much as you ever could. Think of all that came to you in his season."

He thought of the walk with Maggie that afternoon by the Almstead Pool, with the flush of spring on the woods and the charm of her presence in the moment they had seen him, of a December snowfall with the young pines cloaked and bent like Jesuit priests over the dim trail to home, of the sweet, soft bequest of his daughter . . . "Here Daddy . . . hold your grandson."

The old man had been right. "One day you will know," he had said, "but years must pass. It is something I can tell you of myself, but cannot give to you; something that must come to you on your own."

It was in May of the next spring, on a day resonant with the fresh, vibrant green of new life when he and Maggie lay in the lush grass of the meadow by the edge of the creek and watched the mares' tails whisk the sky. Between them, his grandson flailed and shrieked happily over a box turtle. The sun spilled down and butterflies were on the air. His mind drifted with the clouds overhead, mellow with a mix of recollection and reflection.

"Somewhere right now, Maggie," he said thoughtfully, "a buck fawn's being born."

He rolled up on his elbow and looked into the bright, wet eyes of the laughing little boy.

"And one day," he promised, "there'll be another."

Taking A Life

Listen to your years, Old Man," my grandpa would say, upon the rare occasions he blundered right, when the world turned left.

I thought then he was chiding himself, only to find since it was meant for me.

More and more now I pause to honor his bidding, to listen to the lessons of my years. For in the end, life itself is the greatest teacher. I listen to their instruction, can never find folly with their message, but do not always find easy what I hear. Nowhere more difficult than in the conscience of my heart . . .

A venerable friend closed a recent letter with a troubled thought. "We're off to Mattamuskeet tomorrow. We have to shoot steel shot. I can't find any particular fault with that, considering. But I couldn't find any steel shells for my old sixteen and I'm not willing to shoot steel in any of my good doubles. So I think I'll take the middle seat in the blind, just watch and drink coffee. Not a bad idea. I couldn't shoot a swan anyhow – don't want to shoot another goose and don't care a whole lot about shootin' a duck! Wonder what's happening to me – I must hold the boyhood beanshooter record for songbirds and vermin."

I understood perfectly. He wasn't saying he wouldn't shoot, just that it wasn't the first consideration any longer. Such feelings increasingly pervade my own thoughts. By the time I make my friend's vantage, I'm sure my feelings will be as intense as his. I'm not sure, though, that this is cause for worry.

On a bitingly cold morning last fall, I shot a good whitetail buck. Approaching to where he had fallen, I felt swelling inside me the mix of accomplishment and remorse I have almost come to dread. There are no apologies in this. I met him fairly on his own terrain and the kill was clean. Such an experience is gratifying to a hunter, though it involves death.

Yet the day that returns most vividly is another from the same season, when I didn't raise a gun but merely accepted the privilege that made me an observer. That day I was working a field trial dog from horseback. It was unseasonably balmy, with great gusts that roared and bullied their way through the trees in the barren December woods. To gain shelter, I followed a deep-woods property line to a promising beanfield. The wind continued to howl and hearing was impossible above the gale. Halfway there, a tremendous blast nudged my horse forward and lingering oak leaves undaunted by fall were ripped from their deathhold and hurled by in a disorienting swirl. In the same instant I became conscious of a deer. Not just a deer, but an antlered buck. He rose from his bed a scant 30 feet away, took a few bounding leaps and stopped behind a bit of cover.

I could imagine his mind racing, fighting for a signal from his bewildered senses. I rode a few yards farther, for a better line of sight. The buck moved too, but not to bound away as I had anticipated. Instead, he lay down at the base of a huge oak, melting himself into the mute tones of the bark, stretching to full length and dropping his antlers to his neck.

Intrigued, I rode closer, thinking that he was injured and weak. This was not the case. As I neared the tree he started to get up. The movement was quick and coordinated. The eyes were bright. But once again he changed his mind and eased slowly back.

I sat spellbound within six feet of a legal buck with a handsome spread of heavy, eight-point antlers, he looking at me and I at him, each in disbelief of the other. I had never been so close to a live buck of this caliber. His russet coat gleamed with the bloom of peak condition. I admired each polished tine of his antlers as I might a wall mount. I thought of my gun at one point. It rested in the saddle scabbard at my leg. As quickly, I dismissed it. I would not have shot him under the circumstances had he broken every record in Boone and Crockett's book.

The buck made no further move to rise, and I sat watching until my dog doubled back to call me on and I turned to go with her. He remained as I left him until lost from view.

I rode in distraction for several minutes, thinking about what had happened. The wind had robbed the buck of his normal faculties; he took the best alternative at hand. Had I not been watching him, I would have ridden by unaware. The ability of a whitetail to evaporate in sparse cover is uncanny. When the buck changed his mind about leaving the second time, it must have been a submissive action to the horse.

I would never have believed it could happen. I never expect it to happen again.

Over the years, hunters who truly love the woods and wild things come to revere most just such moments of privilege. Often as not, no shot is fired.

Alvin Conner was the closest thing to a mountain man the past century could muster. In body or spirit, he spent every conscious hour somewhere in the Uwharrie backwoods of Randolph County, North Carolina. He died at 87, had hunted doggedly all those years. In his territory his exploits had become fireside tales. A wealth of game had fallen to his gun. Yet in his latter days he spent more time hunting and less shooting. He was bringing along some grandsons. His pleasure was in watching them attempt the things he'd done – in teaching them how. When we talked then, it was different. Rather than dwell on shooting conquests, he would tell me of the duel between a redtail hawk and a gray squirrel on a pristine morning last spring, of watching a doe give a fawn its first lessons in stealth. This relentless man of the quest had mellowed.

Not only that, but the last time I saw Jeff, the eldest grandson, he began our conversation by marveling at a seven-point buck that had spent the morning polishing the velvet off his antlers within a few feet of his stand. The buck he didn't shoot. He could have talked about the one he had taken, because it was among the best that season. He got around to that, as should be. Point is, his priorities were in the right order. Somewhere between Jeff and his grandpa, something was working.

It takes time, character and lessons of life and death to come to Al Conner's perspective. It's born of respect, respect for life and living. Not the least of this is self-respect. If that seems a paradox in one who has chosen to hunt and kill, it's no less true. Hunting, fundamentally, is a life and death proposition. While the urge is almost involuntary, the action is not. There's a conscious decision behind the trigger. Handling it responsibly demands maturity.

I've grown to accept maturity as a product of age, for truly, the years are revealing. It is a point I would not have had time for in the rush of my boyhood, when I too wreaked havoc with a slingshot or BB gun; one I never would have conceded in the cockiness of my teens or even fully appreciated in the growing awareness of my 30s. But it was there, waiting for me.

Things come back now, across the years; my Grandpa again, on the close of a day at quail, telling me, "I know more than a man probably ought to know about the how of things. What I need to know more of is the why."

Inescapably, our middle years become introspective. The edge is off; the fever of youth has become manageable. We can enjoy a few achievements, but can't bask there, for there are miles left in the journey. The questions become larger, the answers more elusive.

Most sobering of all, perhaps, is that for maybe the first time we can look down the road and sense that it has an end. Death becomes a growing presence. We contemplate our own. Suddenly it dawns that life is an extremely precious and fragile thing. Suddenly it is evident that no one ever enjoys clear title to life and living. It's simply an open-ended loan, to be called without notice at Fate's whim. But there are places yet to go, things left to do. Life grows dearer, is guarded more closely, savored more fully. For many who hunt, these revelations bring a deepening quandary. There is a growing reluctance to take a life, faced with the enlightened appreciation of our own.

Feeling so, I ask myself if there will come a time when I quit hunting. The answer must be no. I love the frost of a promising November morning, the slavering excitement of a brace of pointing dogs, the tightness in my throat as I walk to their first point, the unnerving rise of the birds, the tender retrieve of feathers to hand. I love the baying of hounds under a Hunter's Moon, the rustle of fallen leaves under my feet, running with wild abandon through the halflight toward the lure of the tree bark, the riotous din of the dogs, the heft and feel of the burlap sack against my back. I love the careening whine of shearing ice in the pre-dawn of a hard freeze as I clear the way for a waterfowl set, the poetic harmony of a barking skein of geese in the pastels of daybreak, cupped wings over decoys, the shivering retriever against my leg, the loyalty and power of his response at my bidding toward a fallen bird. I love the quest and the conquest, and all the traditions and trappings of the sporting life. Nothing else has so completely captured my soul.

Yet, like my friend, I remain troubled. To hunt is to take a life. Where is the rationale that puts that right with the conscience of my growing years?

The anti-hunting faction has frequently attributed human traits and emotions to gamebirds and mammals in its appeal for support. It is an effective political strategy, but 60 years afield tell me it falls short of fact. The behavior of wild creatures is driven largely by instinct and there is neither the time, need nor inclination for the deep reasoning and contemplation through which human emotion is defined and classified. But neither can I accept the premise that much of the hunting establishment seems to expound – that life other than human is devoid of feeling and is, individually, of small consequence. I abhor the surging tide of crass commercialism that has broadly neutered sporting ethics and, worse, uses game and fish as mere pawns in a scheme of mercenary advantage. The folks I came up with never raised me that way.

What I do believe is that the life of wild creatures has both dimension and sensual fulfillment. I believe the bond between a pair of Canada geese, though not love by human standards, has similar elements and that each finds pleasure, confidence and security in the presence of the other. Are those words too emotionally suggestive? Then perhaps the problem is the limits of our own language in defining behavior that seems so similar to behavior we define with emotional words. Suddenly we border on a challenge to our self-appointed superiority.

The mourning dove softly moaning in the greening of spring is sensuously happy. The whitetail basking in a mountainside "hot spot" on the first clear day after a winter storm is at peace with its world. A black bear with an arrow deep in its chest senses pain. What are the human emotions of love, hate, avarice and greed but sensual experiences that have been set to words?

We stand alone, though, in our ability to contemplate the loss of life, to understand its finality, to comprehend what's forever gone. Out of respect and self-respect, those of us who hunt must apply this greater wisdom on behalf of the wild things we pursue. This is the responsibility decency calls us to acknowledge and practice rather than push aside. For it is inescapable, the wisdom of my years argues. The life we will take is not that different from our own.

The necessity for a kill is never easily explained by one who hunts, as the explanation must be understood by another who doesn't. Surely the urge and the emotion spring from instinct as honestly and purely as do the wiles of the chosen quarry. That these instincts should burn more strongly in some is likely a genetic property. Therein is grounds for neither persecution or apology. In the absence of a kill, there is a void. As the relationship between a man and a woman rarely finds complete expression short of a physical sharing, the hunt is incomplete less possession of the prey. When you boil away the social pretext in either case, the respective behaviors are basic to man's bent for survival and conquest.

The philosophy I hold as truth. The reality of the kill comes harder. What becomes ultimately important is the bridge between.

I'll give you a case in point. Tommy Mock is a comfortable man to share a day with. Being outdoors with him is almost spiritual. He's from rural south Georgia, where a man's religion is important to folks. Tommy's is turkey hunting.

We spent several days after spring gobblers this past April. Most of it was invested in a dominant tom on his strutting zone in a broad expanse of open pasture. He roosted in or around the inundated timber standing in the beaver pond on its eastern edge, and a good bird he was. There were two other mature gobblers in the area, but his authority on this piece of ground had been settled. In the dawning minutes of a new day, he proclaimed it so, his heavy gobbling overpowering the undercurrent of songbird chatter like percussion notes in a woodwind arrangement. Come fly-down time, he simply pitched out and glided into the pasture to his strutting post, demanding that the hens bend to him.

To the south was leased land, beyond our means. West sprawled the barren pasture. The challenge was to call the old gentleman across the pasture to a dark and foreboding edge. We'd have to toll a few hens along to get him started, because he was doing pretty well with the female set where he was.

To me he seemed invincible and I said as much. Tommy didn't answer, but he didn't have to. His wry grin, almost apologetic, was reply enough. The stage was set exactly as he would have it. That's why we were here.

Our commitment was total. Mornings we parked the truck a quarter-mile away and stole to the pasture edge well in advance of day. We took every pain and precaution. First we played it straight. Then we added the hen decoy. Tommy's a better than fair hand on a turkey call. He offered the old gobbler every seductive invitation he could muster. The old man came back with a gobble every beckon. Haughty, swollen and spread under the stage lights of sunrise in the natal swell of spring, he was magnificent. But he wasn't buying. We watched and waited for hours while he put the jakes in their place and bedded the hens, then we tried again. He turned us down cold.

My last morning there, Tommy gave me an option on another bird. But by then I was vested too. Pre-dawn found us at the pasture. This morning something was different. We didn't hear his deep gobble, just the baritones of his rivals. Shortly, they flew out and cautiously advanced into the field. We called and they responded. At least they were on the way, until a trio of hens arrived with a better offer.

"We'd as well try something drastic," Tommy said. "We're not doin' anything like this. I'm goin' way round the beaver pond and come in on those birds from the back side. If we get lucky, one of them may come your way. I don't know where the main man is."

Left with orders to create a diversion of yelps every 15 minutes or so, I'd been through about two runs when the big man opened up, not 40 yards to my left. The first roll of gobbles left me breathing ragged and trying to get my heart down out of my throat. He gobbled steadily for the next half-hour, still hung-up in his roost tree. Apparently the old boy was so close he saw us put the decoy over the fence before daybreak and elected to sit tight. I think the rival birds with his hens finally got his goat.

Tommy had to be somewhere near the gobbling bird. I knew what he would do, but it was a full hour before he was back and I got the story.

"I wasn't 50 yards from him when he gobbled the first time. It made my neck crawl! Took 45 minutes for me to cover the difference, but I made it to the tree. He was in a big oak right on the edge of the pond. Took five minutes more to make him out. I had the gun on him."

"I didn't hear you shoot."

"I probably should have."

"I reckon why you didn't."

He grinned.

Even after all the work and frustration, Tommy didn't want the big tom on those terms. What he wanted was to call him fair and square across that open pasture. Unless and until that happened, the shooting could wait. He was a wise and grand old bird, and if he was brought to bag, it would have to be on a proper field of honor.

I had a long ride back from Georgia. I was traveling alone and had plenty of time to think. I spent hours listening to the dialogue of my restless mind. The experience with Tommy and the gobbler had brought me face to face with a man I'm beginning to recognize again and feel better about. The man is me and maybe I'm not wandering around lost after all.

It's just that I'm becoming more demanding about the conditions of a hunt, about the companions with whom I choose to share it and the dignity afforded whatever we're hunting. It is ever more crucial to me that the moment in which I take a life, while my own continues, be one I can approach and walk away from with self-respect. In the end, I answer to me, no one else.

I'm out about as much as ever, but I don't push quite as hard and I take less game. I never set out to keep score anyhow. It was never in me.

I'm no longer driven to prove myself endlessly. Hell, I've been there. Some of the things that make for a fine day outdoors I'm finding I never even noticed before.

"A vineyard is not judged by the strength of its harvest," my grandpa said, "but by the quality of its wine."

Now I understand.

Chapter 28

Chandler's Wish

Author's Note: *Were life as I could have it, this would be its future.*

I t was the 22nd of April, 2056. Kevin Doughtery was 12 years old and minutes from a dream.

Averting the admonitions of his mother, he rushed his way through dinner, fidgeting as he waited for his father. Across the table his twin sister, Brielle, taunted him with a "goody, have to wait" smirk. He kicked at her and missed, banged his shin on the cross-brace.

Bree loved to rub it in, her trip to Chaleur Bay for salmon. He had to endure the pictures every time he passed her bedroom door.

Gordon Doughtery leaned back from the table, dropped his napkin in the depleted plate of stroganoff, gazed warmly at his wife.

"Divine, dear," he exaggerated.

Carrie laughed. *"Cafferty's,"* she admitted. "I vid-Exed it from work, last thing.

"You know, there's a V-E link now to *Chaumet* in Paris and *Scaturchio's* in Naples?" she exclaimed.

Doughtery stretched and sighed, eyeing his son.

"Time for a nap," he declared.

"D-a-a-d?" Kevin pleaded.

"Better yet," Gordon Doughtery corrected, "Emmy Crawford's on at eight.

"What a woman!"

"She's 45, you know; her mother's in her 80s," Carrie reminded.

"D-a-a-d!" Kevin begged for the second time.

Doughtery paused, smiling, then feigned a lunge toward the hallway.

Kevin burst from his seat, vaulted a robotic serving cart and dashed for the lead.

Braking midway down the hall, he careened past a doorway into a large room dimly but dramatically lit by a melt of liquid crystal colors . . . red, blue, yellow and purple. The exotic illumination emanated from a vast array of idling electronic devices, arranged in a spacious, sensual semi-circle capped with a command console. Immediately the motion sensor kicked up the working lamps, eliciting a diffused influx of white light. The Doughtery's media center occupied fully a quarter of the living space in their Dayton, Ohio home, as did those of the majority of other middle-American households of their mid-50s era. From it, they could initialize each and every facet of commerce or diversion that life in the 21st century could surmise.

Kevin raced directly to the interactive console, plopped into the control station and announced his presence to the command modem. Instantly, the virtualized digital monitor was activated and the life-sized figure of a pleasant young woman in the business garb of the system server appeared. It was the Doughtery's personal assistant, who upon voice recognition and command, facilitated and effectualized any electronic desire. Her name was Amy.

"Good evening, Kevin," she offered in a Kimberly Twain voice. Twain's voice was one of the desktop options. *"Happy birthday!"*

"Hey, Amy," he replied, " . . . thanks."

His dad was behind him now, looking on.

"Good evening, Mr. Doughtery."

"Evening, Amy," Gordon Doughtery returned.

"So, Kevin, what shall we do?" Amy invited.

Kevin was burning with excitement. He had longed for this moment night and day for four years. When he and Bree were six, a friend of his Dad's had suggested they attend the Youth Outdoors Program conducted by the Ohio DNR. It was their first exposure to anything beyond the near facsimile of the classroom, and in the short course of five days both were wonder-struck with the actual touch and feel of the natural world. They had kept Amy busy in the ensuing months, researching and introducing Net sites for anything related. While at the SCI media suite, Amy had found dates for a Hunting & Fishing Education Course to be sponsored by the Ohio state chapter the following summer. The STV (sensual transport) videos of the course content were intriguing and they had attended at the shoulder of their father. Bree had been captivated by fly-fishing; Kevin, more than anything else, was thrilled by the pointing dog demonstrations.

"The Conservancy," Kevin replied brightly.

Amy smiled. It was a familiar site. They had visited the Education Suite many times, which hosted 24-hour interactive programming on a great variety of youth-oriented, sporting heritage topics. And the History Suite, which chronicled likewise the history of hunting and fishing. The Arts & Crafts Suite, which showcased fine guns and knives and rods, trappings of all sorts, and vintage and contemporary sporting art. And now, the latest addition, the Living Literature Suite, which housed the national library collection of sporting literature with daily media-enhanced, on-line readings by famous voices, and classic short stories set to screenplay vignettes.

She pressed the short-cut button and stepped to the left corner of the work space as, behind her, a wash of cobalt blue wallpaper flooded the magna-vis monitor. The audio track cut in with the title theme and one-by-one a montage of a half-dozen active hunting and fishing windows were overlaid onto the screen. A roll-in at the top ushered in the marquee banner behind a wash-in of the foundation logo, then a bright oval window opening to an epic panorama of mountains, valleys and streams – in the foreground the silhouettes of an adult mentor hand-in-hand with two children – a girl with a fishing rod, a boy with a rifle and finally, in large red letters, the herald and the mission: **Conservancy for the Sporting Arts** – *"dedicated to the protection of our natural heritage, the preservation of the great American* *outdoor sporting legacy, and perpetuation of the hunting and fishing arts . . . through youth and discovery."*

"And which suite shall we visit?" Amy inquired, pretending ignorance.

"The Hunting Suite, Amy," the boy replied anxiously, squirming in his seat. "I'm going hunting."

Gordon Doughtery smiled at Amy.

She grinned back and immediately the huge screen scrolled to a grandfatherly man in upland hunting togs, sitting in a big leather chair, a shotgun broken over a knee, a cleaning rod, some rags and a bottle of Hoppe's on a side table. A sleepy setter alongside. Behind them was a flickering fire, around them a room filled with bird hunting and pointing dog memorabilia.

"Happy Birthday, Kevin," the screen facsimile said warmly, *"I'm Joshua Chadwell. Welcome to the Hunting Suite. Amy told me you were coming."*

Kevin looked around at his Dad and smiled, and then turned back to face the video-link which was simul-casting his duplicate to the man on the screen.

"We understand you want to go quail hunting," Josh Chadwell urged. Chadwell was the Conservancy's image mentor for upland bird gunning. There were others for wildfowling, small game and big game.

"Yes sir."

"Sir?" Kevin followed.

"Yes, sir," Chadwell replied whimsically.

"What's your dog's name?"

"This is Jim," the screen mentor answered. At the sound of his name, the setter raised his head. *"He's a four-year-old English setter."*

Kevin smiled and glanced at his dad again.

"So, Kevin, are you ready to start?" Chadwell asked. Kevin nodded enthusiastically.

Three men walked onto the screen and seated themselves around Chadwell. *"Hey, Kevin,"* they voiced mutually.

"Kevin, the man on my right with the big grin is Toby Mock, the two on the left are Gabe Renfroe (Renfroe nodded cordially) and Bobby Briscoe." Briscoe saluted with a finger.

"They're from south Georgia. One of them would like very much for you to come quail hunting with him this fall and for the next few minutes here, they're goin' to take turns telling you and showing you what you could expect. Then, you and your Dad can choose . . .

"Okay."

"Yes-sir," Kevin returned politely.

"Okay! Toby . . . " Chadwell offered.

"Kevin, I'm here for RiverRidge Plantation on the Flint River near Albany. We've been bird hunting RiverRidge for over a 150 years . . . we . . . well, why don't I show you . . ."

Gordon Doughtery watched appreciably as the video unfolded on the screen . . . a merry brace of pointers clipping the piney woods ahead of a plantation quail party, Mock's voice-over torching the excitement, which built to a slap-bang point and a back. His son was beaming, as Bree had been the summer before when she had chosen similarly among the Conservancy's fishing outfitters for the salmon trip.

So was he.

His granddad and grandmother had hunted and fished. He had seen some old 35mm slides. His dad, too, had done a little around the turn of the century. By 2026, though, when he was Kevin's age, there were few places left to go within a convenient radius of the Dayton-Indianapolis-Cincinnati Triad. Fishing maybe, but not hunting. Hardly any private land and the public land was restricted. Hunting was not a permissible activity on much of it. He had grown up a golfer.

Hunting and fishing were just non-entities. The kids loved the nature programs on the education channel and he had often thought he ought to do more with them outdoors. When Monty Tyler had suggested the Youth Outdoors Program, it had seemed a logical progression. Out of it had grown the Hunting and Fishing Course, and then Amy had quickly discovered the Conservancy on the Net, and boy . . . suddenly he had two kids on his hands wild for hunting and fishing.

The Conservancy was the bridge . . . the accessibility it afforded . . . it was unlikely that he would or could have managed it on his own. He had researched the organization – foundation, actually – completely, of course, before he had permitted the kids to attend its summer-side Natural Awakening Rendezvous and afterward, allowed Bree to participate in its fishing program.

It was not only thoroughly legitimate and unsullied. At its heart was one of the most commanding and benevolent endowment funds in America.

Remarkable, its story.

In 2010, an utter stranger had walked into the editorial offices of _Sporting Classics_ magazine in Columbia, South Carolina and, without a preliminary word, placed a cashier's check for $5 million dollars on the desk of its executive editor, Art Carter.

Carter, flabbergasted, had looked at the man – a subscriber to his publication – and then again at the check, uncertain of whether it was Providence or pretense.

"I need your help," the man had said simply and found himself a seat.

The executive editor, astounded still, had waved off his secretary and waited speechlessly for the other shoe to fall.

Jacob Whitaker Chandler was, at 90, a devout traditionalist, whose passions in life were upland birds and small-stream trout. He had grown up hunting and fishing with his father and grandfather among the hardwood forests and limestone rills of rural Pennsylvania, when reverence for woods and water was as unaffected in American youth as grace and goodness. From the Depression he emerged a disciplined and determined young man, who discovered the ache and sweat of corporeal labor long before he found a fortune in pharmaceuticals. Self-made, quiet and unassuming, he was given adamantly to early 20th century values.

America at the Millennium had been an uneasy proposition for Jake Chandler. Time and again, in corporate strife or personal dilemma, his boyhood amid wood and stream, the memory of the simple, homespun people who had been its kith and kin, had been his anchor through stormy seas. That and its legacy – some wild place he could still retreat to, with a gun, a dog and a rod. It was his foremost wish that another child in another century might have the same opportunity . . . to discover the woods and water, the sporting traditions, as he had . . . to embrace them with the same delight and fascination and as similarly, find them touchstones for happiness.

In the year 2009 he had looked earnestly for the semblance of his boyhood and found too little left.

The majority of America's children were growing away from the land, sequestered artificially in urban catacombs, apart from dirt and trees, water and wild things, wandering surroundings so superficial they might never in a lifetime come face-to-face with their souls. Might never be pulled to their knees by the humility of first light on a high mountain bald, returned to their essence by the scream of a bull elk in the chill of dawn or lightened of heart by the dimple of a brook trout on a secret highland pool. The fabric of the family was rent and ragged. Where had the grandfathers gone, the old gentle men who smelled of pipe-smoke and gundog? Who were these impudent, come-lately blurbanites who so arrogantly defiled their memory? Year to year, thousands upon thousands of acres of forests, wetlands and watersheds were being fragmented, desecrated or destroyed by unchecked human replication. In less than another millennium it would consume the vitals of the nation's natural heritage as dreadfully as the innards of some hapless organism amok with a carcinogenic madness.

Wildness was retreating.

Was it the ultimate desire of humankind to live in the artificial environment of a sterile glass bulb, 50 feet above the depleted earth in an ozone-deficient atmosphere of artificial oxygen?

Not Jake Chandler's.

At the turn of the century people were still hunting and fishing, of course. Ironically, hunting and fishing for some species, like deer and turkey, had been temporarily phenomenal. By 2045 Chandler would correctly envision, all that would change over much of the eastern seaboard. And some portions of the Midwest. Nationwide, fragile wildlife populations that had been so delicately restored to fecundity would come push-to-shove with a force more lethally certain than any hunter's gun – the suburban sprawl of a new generation who neither cared nor understood. If you could pay and go, for the next century or so there would be wildness – good hunting and fishing – left somewhere in the world. The majority of American children, left behind in sterile backyards, could neither pay nor go.

But in the year 2009 Jacob Chandler saw other things too. He saw the last great generation of Americans who had come up with the land, the people upon whom had been bestowed the sporting legacy, millions of men and women, as himself, from all walks of life, who cherished it as the pinnacle of their existence, and who in sum comprised the *most affluent* assemblage of sportsman the world had ever known. He saw a generation of sportsmen awakening to the growing uncertainty of their heritage, and wanting both to memorialize its past and make certain its future. A generation who would not, could not, let it pass.

He saw the power beneath the passion!

There was still time. Wild places left. Fifty-eight million youngsters eager for discovery. The future of hunting and fishing and natural heritage depended on sheltered private land, as it always had. A refuge from public political entanglement and protected accessibility to young people and mentors.

So he had walked into the office of Art Carter, the amazed editor of the last sporting magazine most completely dedicated to heritage that September afternoon, with a cause and a conviction, and found himself a chair and said,

"I want to start a foundation, an endowment fund, to preserve the sporting life and the right of every youngster to enjoy it."

And from there the tremendous strength that Chandler had foreseen, the great network muscles beneath the shoulders of the American sporting fraternity, accustomed to quest, inspired by challenge, began to stir.

Carter had a trout-fishing friend, Jack Scofield, in the New Jersey office of Prudential Securities; Scofield had a goose-hunting buddy, Walter Priddy, on Wall Street. In two weeks time Scofield and Priddy had an optimized, hypothetical investment portfolio for five million in endowment principal, with growth scenario extensions to the year 2085. The possibilities were astounding.

Priddy discretely mentioned the proposition to a deer-hunting friend he happened to know with a national beer distributing company. Before the fund even went public, Anhauser-Busch, long a conservation leader, had upped the ante by an additional million.

Carter made other discreet calls to respected companions in the sporting industry. One to Bill Ruger. Another to Bill Jordan. A third to Johnny Morris at Bass Pro Shops.

In its January-February issue, Volume XXI, Issue 1, dated 2011, now a premier collector's item, *Sporting Classics* tested the waters with a four-color, four-page ad announcing the establishment of the National Sporting Heritage Foundation and its working arm, the Conservancy for the Sporting Arts, to be supported by a $12 million Endowment Fund. Dedicated solely to the perpetuation of the hunting and fishing arts and their associated traditions, its focus would be youth programs. The declaration was accompanied by an initial list of benefactors and a mission statement tracking Jake Chandler's vision. Donations were welcomed.

It was an idea that had found its time.

By mid-June, of 2011, Carter and the staff at *Classics* had been overwhelmed by an avalanche of inquiries and an impressive accumulation of contributions. At Carter's S.O.S., the head of a respected national promotions firm, an avid big game hunter, stepped in, volunteering responsibility for the "marketing" account, gratis. An attorney and corporate officer at Merrill Lynch, a keen bass fisherman, convinced his partners of the pro-bono wisdom in stewarding the growing investment portfolio. At Earnst & Earnst, a saltwater fly-fishing executive persuaded his firm to certify the integrity of the account.

By 2014 the Conservancy was on its way as a tax-exempt 501(c)(3) organization, with an initial Web address, a board of directors comprised of twelve of the most highly regarded and influential men and women in the sporting world, and a lean but diligent administrative staff.

By 2015 the investment principal had grown to $17.8 million and early interest/dividend earnings had enabled the first of the Conservancy's natural awakening seminars, a series of camps and expositions, which sought simply to place kids 6-11 amid woods, water and wild things. To instill in them a respect for life and the living, to awaken an innate fascination for the outdoors, all things great and small. From this base, through developing perpetual heritage programs, they would learn of their sporting legacy, the ethics and responsibility expected of those who pursue it, and the proper fit of the sportsman in the continuum of nature. Also that year, 347 children, ages 12-16, went hunting or fishing for the first time of their lives under inaugural "Come Along" invitations by coordinated arrangement with volunteer mentors, private landowners and outfitters.

Throughout the following decade, contributions to the Foundation ascended astonishingly, as America's 50 million hunters and anglers, united heart, spirit and wherewithal, embraced the Conservancy and its mission. From Dallas, a Jaguar-Benz-Land Rover dealer mailed a bank draft for $20,000, dated the birthday of his newborn son. "Another duck hunter," he announced. While, from West Virginia, a 79-year-old grouse hunter on social security, equally sincere, sent a check for $20 "in memory of his father and Jack, his first spaniel." In a brown cardboard box from a Wyoming widow came a split-cane rod and a vintage fly reel. "Maybe one day you can start a museum," she wrote. Taped to the reel was a tightly folded money order for $250. Nationwide, from pensioner to millionaire, the response was as earnest and enthralled.

And in 2021, the great American hunting and fishing industry, turning more than $75 billion annually in the national economy, had responded in kind, for the second time in a hundred years. Not everyone of his generation knew, Gordon Doughtery mused, that the industry the antis viewed as largely avaricious had, 70 years before, voluntarily moved to tax itself by congressional excise in the interest of wildlife conservation. Some say Bill Ruger, Jr. had spurred the initiative in this century, others Jay Crowell at the Brunswick Corporation. No doubt, many were involved. What mattered was the consensus, that with the Foundation and the Conservancy lay the second great conservation movement, this time to preserve the nation's hunters and fishermen themselves. Industry leaders had readily acceded that a second measure no less profound than the first was not only warranted but imperative, dedicating for "perpetuity" one percent of gross national profit in each year to the Foundation and its programs.

Between 2015 and 2025, with the working endowment well beyond $300 million and growing geometrically, the Conservancy, accepting Chandler's wisdom that protected accessibility was ultimately the key to the perpetuation of the sporting heritage, began sheltering woods, marshes and waters through direct acquisition, gifts and bequeaths. Modestly at first, a half-mile of native trout water in West Virginia, a 300-acre wetland in Louisiana, 450 acres of prime elk range abutting the Gila National Forest in New Mexico. Then acres by the accruing thousands nationwide, acres that would forever be protected from development, from government manipulation and parafadoodle, from rapacious political whims, from harassment through public levers by opposition fanatics. Free and wild, forever and accessible . . . accessible to children of all generations and the responsible and dedicated adults who would be their mentors.

Just recently, he had read, the Foundation's holdings were reported in millions of acres, with a Conservancy Chapter in every state of the union devoted to stewarding, expanding and facilitating its utilization within the program mission. It's net worth and national influence, it was alluded, was beyond speculation. Under the shelter of its umbrella were the many associative arms: The National Rifle Association, Ducks Unlimited, The National Wild Turkey Federation, The Rocky Mountain Elk Foundation, Safari Club International, the National Shooting Sports Foundation. Web visits exceeded 30,000 hits a day.

Remarkable indeed, Gordon Doughtery thought.

And now his son was going hunting and Bree was already looking forward to her next fishing trip, for Montana rainbows, just two of thousands upon thousands of kids across the country who otherwise would never have known the joy, who now had a perpetual, living outdoor heritage.

The screen trio from south Georgia had finished their presentations. Kevin was aglow.

"So which of these gentlemen do you want to share a mule wagon with this November, Kevin?" Josh Chadwell asked, a curl of smoke ascending from the pipe in one hand, the setter's ear tousled by the other.

Kevin turned to his Dad, his face contorted with dilemma.

"It's your call, Kev," Gordon Doughtery said. The boy's face screwed into a wrinkle again.

Squirming, he turned to Josh Chadwell again, and the setter. "I think Mr. Toby Mock," he answered meekly.

From the screen, Mock grinned broadly, stuck up a thumb. *"Next time, Kev,"* Briscoe and Renfroe conceded.

"Okay, Kevin, you and your Dad be getting ready. Your hunt will be the 20th to the 23rd. We'll send the tickets and particulars soon. Your hunting partners will be Tim Parks and his dad, from St. Cloud, Minnesota. He's 12 too.

"Drop in on me and Jim again soon, okay."

"Yes-sir."

"And, oh yes . . . Kevin!"

"Yes-sir."

"Drop in on Federal Cartridge, Filson, Boyt and Cabela's before you go to. They want to send something along for your hunt."

Kevin was glowing again.

"Yes-sir," he repeated. "Thanks, sir . . . "

Josh Chadwell leaned back into his chair; with a catchy prompt-tone the screen rolled out of the Hunting Suite, back to the marquee window and the main menu.

Gordon Doughtery laid a hand on each of his young son's shoulders. The boy looked up at him, his face full of life and joy.

"Come with me to the study a minute, Kevin," he said, eyes welling. "I have something for you too."

The little Beretta 20 waiting on the couch he might not have considered before the Conservancy . . . Carrie either. But that was before.

Gordon Doughtery turned and started for the door. Kevin bounced up and ran after him.

"Hey, Kev," somebody called.

The boy pulled up and whirled. It was Amy. She did a funky little rock step, then shot up a palm and five fingers, waiting.

Turning, rushing back, Kevin Doughtery cocked a jubilant five in return. Bracing, mouths set, teeth clenched with triumph, they hurled their palms together with a resounding clap.

Then the boy dashed away to catch his Dad, as behind him the magna-vis screen exploded in a cannonade of sound and color.

Chapter 29

Come Tell Me

In the years of my boyhood, as winter waned, my Aunt Louise would call us kids together and ask a simple favor.

"Come tell me," she would say, "when spring is here. Not by the calendar, but by your heart."

One by one we would come, when we were so overtaken with life and renewal that our hearts said it was time.

And she would say to each of us, "Tell me how you know."

Exhilarated, we would tell her of the first, faint blush of pink upon the woods-line, of buds that burst overnight into mint-green leaves, of basking against a fence rail in the growing sun and listening to the birds rejoice, of finding the first trillium, of spirits that ran as free again as the March winds. She would listen with her eyes closed, savoring every word, for she loved the season above all others. Multiplying her enjoyment by each account, she kept it as fresh as childhood.

As I grow older, it is a sentiment and a ritual that I relish ever more. Though my heart resides in a different season, I am coming to understand how painfully precious each renewal becomes, and how crucial it is to wellbeing that I savor every possible moment. For each grows a little less certain than the last and increasingly ephemeral.

As she loved spring, I cherish the bittersweet mix of amity and melancholy that is autumn and most of all, the rare, perfect height of its maturity, when it has distilled to its essence. In it are the things that replenish my being, that see me through another year.

It seems uncertain now whether I shall have the privilege of a grandson. But should it come to pass, I will call him to me on a proper occasion, when he is old enough to understand, and say to him,

"Come tell me, boy, when November is here again."

I want to live it through his eyes as well as mine. Perhaps there is something I have missed. I want to hear it in the words from his heart as I have listened to those from my own. Perhaps there is something I have not heard. I long for the day that we will talk of it together.

I hope he will say to me,

"How will I know?"

I want the pleasure of explaining to him what he should look for. With all the wisdom and patience I can muster, I want to be the one to tell him how he would know.

For 30 days, I will explain to him, Heaven will touch Earth.

The world will be so perfectly focused, the sky so deep and clean, the separation between earth, trees and forever so brilliantly cut that its clarity will overwhelm you. The colors on the hills will be so vibrant they live and breathe. And regardless of your recorded birthdate, you will be born then – here, now.

Nights will be cold, mornings will find the green plumes of the pines hoary with frost, and midday will be mood-stained and mellow. Twilight will huddle to earth under the make of a Hunter's Moon so gorged it can scarcely best the horizon.

Each minute of each golden day will make your heart beg for completion. You'll find it in the medley of your soul.

In it will be a gun and a dog, the woods, waters and wild things, the wistful fragrance of chimney smoke at dusk, the distant lights of home across the fields under the chill of evening. In it will be the bounce in the old setter's step again, the crack to her tail, the conviction in the way she grabs the long, winding edges. In it will be the belonging of the gun across your shoulder, the perfect nestle of its stock in your hand and the soft rattle of shells in your pocket. The clamor of rising quail against dry ragweed . . . a whisper of passing wings high above a frozen marsh before dawn . . . the shadowy flutter of a woodcock from the alders . . . the lay of spent powder on the dank, still breath of impending snowfall . . . all will be a part of it. With your dearest friend and hunting companion you will find and share at length the small, wonderful things that will come to compose the sum and substance of your existence.

In it will be Thanksgiving, the succulence of yesterday's turkey hunt, pumkin' pie, the people you love and the promise of the deer you will hunt on the morrow.

You will come to yearn for it as you yearn for the woman you will love, and each time it arrives you will seek to enjoy it as you have never before, to give yourself to it so completely that, should there never be another, there can be small room for regret.

And then, as the days pass, wild, wet nights of bluster and storm will come, nights that will wring leaves from even the hardiest oaks.

Gone will be the flamboyant heraldry on the hills . . . the effrontery of the maples, dogwoods, gums and poplars . . . the defiant scarlets, pulsing vermilions, vibrating oranges and electric yellows . . . renounced for the stoic, quiescent hues of reticence and maturity. The great shoulders of the oaks will be draped with mantles of maroon and the hickories will pull on coats of aged tobacco gold. Summer will finally surrender. The first heavy frosts will fall. It will happen while you are so taken with life that you will not immediately sense the change.

Across the land about you the verdant thatch of the growing season will lie withering and the bare, gaunt fields will comply in solemn tones of gray, umber and fawn. On their fringes will be a beard of grizzled whiskers, in their corners a gather of hedge and brier. With growing fury north winds will hurl punishing gusts to press a frigid warning, while all creation takes notice. The year will feel the initial shiver of winter and admit for the first time that it is growing old. There will be a personal inference you will wish to avoid, and cannot.

In paradox, it will be old age at its best, bringing a penchant for tarrying at length with simple pleasures and the wisdom not to fight it. Within it will be a place and time called Indian summer, and you will know it as a golden state of mind between yesterday and tomorrow, and you will wish to remain there forever. In it will be days so brilliantly rich with life and living that grouse will drum on the mountain of sheer exhilaration. In it will be invigorating, flawless mornings that restore your spirit, aimless noonings of lying on your back and wondering into faultless blue skies, and pensive meanderings about afternoons strangely tinged with sadness. In it will be nights so brittle, pure and honest that the stars will cry.

Later, when the gray is on your temples, you will strain to savor every fleeting moment, saddled with the infinite monody that all good things must end, yet striving with all your might to defy the truth of it. Despite your best efforts at detaining it, it will refuse to abide. Perhaps that is the greatest sadness of all. It will scurry past like stolen time, as swiftly as your own life, aging prematurely into its final days . . . and leave you with the same anticipatory morbidity you used to feel a millennium ago when you were a school kid in his last week of summer vacation. And suddenly one day you will realize, how closely similar the two of you have become.

And for all of that, at its close will be the satisfaction that whatever is left to be, for once you have lived life to its fullest, tasted the earth at its richest.

That, my son, will be November.

Then, best of all, in the time we would have together, I would say to him, "Come, boy, let me show you, so that you may come to love it as your own."

I will not expect him to comprehend at once, or for a time, maybe even the extent of my days. But he will listen to my words and if he does not fully sense their letter, he will remember their lesson. Whether I am still of this world or another will be of little matter. For each time that he returns to me as a man in another autumn, with a gun over his arm and a dog at heel, and says with his heart . . .

"Grandpa, it's here,"

I will know that I succeeded.

Chapter 30

A Dog Shines Through It

It is not ours to know what ethereal timbers, if any, bridge the Here and Hereafter, only that there are occasions we are driven strongly to wonder.

For the 89 years of my mother's life – from the bedroom of her birth in an agrarian clapboard home, to the house of hope she and my dad built and abided in for 58 years, to the dim, contrived cubicle of her deathbed in a sterile, urban nursing ward – there resided close to hand and heart a homespun country painting. It was her most beloved, in an existence completed by an infinite passion for flowers and a boundless adoration for traditional pastoral art.

So it was that I played and grew up among butterflies and bees, among brilliant and blissful gardens of buttercup and hyacinth, snap dragons and forget-me-nots, columbine and cocks-comb. And that she would call me to her knee – even through the years as a grown man – stooping to show me in great delight again the tiny rabbits that lived in the bloom of larkspur, the pretty little faces of the petunias, the old man and his beard that habited the white ash.

As it was, also, that she took me to the woods and meadows, to hunt for the bridal white trilliums that sprouted in springtime among the green ferns along the gurgling little creeks, to spy the pink lady's-slippers that peeked from the rotted oak leaves on the hillsides, to appreciate the coarse purple blossoms of even the homely thistle. Never satisfied until I knew and would always remember the hundreds of tiny wonders that Nature has hidden into the mystery of a pistil and a petal.

In the rising loneliness of a summer's evening, when the day lapsed a bit scary, she would take my hand and I would toddle along beside her down a quiet rural path, breathing deeply the loveliness of gardenia and jasmine, honeysuckle and wild rose, wisteria and Sweet Betsy.

"Now, now, little man, forget your tears. See how wonderfully the world smells."

Thus it was, as well, that I grew up with plow horses and shepherd dogs and laying hens, around a house wherein every wall was a fascination of country fantasies, cultivated from the mind and mist of an artist's palette. Where pictures were squeezed shoulder-to-shoulder until there was no more hanging room. Bucolic scenes of farm mules and wagons, horses and hanes, chickens and ducks and biddies, kittens and roosters and pigs. Portraits of stately Grecian mansions that lived alongside sketches of back-40, share-croppers' shacks, outhouses that kept company with cribs. Farm-table settings and still-lifes. Bonnets and bouquets. Christmas trees, snowfall and sleigh-bells. Holly berries and hayfields. And always and ever, children and dogs. Terriers and bulldogs, harriers and hounds, collies and fiests, in old-time hunting scenes or hearth-side repose, erstwhile companions of my many dreams.

But above all, there was the one. In my mother's bedroom, close by her bed above her reading chair. A vintage painting of a little girl and a Jack Russell terrier. The Jack is in the foreground, properly sassy, the little lass – charming as they come – behind, her face and eyes a melt of adulation for her dog. Unique the composition, exquisitely done. She cherished it beyond her being.

"That's me and Priss," she would tell me time and again . . . she and the terrier she loved as a child. Gone, before the several others I knew, coming along a boy. The ones I squirrel hunted over with my grandpaw – my mother's father – about the golden hickory hills.

But there was more. I sensed it in her eyes. Later, I knew. The little dog in the picture was her strength, the thing that helped her past the night.

Sixty years and more have passed since those halcyon days of my childhood, two long winters, even, since my mother left.

Though it was only two months ago, Mother's Day coming – with the wisteria in fragrant bloom and trouble in my life – that Loretta walked routinely to the barn for the morning's chores. Finding in her path a Jack Russell dog. A small female, lemon-and-white, wearing a double mask that traversed both ears and a patch about her tail. Typically Jack, she volunteered a hello to Retta, then sallied off to the barn to prospect for mice. Later she cornered a toad and afterward, fetched up a gray fence lizard. There was something between us, she and I, first time we met.

In the time since we have searched high, low and between for an owner. I do not believe, now, we will find one.

"She was just suddenly there," Loretta has said to me, time and again, wonder in her voice. Already the inference was building. The more, when we carried her to the vet, and she was utterly free of ill-health or parasites. Uncommon for a cast-off or stray.

We call her Lottie. She's dozing, now, as I write this, in the chair beside my desk, where she has been content to quietly spend my work mornings every day since she came. From the beginning she has doted on me. Afternoons, she's all Jack – straight-wired – treeing the squirrels on the back hill, watching them through the trees, just like grandpaw's did. No mistaking. Somehow, some way, she's a squirrel dog. And this fall when the leaves age red and yellow, we'll drop back a few years, take up the .22 and go chase up a few bushytails.

I visited my father recently, assisted with living now himself. Mother's painting hangs in his apartment, on a bedroom wall. Randomly as I was leaving, I thought of it. I had not seen it since mother died; the image was vague. Suddenly it was imperative that it be clear.

Dumb-struck, I stood before it in a trance, as if I was being transported outside myself, to a dimension strange and deep. The little girl was adorable, much as I remembered. But it was the Jack that was transfixing. It was a little female. I know. A lot of living with dogs, the softness about her face and eyes, told me so. But it was the more . . . she was lemon-and-white, marked to a hair, to the tail patch, to the cock of her ears . . . as Lottie.

The inquisition of the moment was searing: What more telling gift could she have returned with, than a small terrier dog?

I am not the only one bent to gauge fathomless waters.

What brought a perfectly, heart-shaped oak stump, never-before noticed, to be found within the favorite cover of a hard-bitten grouse hunter – a grouse to take flight at the moment of its discovery – prompting him to remember that his lately departed Belle, the greatest pointing dog of his years, loved that place most as well? What caused Jack, a mannered English setter, to abruptly yowl at the middle of a funeral service, so mournfully it raised every hair on every head in the congregation? Was he bid to witness the departure of his master's soul? What brings the one thing, en route to its eternal shrine and surviving a horrific trailer accident demolishing every other scrap of cargo, to be the unscathed, fragile urn containing the ashes of Giz, a treasured retriever?

I do not know. I only know, from others, that it happened.

An old and dear friend has exacted a promise. For we have marveled deeply of such things.

"If there's any way back," she has said, "I will bring you a sign. Vow to me the same. So that whoever goes first, the other will come to know."

And I have. I will not divulge the explicit elements of disclosure, for that is sacred trust. But we have agreed that it will be some small and happy thing, something from the outdoors, that the either of us has especially loved. Delivered in such remarkable context as to be unmistakable.

Will it be within our means to pilot even so small and incidental an inference of our after-fate? Or must we bow, forever, to the guarded ambiguity of the unknown? Should I be the survivor, what really shall come to be? Will there be a brief, enlightened moment of joy to illuminate an eternity of darkness?

I'll know all, I suppose, or nothing at all.

But if there's truly the way, I'll not be surprised if . . . on some day, from beyond the gray . . . a dog shines through it.

Chapter 31

I Don't Look Good
Nekid Anymore

I don't look good nekid anymore.

I mean the other day it was July hot and sticky, and I left the truck by the bridge, and meandered my way a mile-an'-a-half and sixty years back down Taylor's Creek to the swimming hole. Where when I was 13 I discovered Janey Presnell did. Look good nekid, that is. Awfully good. Anyhow, there wasn't nobody around, so I stripped off and stretched out on a big flat rock, like a lizard on a fence rail.

Suddenly it wasn't hot anymore, just covertly pleasant like I remembered it to be. The sun was soft as a lover's kiss and there was the same careless breeze and it tickled the gray hairs on my chest, and those in a few other manly places. And that was different, cause back then I didn't have none to tickle. But I could still look up through the trees and trace the long wispy mare's tails in a milky blue sky, and way-up-high the loaf-along circles a big black buzzard was cuttin' on the wind.

The water still babbled through the little stone rapids beneath the pool and above its voice you could still hear the trill of the prothonotary warblers that hid amongst the maple leaves. Once even, I'd seen a tanager in the top of a sweetgum tree. Lady, my little girl beagle wasn't there, and always she had been. Nor the little single-chance Winchester .22. But if I closed my eyes and squeezed real hard, thought about box turtles, water snakes and dragonflies, I could almost make them be.

All-in-all, it felt a shake like it oughta feel – a lot like 1955 – a lot like free – and not a meddling soul around to go fooling with it. I remembered it had always felt that way after a while, once you escaped civilization and got back to natural. What it felt like actually was going swimmin', and I didn't wait a minute longer.

It was when I stood up I most noticed the difference. The water immediately caught my sunlit reflection, and it had been a long time since I took stock of myself so starkly in that particular mirror. Last I had looked there had been this nut-brown, tow-headed, lissome and lean kid with stomach muscles knotted like roped hemp, over the blossoming red-acorn hopes of manhood. Now there was just a pale, wrinkling and saggy old character with ash in his hair, that looked a lot like a mushmelon gone to seed.

It reminded me of just how pidly an excuse a human being is in the world wild – not one gay dab of plumage, not a silky strand of fur – only a bland, straight-in-your-face, mostly painful spectacle of barren flesh. All the wild critters unfortunate enough to be born that way are given the good sense and grace to grow out of it. At least when they get old, they naturally got coat or feathers to cover some of the ugly. If a man raises pelage, it's either a brierpatch or a sorrowful crop. Without the cotton loom, I figure at least three-quarters of mankind would have died of embarrassment two years past the Renaissance.

They say the Good Lord created man of his image. God only knows why he would admit it.

"Listen, Lord, we could've been an elk, or a wood duck, or a kudu, or a grizzler bear?" Somethin' pretty or fierce. Nobody would ever have guessed. As it is, ain't nobody can stand us but ourselves.

"Whoooohaw!"

There wadn' a fig leaf around big enough, so I piled off butt-first and into the pool, and that way I didn't have to look at myself any longer cause everything below my neck was hidden to Eden. First the water was so cold my teeth chattered and then gradually so loverly it felt like I could remember it used too once the rose blushed.

Memory is a beautiful thing, until it turns on you. I was just to the point of lolling back and giving myself to the Lady of the Lake when I recollected, once, not long enough ago, Loretta had told me I stunk.

"You stink," she decried, "smell bad."

Well, maybe along then I had hung out a spell too long with Meg and Sir, my 12-year-old setters, but it had only been a four-day trip – down to Six Runs, for old times sake. There wasn't occasion to bathe a lot. It wasn't entirely unpredictable that Meg would wallow in a defunct hog at the edge of Briley Baxter's pasture, or that Sir would suffer the recurring, come-lately indignity of dribbling on his leg feathers. If I'm not careful these days, I dribble on mine. I did spill pork-and-beans on my pants one night, an' there weren't the need to carry but the one pair. I wiped them off careful with an old floundering rag I found under the front seat. Then, one night comin' back, Ed Boyette had invited us catfishing on the river. The chicken livers, Ed said, were three days fresh.

Who'da knowed, after 40 years, she might take on that way.

I shrugged it off, went ahead and skinned my catfish, mucked the manure out of the stable, then aerated my worm bed.

Later, though, when she said it again, I thought to pay attention. Well . . . first I did, and then I didn't. Finally I decided there weren't no use worrying about it.

After a point I reckoned – lying there in the creek and lettin' the crawfish nibble my toes – there ain't but so much a man can do about it noway. Bobby Ruark caught the heifer in the haymow, 'bout the time he wrote *The Old Man and The Boy*. It wasn't just the Old Man he was talkin' about, you suppose, when he allowed "Old Dogs and Old Men Smell Bad."

I never took no offense to the proposition. Nowadays, I gather it a compliment. My grandpa smelled bad and that was good. It was acause of pipe smoke and ceegars, chewing tobacco and good scotch whiskey, inverted catalpa worms and gun solvent and canned sardines. You might even say it was a public service, since it covered up the really old man smell of souring yeast you can't bathe off at that fine juncture of life, no matter how much you scour.

Reckon they's worse things than looking old or smelling bad anyhow. A man can look at it as kind of a trade. Fair bargain-and-the-miles for all the dreams he dreamed layin' there nekid on that flat rock, in the sun on the creek, back when he was fresh as spring clover and a lad of 13. All the imaginings that, somehow, someway, fared true.

The sun was failing and I pulled myself out of the water, back atop the warm rock, dried a few minutes and tugged on my duds. Piddling my way back to the bridge, I lay hold of a thing or two. You go thinking of yourself as The Boy for so long, and it gets in your nose to be a man so long, that when you finally pass ripe on the other end you're too familiar with yourself to know it. A skunk never knowed he stunk without somebody come along and thunk he stunk.

I guess how I smell is a lot like I be these days, and if it means givin' up any of the things I love, like marsh mud and Labs in the bunk, remember, I been a long time earning it. I figure it's who I am, and a body'd play hell now tryin' to scrub it off.

Though I do believe Master Ruark could just have stopped at the gist of the thing: "The Old Man knows pretty close to everything and mostly he ain't painful with it."

That way a body gets by with a little respect, and only the womenfolk leave worry the illogicality between wisdom and washing.